Rome

WHAT'S NEW | WHAT'S ON | WHAT'S BEST

www.timeout.com/rome

Contents

Don't Miss

Itineraries

Rome by Area

Essentials

Published by Time Out Guides Ltd
Universal House
251 Tottenham Court Road
London W1T 7AB
Tel: + 44 (0)20 7813 3000
Fax: + 44 (0)20 7813 6001
Email: guides@timeout.com
www.timeout.com

Managing Director Peter Fiennes
Editorial Director Ruth Jarvis
Business Manager Daniel Allen
Editorial Manager Holly Pick
Management Accountants Margaret Wright, Clare Turner

Time Out Guides is a wholly owned subsidiary of Time Out Group Ltd.

This edition first published in Great Britain in 2011 by Ebury Publishing
A Random House Group Company
Company information can be found on www.randomhouse.co.uk
Random House UK Limited Reg. No. 954009
10 9 8 7 6 5 4 3 2 1

Distributed in the US and Latin America by Publishers Group West (1-510-809-3700)
Distributed in Canada by Publishers Group Canada (1-800-747-8147)

For further distribution details, see www.timeout.com

ISBN: 978-1-84670-252-5

A CIP catalogue record for this book is available from the British Library.

Printed and bound in Germany by Appl.

The Random House Group Limited supports The Forest Stewardship Council® (FSC®),
the leading international forest certification organisation. All our titles that are printed on
Greenpeace approved FSC® certified paper carry the FSC® logo. Our paper procurement
policy can be found at www.randomhouse.co.uk/environment.

Time Out carbon-offsets all its flights with Trees for Cities (www.treesforcities.org).

Rome Shortlist

The **Time Out Rome Shortlist** is one of a new series of guides that draws on Time Out's background as a magazine publisher to keep you current with what's going on in town. As well as Rome's key sights and the best of its eating, drinking and leisure options, the guide picks out the most exciting venues to have recently opened and gives a full calendar of annual events. It also includes features on the important news, trends and openings, all compiled by locally based editors and writers. Whether you're visiting for the first time, or you're a regular, you'll find the *Time Out Rome Shortlist* contains all you need to know, in a portable and easy-to-use format.

The guide divides central Rome into six areas, each of which contains listings for Sights & Museums, Eating & Drinking, Shopping, Nightlife and Arts & Leisure, with maps pinpointing all their locations. At the front of the book are chapters rounding up these scenes city-wide, and giving a shortlist of our overall picks in a variety of categories. We include itineraries for days out, plus essentials such as transport information and hotels.

Our listings give phone numbers as dialled within Italy. Rome's prefix is 06; you must dial this prefix even if you're calling from on in the city. The international code for Italy is 39. When calling from outside Italy, do not drop the initial '0' of the Rome prefix. Listed numbers beginning with '3' are mobiles.

We've noted price categories by using one to four euro signs (€-€€€€), representing budget, moderate, expensive and luxury. Major credit cards are accepted unless otherwise stated. We also indicate when a venue is **NEW** and give **Event highlights**.

All our listings are double-checked, but places do sometimes close or change their hours or prices, so it's a good idea to call a venue before visiting. While every effort has been made to ensure accuracy, the publishers cannot accept responsibility for any errors that this guide may contain.

Venues are marked on the maps using symbols numbered according to their order within the chapter and colour-coded according to the type of venue they represent:

- ❶ Sights & Museums
- ❶ Eating & Drinking
- ❶ Shopping
- ❶ Nightlife
- ❶ Arts & Leisure

Map Key	
Major sight or landmark	▬
Railway station	▬
Park	▬
Area name	TRIDENTE
Metro line	✕
Hospital	H
Church	⛪

Time Out **Rome** Shortlist

EDITORIAL
Editor Anne Hanley
Deputy Editor Dominic Earle
Proofreader John Shandy Watson

DESIGN
Art Director Scott Moore
Art Editor Pinelope Kourmouzoglou
Senior Designer Kei Ishimaru
Group Commercial Designer Jodi Sher

Picture Editor Jael Marschner
Acting Deputy Picture Editor Liz Leahy
Picture Desk Assistant/Researcher
  Ben Rowe

ADVERTISING
New Business & Commercial Director
  Mark Phillips

International Advertising Manager
  Kasimir Berger
International Sales Executive
  Charlie Sokol
Advertising Sales (Rome)
  Margherita Tedone

MARKETING
Senior Publishing Brand Manager
  Luthfa Begum
Group Commercial Art Director
  Anthony Huggins
Guides Marketing Manager
  Colette Whitehouse

PRODUCTION
Group Production Manager
  Brendan McKeown
Production Controller Katie Mulhern

CONTRIBUTORS
This guide was researched and written by Anne Hanley, with the exception of Rome
on Film, Baroque's Bad Boy, Bedazzling Baroque, Proceeds of crime and Top notes
(all Julia Crosse). The editor would like to thank all the writers of *Time Out Rome*
on which this guide is based.

PHOTOGRAPHY
Pages 10, 20, 21, 23, 24, 26, 56, 59, 75, 84, 88, 100, 106, 111, 112, 117, 121,
126, 128, 133, 134, 137, 139, 152, 161, 168, 174, 179 Alessandra Santorelli; page 30 Marco Caselli Nirmal; page 32 Michele
d'Annibale; pages 41, 53, 178 Agnese Sanvito; pages 42, 44 (bottom) Denis Babenko;
page 43 Vladimir Mucibabic; page 44 (top) Offscreen; pages 46, 50 Khirman Vladimir;
pages 47, 55, 144 Losevsky Pavel; page 48 Clara; page 62 Matej Hudovernik; page
67 alarik; page 72 Circumnavigation; page 143 Collpicto; page 159 (top & bottom
right) imagestalk.

The following images were provided by the featured establishments/artists: pages 8, 29,
35, 36, 39, 78, 163, 164, 177.

Cover photograph: Vatican City, Rome. Credit: Photolibrary.com.

MAPS
LS International Cartography, via Decemviri 8, 20138 Milan, Italy (www.mapmovie.it).

About **Time Out**

Founded in 1968, Time Out has expanded from humble London beginnings into the
leading resource for those wanting to know what's happening in the world's greatest
cities. As well as our influential what's-on weeklies in London, New York and Chicago,
we publish nearly 30 other listings magazines in cities as varied as Beijing and Mumbai.
The magazines established Time Out's trademark style: sharp writing, informed
reviewing and bang up-to-date inside knowledge of every scene.

   Time Out made the natural leap into travel guides in the 1980s with the City Guide
series, which now extends to over 50 destinations around the world. Written and
researched by expert local writers and generously illustrated with original photography,
the full-size guides cover a larger area than our Shortlist guides and include many more
venue reviews, along with additional background features and a full set of maps.

   Throughout this rapid growth, the company has remained proudly independent,
still owned by Tony Elliott four decades after he started Time Out London as a single
fold-out sheet of A5 paper. This independence extends to the editorial content of all
our publications, this Shortlist included. No establishment has been featured because
it has advertised, and no payment has influenced any of our reviews. And, for our critics,
there's definitely no such thing as a free lunch: all restaurants and bars are visited
and reviewed anonymously, and Time Out always picks up the bill.
For more about the company, see www.timeout.com.

Don't Miss

MAXXI

Sights & Museums

If you come to Rome with a neat list of things to do, make sure it includes 'sitting at pavement cafés watching people go by' and 'strolling aimlessly through the alleys of the *centro storico*'. Of course, the city's museums, galleries and archaeological gems are second to none. But so is the spectacle that plays out on its streets 24/7.

It pays to approach the Eternal City knowing that you won't be able to see everything: you can live here for decades and keep on being amazed by new finds. To fully appreciate Rome's treasures and its unique urban landscape, you'll need to walk, so bring comfortable shoes. You'll also need to lounge; although sitting at a pavement café may crank up the price of your cappuccino somewhat, a front-row seat at the spectacle that is Rome is cheap at any price.

The streets of the *centro storico* are looking grimier now than they were just a few years ago, and graffiti in the city is endemic. But this only distracts slightly from the restored and gorgeously illuminated *palazzi*, and the streets and squares – some of them pedestrianised – repaved with traditional *sampietrino* cobbles.

Ancient sites

The area of the city with the greatest density of remains lies between the Palatine, Capitoline, Esquiline and Quirinal hills. Located here are the Colosseum (see p58), the Roman Forum (see p63) and ancient Rome's most desirable residential area, the

Palatine (see p63). But ancient Rome doesn't stop there: the Museo Nazionale Romano group (Palazzo Massimo alle Terme, see p101; Palazzo Altemps, see p79; Crypta Balbi, see p68; and the Baths of Diocletian, see p101; for all, see www.archeorm.arti.beniculturali.it) houses a positively mind-boggling collection of ancient statuary. There is plenty more to admire in the Vatican and Capitoline museums (see p146 and p58) too. And the Pantheon (see p79) is a work of art in itself.

Churches

Down the centuries, popes, princes and aristocrats all commissioned architects and artists to build and adorn their preferred places of worship, with the result that central Rome is home to more than 400 churches, containing endless artistic treasures.

Churches are places of worship; although only the Vatican imposes its dress code rigidly (both in St Peter's and in the Vatican Museums), very short skirts, bare midriffs, over-exposed shoulders and shorts are all frowned upon. Churches ask tourists to refrain from visiting during services.

A supply of coins for the meters to light up the most interesting artworks is very handy, as is a pair of binoculars.

Museums & galleries

Rome has long boasted some of the world's greatest galleries and museums, but the last few years have seen a rash of new permanent exhibits, and there are new showcases for old ones.

The ancient, Renaissance and Baroque dominate, of course; but venues such as MACRO and MAXXI (for both, see p99) mean

SHORTLIST

Ancient monuments
- Ara Pacis Museum (see p85)
- Colosseum (see p58)
- Crypta Balbi (see p68)
- Imperial Fora Museum (see p61)
- Pantheon (see p79)
- Roman Forum and Palatine (see p63)

Grand masters
- Capitoline Museums (see p58)
- Doria Pamphilj Gallery (see p77)
- Galleria Borghese (see p92)
- Palazzo Barberini (see p96)
- Vatican Museums (see p146)

Bustling piazze
- Campo de' Fiori (see p67)
- Piazza di Spagna (see p89)
- Piazza Navona (see p79)
- Piazza del Popolo (see p84)

Contemporary architecture
- Ara Pacis Museum (see p85)
- MACRO (see p99)
- MAXXI (see p99)

Leafy parks
- Villa Borghese (see p91)
- Villa Torlonia (see p99)

Roman sculpture
- Capitoline Museums (see p58)
- Palazzo Altemps (see p79)
- Palazzo Massimo alle Terme (see p101)

Stunning views
- From the dome of St Peter's (see p145)
- From the Gianicolo hill (see p138)
- From the lift at the Vittoriano (see p65)

DON'T MISS

Roman Forum p8

that contemporary art is, finally, well represented and displayed.

Hours & information

In our listings we have given winter opening hours (*orario invernale*). In summer, opening hours may be extended significantly, with some major museums and sites keeping their doors open as late as 11pm in high season. Many museums – though not churches – are closed on Mondays.

Note that ticket offices at many museums, galleries and ancient sites stop issuing tickets up to 75 minutes before the gates shut.

Church opening times should be taken as rough guidelines. Whether doors are open or not

often depends on anything from priestly whim to the availability of volunteer staff.

Regularly updated information – including timetable information – on all Rome's sights, shows and entertainments in general can be found on the excellent, exhaustive website www.060608.it. Alternatively, call 06 0608 for information on just about anything that might interest visitors to Rome; all operators speak passable English. This phoneline will also arrange bookings.

Tickets

Entrance to publicly owned sites and museums is free (*gratuito*) or reduced (*ridotto*) for EU citizens (and citizens of other countries with bilateral agreements) aged under 18 or over 65; you must show photo-ID (for children too) at ticket offices to prove that you are eligible. Under-25s in full-time education may also be eligible for discounts, as may journalists, teachers, motoring association members and others. Carry a range of ID just in case.

Note that many venues now levy an extra charge, generally of around €1.50-€3, when special exhibitions are taking place inside; visitors are given no option other than to pay the ticket plus exhibition price, and some sights seems to have extra-levy shows on more or less constantly. In all cases, however, we have given the basic price in this guide.

Booking

Booking is mandatory for the Domus Aurea (see p101; 06 3996 7700, closed at the time of writing) and Galleria Borghese (see p92; 06 32 810). It is also a good idea for big one-off shows, if they have opened very recently.

Booking is possible – though really not necessary except for large groups – for many other sites and museums. Note that agencies charge a booking fee that further bumps up the price of tickets.

The official booking agencies for Rome's major sites are Pierreci (06 0608, www.060608.it or www.pierreci.it) and Ticketeria (06 32 810, www.ticketeria.it). Both accept MasterCard and Visa.

Discounts & passes

The Roma Pass is a multi-entrance card that costs €25 and is valid for three days. It gives free access to any two sights, reduced entry to all others, plus unlimited use of the city's public transport system. For further information, see www.romapass.it.

The following tickets can be bought (cash only) at any of the sites involved or online from www.ticketclic.it, which charges a €1.50 booking fee.

Appia Card (€6, €3 reductions, valid seven days) covers the Baths of Caracalla, Tomb of Cecilia Metella and Villa dei Quintili.

Archeologia Card (€23, €13 reductions, valid seven days) covers the Baths of Caracalla, Baths of Diocletian, Colosseum, Crypta Balbi, Palatine, Palazzo Altemps, Palazzo Massimo alle Terme, Tomb of Cecilia Metella and Villa dei Quintili.

Capitolini Card (€8.50, €6.50 reductions, valid seven days) covers the Capitoline Museums and Centrale Montemartini.

Museo Nazionale Romano (€7, €3.50 reductions, valid for three days) covers the Baths of Diocletian, the Crypta Balbi, the Palazzo Massimo alle Terme and the Palazzo Altemps.

Tours

Trambus's 110 Open bus (06 684 0901) leaves Termini station every 15mins (8.30am-8.30pm) on its two-hour circuit. Tours include commentary (in eight languages); an all-day stop-and-go ticket is €15. There's also a €50 family ticket.

The Archeobus passes by the Baths of Caracalla (see p117) and along via Appia Antica (Appian Way, see p151), leaving Termini station about every 30mins from 9am to 4.30pm. Stop-and-go tickets cost €10; without stops, the trip takes about one-and-a-half hours.

Tickets for both can be bought at the booth in front of Termini, on board or online (www.trambusopen.com).

IN THE HEART OF ROME, IN THE CENTER OF THE WORLD!

Four Hotel, two Restaurants, two Roof Gardens, located in the heart of Rome, a few steps from Termini Railway Station, near the central hub of public transport, nearby the major monuments like the Colosseum, the Pantheon, the Trevi Fountain, the Roman Forum, the Opera and National Museum.

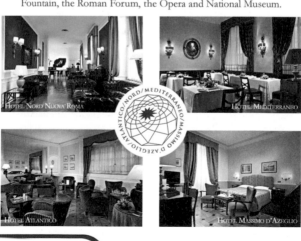

HOTEL NORD NUOVA ROMA

HOTEL MEDITERRANEO

HOTEL ATLANTICO

HOTEL MASSIMO D'AZEGLIO

Grano p82

Eating & Drinking

Time was when your average Roman family thought nothing of eating out a couple of times a week, mostly in the local pizzeria or trattoria *sotto casa* (downstairs), with a fling at something more upmarket for special occasions. But the shock of the credit crunch, coming on the heels of sharp price rises with the introduction of the euro, left Italians feeling much poorer. Few eateries feel cheap any more, and few Romans cheerful. But when they do go out, they are as determined as ever to get value (and that means quality) for money.

The shabby neighbourhood bar with its excellent coffee and *cornetti* (croissants) remains a favourite, however. And where the local trat has stuck it out and kept prices in check, it will still attract local diners. If, however, you're in the Eternal City to banish financial woes for a while, there's a host of addresses for sipping and dining in style. And if prices are now on a par with, or higher than, many other European cities, the quality and authenticity of what's on offer are hard to beat.

Eating

Designer restaurants continue to open in Rome – and they close, too, with alarming regularity. The survivors, as a rule, are those that offer real culinary excitement, rather than just a few twigs in a vase and the chance of spotting a once-famous TV starlet. Substance always counts for more than style.

The growing demand for value, however, means that *trattorie* and *osterie* are weathering the storm much better. Some are

Offset your
flight with
Trees for Cities
and make your
trip mean
something for
years to come

www.treesforcities.org/offset

Trees for Cities
Charity registration number 1032154

unreconstructed family-run operations; others are recently opened places that take the trattoria formula and give it a twist by upping the creativity quotient in the kitchen.

What now sets Rome apart is the focus on raw materials. Foodie enthusiasm has upped quality no end; the trickle-down effect of this means that even the most basic trat now generally offers decent extra-virgin olive oil with which to dress your salad and more-than-drinkable house wine.

Another recent novelty is the increasing variety. Once, the choice was between posh restaurant, humble trattoria or pizzeria. Today, there are wine bars, salad bars, gastropubs and deli-diners. Even the unchanging pizzeria has been shaken up by the arrival of gourmet pizza emporia. Rome now has more decent Japanese and Indian eateries than ever before too – although moves by some councils in northern Italy to maintain culinary purity by banning the opening of 'foreign' food outlets showed a worrying tendency towards food protectionism.

It pays to be adventurous when eating in Rome; most of the best places don't have menus in six languages, and may not look like much on the outside. It's also worth getting away from the most heavily touristed parts of the *centro storico* to outlying areas such as Testaccio, San Lorenzo or Il Pigneto, where you'll find some of the city's best-value, most creative *trattorie*.

Going the course

Traditionally, an Italian meal goes *antipasto* (starter), *primo* (usually pasta, sometimes soup), *secondo* (the meat or fish course) with optional *contorno* (vegetables or salad, served separately) and *dolce* (dessert). But locals these days

S H O R T L I S T

Health food & veggie
- Città dell'Altra Economia (see p125)
- RistorArte Il Margutta (see p90)

Ice-cream to remember
- Gelateria del Teatro (see p82)
- Il Gelato (see p120)
- Il Gelato di San Crispino (see p98)

Lunch on the run
- 00100 (see p124)
- Antico Forno Roscioli (see p73)
- Cinecaffè (see p94)
- Il Seme e la Foglia (see p125)

Perfect pizza
- Bir & Fud (see p132)
- Da Francesco (see p81)
- Isola della Pizza (see p149)
- Remo (see p124)

Roman traditions
- Checchino dal 1887 (see p124)
- Da Felice (see p124)
- Matricianella (see p90)
- Sora Margherita (see p74)

Tradition shifts up a gear
- Agata e Romeo (see p105)
- L'Asino d'Oro (see p107)
- Grano (see p82)
- Pastificio San Lorenzo (see p115)

Sipping wine with a hip crowd
- Etabli (see p82)
- Freni e Frizioni (see p135)
- Hotel Locarno bar (see p90)
- Salotto 42 (see p82)
- Société Lutèce (see p82)
- Time Seafood Café (see p95)

rarely manage the whole routine, and you're under no obligation to order four courses either. It's perfectly normal to order a pasta dish followed by a simple *contorno*.

Top-flight restaurants will occasionally offer a special *menu degustazione* (taster menu), but any place with a *menu turistico*, especially one translated into many languages, should usually be avoided.

Drinks
One of the biggest changes over the last decade has been the way even humble eateries have started to have decent wine lists. More and more establishments are now offering a good selection of wine by the glass (*al bicchiere* or *alla mescita*). In pizzerias, the drink of choice is *birra* (beer) or soft drinks. Mineral water – *acqua minerale* – comes either *gassata* (sparkling) or *naturale* (still) and is usually served by the litre.

Prices, tipping & times
Places that add service to the bill are still in the minority; if in doubt, ask, *'il servizio è incluso?'* A good rule of thumb is to leave around five per cent in humbler places, or up to ten per cent in smarter eateries. If service has been slack or rude, you should have no qualms about leaving nothing – or checking the bill in detail, as there is still the occasional restaurateur who gets his sums wrong when dealing with foreigners. Most restaurants accept credit cards, but if there is no sticker on the door, ask, *'prendete le carte di credito?'*

Where we have specified '**Meals served**', this is the opening time of the kitchen: the establishment may remain open long after. In the evening, few serious restaurants open before 7.30pm. Pizzerias begin serving earlier, generally by 7pm.

In this guide, we have used the euro (€) symbol to indicate the average price range for a three-course meal without wine for one:

    € – €25 or less
    €€ – €26 to €35
    €€€ – €36 to €50
    €€€€ – over €50

Children, women & (no) smoking
Taking children into restaurants – even the smartest – is not a problem in Rome. Waiters will usually produce a high chair (*un seggiolone*) and are generally happy to serve *una mezza porzione* – a half-portion.

Women dining alone will rarely encounter problems, though you have to get used to the local habit of staring. Single diners of either sex can have trouble getting a table at busy times: few proprietors want to waste a table that could hold four.

Smoking is now illegal in all restaurants except where there is a designated smoking area that meets stringent regulations.

Booking is recommended for Friday or Saturday evening or Sunday lunch, even in the more humble-looking places.

Pizza
Traditional Roman pizza is thin; Neapolitan pizza is puffier. Either way, make sure it comes from a wood-fired oven (*forno a legna*).

Pizza toppings are strictly orthodox: don't expect pineapple. Note that pizza is an evening thing – very few places serve it for lunch.

Wine bars
Neighbourhood *enoteche* (wine shops) and *vini e olii* (wine and oil) outlets have been around in Rome since time immemorial. Recently, a number of upmarket, international-style wine bars have also sprung up, offering snacks and even full meals to go with their wines.

Get the local experience

Over 50 of the world's top destinations available.

Snacks

The city's snack culture lurks in unlikely places, such as the humble *alimentari* (grocer's), where they'll fill a crusty white roll (*rosetta*) or a slice of *pizza bianca* (focaccia) with ham, salami or cheese. *Pizza rustica* outlets serve pizza by the takeaway slab, while most bars have a range of sandwiches and filled rolls on offer.

Vegetarians

Rome has few bona fide vegetarian restaurants, but even in traditional *trattorie* there are plenty of meat-free options to try, from classic *penne all'arrabbiata* (pasta in a tomato and chilli sauce) through to *tonnarelli cacio e pepe* (thick spaghetti with crumbly sheep's cheese and black pepper) to *carciofi alla giudia* (deep-fried artichokes). If you are at all unsure about the ingredients of any dish, ask if it has meat in it ('*c'è la carne?*').

Pasticcerie & gelaterie

Most *pasticcerie* (cake shops) are bars where freshly baked goodies can be consumed *in situ* with a drink, or taken away.

Many bars have a freezer cabinet with a sign promising *produzione artigianale* (home-made ice-cream). This is often a con: it may mean industrial ice-cream mix whipped up on the premises. While this doesn't mean the ice-cream will be bad, you'll need to be selective when seeking a truly unique *gelato* experience (see box p97). If the colours seem too bright to be real, then they aren't. Banana should be creamy-grey, not electric yellow.

As well as the two main choices of *frutta* or *crema* (fruit- or cream-based ice-cream), there's also *sorbetto* or *granita* (water ices). When you've exhausted these, sample a *grattachecca*, a rougher version of water ice.

Drinking

Cafés & bars

The average Roman starts his or her day with a coffee in a local café or bar (in Italy these amount to the same thing, since alcohol and coffee are served all day long in both). They will also have snacks, maybe cigarettes and bus tickets, and fabulous, cheap coffee.

In the touristy *centro storico*, things are different. Standing at the counter like the locals to knock back your tiny cupful is one thing; but occupy a table or, worse, a pavement table, and the bill will double or even treble. Of course, there are moments when nothing is more beguiling than sitting outside with a view of the Pantheon; just be aware you'll pay for the luxury.

Besides the many variations of *caffè* (espresso) and cappuccino, most bars offer *cornetti* (croissants), *tramezzini* (sandwiches) and *panini* (filled rolls; one is a *panino*). A small bottle of still or sparkling mineral water (*acqua minerale naturale* or *gassata*) costs around €1.

By law, all bars must have a *bagno* (lavatory), which can be used by anyone, whether or not they purchase anything. Bars must also provide dehydrated passers-by with a glass of tap water, free and with no obligation to buy. Smoking is forbidden inside all bars and cafés.

Pubs & enoteche

Many of Rome's *enoteche* and *vini e olii* have recently become charming places to grab a drink and a slice of the *vita romana*. Some of these are chic venues with a *dopocena* (after-dinner) scene and a beautiful, see-and-be-seen crowd.

Rome's pubs are divided between a handful of long-standing British- and Irish-style institutions and a host of newer casual joints.

Galleria Alberto Sordi

Shopping

Shopping habits among Romans have changed considerably in recent years, as locals head in droves for outlet malls in the city's hinterland peddling cut-price designer names. Regular malls with high-street fashion and household brands, plus the odd hypermarket or two, are also increasingly popular. And yet, Rome's *centro storico* shopping streets continue to teem with people. In the Eternal City, there's something for all tastes.

As a visitor, you'll probably shop exclusively in the *centro*, where the first thing that will strike you is the dearth of malls and familiar chains (give or take a Benetton or two). Instead, there are corner grocery shops, dark and dusty bottle-lined wine shops, one-off boutiques catering to every imaginable taste… and, of course, the opulent outlets of Italy's fashion aristocracy.

Traditionalists can draw comfort from the fact that, for now, tiny boutiques and family-run stores are managing to retain their presence in Rome's retail sector. Just.

Because, in fact, the 'uniqueness' of Rome's shopping is skin-deep. Here, as elsewhere, the corner shop is being driven out by big-name mini-markets; there *are* clothing chains – it's just that they have different names here; and major international brands are colonising the Roman high street at a distressing pace.

Where to shop

Milan retains its crown as fashion centre, but the Eternal City is

SHORTLIST

Clothes with class
- Abito – Le Gallinelle (see p107)
- Arsenale (see p83)
- Maga Morgana (see p83)
- Momento (see p76)
- Le Tartarughe (see p83)
- Tina Sondergaard (see p107)

Divine confectionery
- Moriondo e Gariglio (see p83)
- Valzani (see p136)
- Vino e Cioccolata (see p132)

Flea (etc) markets
- Micca Market at Micca Club (see p114)
- Porta Portese (see p136)
- La Soffitta Sotto i Portici (see p91)
- Testaccio (see p125)
- Via Sannio (see p113)

Produce markets
- Campo de' Fiori (see p67)
- Ex-Piazza Vittorio (see p107)
- Testaccio (see p125)

Reading matter
- Almost Corner Bookshop (see p136)
- Feltrinelli International (see p107)
- Libreria del Cinema (see p136)
- Palazzo delle Esposizioni – basement shop (see p101)

Shoe heaven
- Borini (see p74)
- Loco (see p76)

Take-home treats
- Bottega dei sapori della legalità (see p91)
- Castroni (see p150)
- Città dell'Altra Economia (see p125)
- Volpetti (see p125)

unquestionably a more picturesque place to shop. The major Italian names in *alta moda* are huddled around piazza di Spagna and via Condotti, in the Tridente. The main streets are often packed, so instead wind your way through the pretty side streets and check out the smaller – though rarely less costly – boutiques dotted around. Slicing through the Tridente from piazza del Popolo to piazza Venezia is via del Corso, which is home to mid-range outlets for everything from books and music to clothing and shoes.

Further south along via del Corso, the Galleria Alberto Sordi, a restored early 20th-century arcade, is one of the *centro*'s prime shopping and meeting points. As well as the 20 retail outlets, there are a couple of *aperitivo* bars and frequent 'happenings' of a musical and artistic nature, all under one beautifully coloured glass roof.

There are more high-street clothing retailers along traffic-clogged via Nazionale; while

Campo de' Fiori p67

this street itself is no charmer, the nearby Monti neighbourhood packs in a decent selection of boutiques and hip originals.

Across the river, beneath the Vatican walls in the Prati area, via Cola di Rienzo is a shorter and marginally less crowded version of via del Corso, with major retail chains and some great food shopping.

For independent designers and a look at the city's best vintage gear, on the other hand, you need to head west of piazza Navona to via del Governo Vecchio.

In order to sample those outlet malls, you'll need your own car. The largest are Castel Romano (www.mcarthurglen.it/castel romano) south of the city, Valmontone Fashion District (www.fashiondistrict.it) off the A1 motorway heading south, and Soratte Outlet (www.soratte outlet.it) off the A1 motorway just north of Rome.

Opening times

Many Rome shop owners forgo the sacred siesta in favour of '*no-stop*' opening hours, from around 10am to 7.30pm, Monday to Saturday. The odd independent still clings to the 1-4pm shutdown. In the centre, lots of stores now open on Sundays.

Times given in this guide are winter opening hours; in summer (June to September), shops that opt for long lunches tend to reopen later, at say 5.30pm, until around 8pm. Most food stores close on Thursday afternoons in winter, and Saturday afternoons in summer. The majority of non-food shops are closed Monday mornings. Many shops shut for at least two weeks in summer (usually in August) and almost all are shut for two or three days around the 15 August public holiday. If you want to avoid finding a particular shop *chiuso per ferie* (closed for holidays), be sure to ring ahead.

Service has improved a little, but many shop assistants still seem hell-bent on either ignoring or intimidating customers. This is no time for Anglo-Saxon reticence; perfect the essential lines *'Mi può aiutare, per favore?'* ('Can you help me, please?') and *'Volevo solo dare un' occhiata'* ('I'm just looking') and you're ready for any eventuality.

For bargains, visit during the sales: prices drop for six weeks from 6 January, and from the first Saturday in July.

Prices & paying

Italians bemoan the advent of the penury-inducing euro, but for Brits with much-devalued pounds, Italy may seem even more expensive than it does for euro-wielders. Home-grown designer names are still a little easier on the wallet here than abroad, however. Haggling belongs firmly at the flea market.

You should always be given a *scontrino* (receipt). If you aren't,

then ask for it: by law, shops must provide one, and they and you are liable for a fine in the (wildly unlikely) event of your being caught without it. Major credit cards are accepted just about everywhere, but do check before getting to a till.

The rules on returning purchases are infuriatingly vague. Faulty goods, obviously, must be refunded or replaced. Many shops will also accept unwanted goods that are returned unused with a receipt within seven days of purchase, though this is not obligatory.

Tax rebates

Non-EU residents are entitled to a sales tax (IVA) rebate on purchases of personal goods worth over €155, if they are bought from a shop with the 'Europe Tax Free' sticker. The shop will give you a receipt and a 'Tax Free Shopping Cheque', which should be stamped by customs before leaving Italy.

Libreria del Cinema p136

The Place p150

Nightlife

After a bright start to the millennium, Rome's arts and entertainment scenes have entered a less jubilant phase as the damper cast by the city's new right-wing administration – especially over anything vaguely 'alternative' – begins to be felt: it's not a good time for experimental endeavours in the Eternal City.

Nonetheless, those few years of frenetic activity have left the city an important heritage. Highbrow entertainment continues to thrive, especially around the Auditorium (see p99). And there are still plenty of opportunities for dancing to the best international DJs and hearing the latest bands. You will, however, need some inside information to avoid the Eurotrash dished out by the plethora of commercial venues.

Where to go, when to go

Compulsory closing times forcing most *centro storico* bars to shut up shop at 2am have cancelled the unwritten 'open until the last punter stumbles out of the door' rule that long gave Roman nights their relaxed feel.

Discos and live venues still stay open until the small hours, though, allowing Romans to maintain their habit of starting the evenings late and ending them even later.

Rome's nightlife venues tend to be concentrated around a few easily accessible areas.

In Testaccio, nightlife action happens around Monte Testaccio (see p120): just walk around until you find the vibe you're after.

The area around via Libetta, off via Ostiense, teems with trendy clubs and will, one day, become even more crowded: the whole area is (very) slowly being developed as an arts hub.

Fashionistas head for the *centro storico*: spend an evening in the *triangolo della Pace* around via della Pace and you're part of trendy Roman life. The campo de' Fiori area, once another fashionista meeting spot, has become increasingly chaotic and, as the evening progresses, it gets seriously squalid.

Trastevere has lovely alleys packed with friendly, crowded bars, where English is the lingua franca. Note, though, that around piazza Trilussa, it can get pretty seedy in the wee hours.

Slightly further from the *centro*, artsy, studenty San Lorenzo is altogether less pretentious: drinks are cheaper, and there's always something interesting going on.

Not far from here, but further out still, is Il Pigneto (see p116), fast becoming Rome's hippest nighttime hang-out. With only a couple of clubs – Circolo degli Artisti (see p116) and Fanfulla 101 (via Fanfulla da Lodi 101, www.fanfulla.org) – the real attractions here are the great restaurants, late-night bars and vibrant atmosphere. Don't hang about too late though: it's a tough area, and after 2am you may be made to feel unwelcome.

Clubbing

When picking a club, bear in mind that many of Rome's mainstream venues play commercial house or 1980s retro on Fridays and Saturdays. Established places such as Goa (see p127), La Saponeria (see p127) and Micca Club (see p114) offer high-quality DJ sets; the focus in the last is on 1950s and '60s beats.

For something a little more alternative, try dancing the night away at Screamadelica (Saturday at Circolo degli Artisti, see p116), where global live acts are topped by DJs playing rock, pop and indie. On Tuesdays, DJ Andrea Esu and international guests spin their electro-house and tech sounds at L-Ektrica (Akab, see p125).

Muccassasina at Qube p116

Vintage enthusiasts strike gold at Twiggy, Rome's best '60s night, where Italy's top bands introduce DJs Luzy L and Corry X (usually at Mads, see p115, but check www.myspace.com/twiggy60sparty for updates). Micca Club (see p114) changes its events frequently but whatever's happening, it's bound to include gigs and DJ sets.

Going live

Eclectic programming at the Auditorium – Parco della Musica (see p99) has helped to seduce music-shy Romans into making live sounds a regular diary fixture.

But Rome's live-music scene is also being boosted by a string of smallish clubs. In 2005, the city-sponsored Casa del Jazz (see p120) opened in a villa confiscated from a local mobster. The cool Teatro Palladium (see p127) hosts a daring programme too. And City Hall continues – for the moment – to fund the prestigious RomaEuropa Festival (see p40), although the right-wing administration seems slightly less willing to stump up for free mega-concerts in grand settings than its predecessor.

Concerts by huge international names are rare, but when they do happen, it's often in atmosphere-lacking mega-venues such as the Stadio Olimpico (see p99) or the PalaLottomatica in the suburb of EUR (see p155).

Until not so long ago, much of Rome's alternative live action centred on very low-cost events hosted by *centri sociali* – disused buildings that were occupied by dissatisfied youth and transformed into spaces for art, music and politics. Of the remaining few in the city centre, the very active Villaggio Globale (www.vglobale.biz) in Testaccio offers a good programme of live events.

SHORTLIST

Alternative happenings
- Dimmidisi (see p115)
- Locanda Atlantide (see p115)
- Villaggio Globale (see left)

Going live
- Circolo degli Artisti (see p116)
- Dimmidisi (see p115)
- Mads (see p115)

Late late bars
- Al Vino al Vino (see p105)
- Caffè della Pace (see p81)
- Ombre Rosse (see p136)
- Oppio Café (see p107)
- Salotto 42 (see p82)

Dance 'til you drop
- Akab (see p125)
- Alpheus (see p127)
- Anima (see p83)
- Micca Club (see p114)
- La Saponeria (see p127)

Best gay venues
- Coming Out (see p114)
- Hangar (see p108)
- Skyline (see p114)

Best gay one-nighters
- Gorgeous I Am at Alpheus (Sat; see p127)
- Muccassasina at Qube (Fri; see p116)
- Omogenic at Circolo degli Artisti (Fri; see p116)
- The Venus Rising at Goa (women-only, last Sun of month; see p127)

Jazz, Latin & blues
- Alexanderplatz (see p150)
- Big Mama (see p138)
- Caruso-Café de Oriente (see p127)
- Gregory's (see p95)
- The Place (see p150)

Summer in the city

Rome gives its best during the long summer: you'll be spoilt for choice between festivals, concerts, open-air cinema, theatre and discos, most of which come under the Estate Romana (see p38) umbrella.

Gay Rome

Rome's gay community has been on an emotional roller-coaster over the past few years: civil unions almost became a reality, then didn't – thanks, many suspect, to Vatican intervention. And a traditionally gay-friendly (or at least gay-tolerant) attitude has been clouded by some truly nasty attacks – arson and otherwise – on the gay community and its favourite haunts.

Undaunted, gay life in the capital goes on, and continues to be mainstream, with new venues, organisations and facilities popping up. The historic Mario Mieli (www. mariomieli.org) group, flanked by the newer, hyperactive Di'Gay Project (www.digayproject.org), continues to add more social goodies to the shopping trolley.

Likewise, the gay going-out scene continues to diversify and cater for distinct clienteles, with restaurants, pubs, clubs and bars attracting punters of all ages. A proliferation of mixed one-nighters also mirrors the increasing number of places where men and women can have fun under the same roof. Or, for that matter, outdoors: one of the most notable successes in the Roman calendar – despite obstructionism from City Hall – is the summer Gay Village (see p38). The website (www.gayvillage.it) is also a great source of year-round events info.

Many gay venues ask for an Arcigay card (€15 for annual membership). The card can be bought at any participating venue.

Getting in

Getting into Rome's fashionable mainstream clubs can be stressful, no matter how well you're dressed. Intimidating bouncers block your way, while PR luvvies smirk as they whisk supposed VIPs past lines of frustrated would-be clients. But persistence and patience will get you in eventually.

Clubs and disco-bars generally charge an entrance fee at weekends but not on weekdays; be aware that on your first visit you will often have to buy a *tessera* (membership card) on top of, or sometimes instead of, the entrance fee. Tickets often include a 'free' drink, but you can expect the drinks you buy thereafter to be pricey. Another popular formula is to grant 'free' admission while forcing you to buy a (generally expensive) drink. To get out again you have to hand a stamped drink card to the bouncer, so hold on to whatever piece of paper staff give you or you'll be forced to pay twice.

Where we haven't specified a price for entrance, admission is free.

Finding out

For details of upcoming events, consult the listings magazines *Trovaroma* (Thursday with *La Repubblica*), *Roma C'è* (Wednesday) or *Zero6* (monthly, free in shops and pubs; http://roma.zero.eu). Or visit www.romastyle.info, which is good for techno and drum 'n' bass, and http://roma.2night.it or www.musicaroma.it for the latest gigs. Fans of indie and punk rock should take a look at www.myspace.com/romecityrockers and www.pogopop.it (in English, after a fashion).

Rome International Film Festival p31

WHAT'S BEST

Arts & Leisure

A spell of big arts spending after the turn of the millennium has now tailed off, with a less culture-friendly mayor installed in City Hall, and the national government cutting arts funding at a terrifying rate. Still, the after-effects of that golden age are still being felt, and Rome continues to offer a reasonably healthy selection of performing arts options.

Fine arts – of the contemporary, commercial variety – shifted up through several gears when top art dealer Larry Gagosian opened a gallery here in 2007. Now, with the inauguration in 2010 of the extraordinary MAXXI (see p99) and the hugely enlarged MACRO (see p99), the contemporary art scene is being given the kind of attention never before received in the Eternal City.

Music

If Rome still enjoys a place on the music-lovers' map of Europe, this is thanks mainly to activities at the Auditorium – Parco della Musica (see p99).

Inaugurated in 2002, this huge complex of exhibition and concert spaces, designed by Renzo Piano, has been immensely successful, enticing Romans of all tastes with a programme of such dazzling breadth it is second only to New York's Lincoln Center for the variety of its offerings. This democratic eclecticism has cast its spell over citizens who had never previously set foot in a classical music venue in their lives.

But it is not the only venue in Rome for music. Many of the more traditional concert halls and locations also benefited from the surge of energy, and many of them offer high-quality programmes.

Opera is one branch of the arts that continues to languish, with dull programmes and generally rather mediocre productions. But like many other musical offerings in Rome, the settings for opera – the Teatro dell'Opera (see p108) and the Baths of Caracalla (see p117), where the summer season is staged – are so glorious that the quality doesn't always matter.

La Stravaganza (06 7707 2842, www.lastravaganzamusica.it) organises delightful chamber music concerts in the throne room of the Palazzo Doria Pamphilj (see p77). On Sundays, there are noon recitals in the sumptuous Cappella Paolina of the president's residence, Palazzo del Quirinale (see p96). There are also frequent concert seasons at the Museo Nazionale degli Strumenti Musicali (piazza Santa Croce in Gerusalemme 9A, 06 701 4796, www.museostrumentimusicali.it); during some performances, items from the museum's collection of antique instruments are played. And at the church of Sant'Anselmo (piazza Cavalieri di Malta 5) on the Aventine, Benedictine monks sing Gregorian chant evensong daily at 7.15pm. All musical events held in churches, and many held elsewhere, are free.

Theatre

If you're thinking of an evening at the theatre, don't expect daring performances: the Italian school of drama, with its stiff style imposed by the stuffy dramatic arts academy, still holds sway.

One interesting project is the Casa dei Teatri (06 4544 0707, www.casadeiteatri.culturaroma.it), in a *palazzo* in the Villa Pamphili

RomaEuropa

public park. This centre integrates performances with workshops and research. The Teatro India (www.teatrodiroma.net), and the Teatro Palladium (see p127), both in the southern suburbs, can be relied on to come up with more challenging performances.

Dance

This Cinderella of Italian arts is allowed out of the kitchen more often nowadays, and features in seasonal programmes and festivals such as RomaEuropa (see p40).

Galleries

Rome's commercial contemporary art world has been striving for some time to rival Turin and Naples, with limited success. But Larry 'Gogo' Gagosian's temple to art dealing on via Francesco Crispi (no.16, www.gagosian.com) draws the occasional international buyer.

Film

Italian dubbers are recognised as the world's best, but that's little consolation if you like to see films in the original language (*lingua originale* or *versione originale* – VO in listings). Little is left untampered with, but there are a handful of cinemas where some VO offerings appear on programmes. The Nuovo Olimpia (see p91), just off via del Corso, is the best bet for recent releases. There are VO screenings at the Alcazar (via Merry del Val 14, Monday) and at the Nuovo Sacher (largo Ascianghi 1, Monday and/ or Tuesday). The Warner Village Moderno (piazza Repubblica 43-45) also hosts the occasional blockbuster in VO.

The Casa del Cinema (largo M Mastroianni 1, www.casadel cinema.it), inside Villa Borghese (see p91), screens an interesting selection of films for free.

Rome's annual film festival, Festa Internazionale del Film di Roma (aka Rome International Film Festival; see p40), launched in 2006 and held in October, provides a good chance to catch some pre-release treats.

Sport

Many Romans have an aversion to physical activity, but they are passionate supporters of sport.

Rome is home to two first-class football clubs: AS Roma (www. asroma.it) and SS Lazio (www. sslazio.it). The two teams share the Stadio Olimpico (see p99). Buy tickets from www.listicket.it or specialist outlets.

Since 2000, the national rugby side has been in the Six Nations' Championship, with home games played at the Stadio Flaminio (viale Tiziano, 06 3685 7309, www.federugby.it).

SHORTLIST

Alfresco music
- Roma Incontra il Mondo world music festival (see p38)
- Teatro dell'Opera Summer Season (see p38)
- Villa Celimontana Jazz Festival (see p38)

Eclectic offerings
- Auditorium – Parco della Musica (see p99)
- Teatro Palladium (see p127)

Unmissable festivals
- Estate Romana (see p38)
- RomaEuropa Festival (see p40)
- Rome International Film Festival (see p40)

Films in English
- Alcazar (see left)
- Nuovo Olimpia (see p91)
- Nuovo Sacher (see left)

Virtual Rome
- Palazzo Valentini (see p63)
- Rewind Rome (see p108)
- Terme di Diocleziano (see p101)
- Time Elevator (see p78)

Sensuous spas
- Acquamadre (see p76)
- Kamispa (see p99)

Sporting fixtures
- Football at the Stadio Olimpico (see p99)
- Rugby at the Stadio Flaminio (see left)

Theatre & opera
- Teatro dell'Opera di Roma (see p108)
- Teatro India (see p30)
- Teatro Palladium (see p127)

DON'T MISS

WHAT'S ON
Calendar

Romans love their holidays, and are experts at making the best of whatever spare time comes their way. Any crisp, sunny winter weekend is good for a *scampagnata* (jaunt to the countryside); a mid-week public holiday can be made into a lengthy break by doing what is known as *un ponte* (a bridge), or taking off the days between the holiday and the nearest weekend. If the current ten annual public holidays look rather paltry next to the ancient Romans' 150 (see box p34), citizens of the Eternal City will make them feel like far, far more.

Religious holidays (and the Easter week in particular) turn the city centre into a heaving mass of visiting humanity; only *Ferragosto* (the Assumption) on 15 August shuts the city down. Different districts of Rome hold smaller-scale celebrations of their own patron saints in their own way, from calorific blowouts and costume parades to extravagant fireworks displays.

Throughout the year, Rome offers small-scale independent festivals and big-budget citywide events that make ample use of the city's seemingly endless supply of photogenic venues.

Keep an eye on local press and posters for the occasional huge free concert, and also major exhibitions, which tend to be announced at short notice. The websites of the cultural heritage ministry (www.beniculturali.it), the Rome city council (www. comune.roma.it), the city's official information site (www.060608.it) and the Rome tourist board (www.turismoroma.it) are all useful sources of information.

Dates highlighted in **bold** are public holidays.

Rome Marathon p37

Roman holidays

If you've ever tried to calculate with Roman numerals, you will know just how complicated the ancients made some aspects of their lives. The Roman calendar was no simpler.

The day of the new moon, the first of the month, was *kalends* (hence our word calendar); *nones* fell about seven days later, on the quarter moon; the full moon, between 13 and 15 days into the month, was *ides*. All other days were counted up to or down from these.

Romans had no weeks (or weekends) until early in the Christian era but official calendars, posted in public places, assigned functions to certain days: market days, trial days, voting days and feast days... many, many feast days.

In Febuary, Lupercalia allowed strapping youths to run through the streets dressed in nothing but skins from sacrificed goats, whipping by-standers to banish impurity and infertility.

In May, Bona Dea fertility celebrations led by Vestal Virgins gave Rome's women the chance to do their own sacrificing (usually reserved for men) and consume a lot of strong wine.

In September, the *Ludi romani* (Roman games) saw factions face off in chariot races, and the city's youth compete for a laurel crown in horseback, running and boxing events.

During Saturnalia in December, slaves could cheek their masters (within reason), eat in their masters' presence and indulge in forbidden activities such as gambling.

January

1 Capodanno
New Year's Day.

6 Epifania – La Befana
Piazza Navona (see p79)
From mid December all the way to Epiphany itself, piazza Navona hosts a Christmas fair, with market stalls peddling sweets and cheap tat. The fair is dedicated to *La Befana* – a present-bearing old witch – who brings Epiphany treats for all the children.

17 Sant'Eusebio
Sant'Eusebio, via Napoleone III
Animal lovers have pets blessed.

February

Feb/Mar (date varies) **Carnevale**
Around the city centre
In the Middle Ages, this riotous last fling before the rigours of Lent was celebrated with wild abandon on Monte Testaccio. Nowadays, kids dress up and throw confetti.

March

9 Feast of Santa Francesca Romana
Monastero Oblate di Santa Francesca Romana, via Teatro di Marcello 32 & 40
A rare opportunity to visit this medieval nunnery; Romans have cars blessed at Santa Francesca Romana church in the Roman Forum.

16 Palazzo Massimo alle Colonne
Corso Vittorio Emanuele 141
Once-a-year opening of the patrician Massimi family's fabulous palace, 8am-1pm.

19 Feast of San Giuseppe
Around via Trionfale
Partying and batter-ball eating in this northern district to mark St Joseph's day. In the run-up to the feast, the city's *pasticcerie* are piled high with the deep-fried batter-balls.

Gay Village p38

Rome International Film Festival p40

DON'T MISS

Late Mar **Maratona della Città di Roma**
Around the city centre
www.maratonadiroma.it
The marathon begins and ends in via dei Fori Imperiali. There's a 5km fun-run for those not up to the whole 42km. The race is usually held on the third Sunday of the month.

Late Mar **Giornate FAI**
Various locations
www.fondoambiente.it
For one weekend each spring, the Fondo per l'Ambiente Italiano (FAI) persuades private and institutional owners of interesting historic properties to throw open the spectacular interiors to the public.

April

21 **Natale di Roma**
Campidoglio (see p58)
Rome celebrates its birthday (its 2,765th in 2012) with an immense display of fireworks.

1-8 Apr **Settimana Santa & Pasqua (Holy Week & Easter)**
Vatican (see p145), Colosseum (see p58)
Tourists and pilgrims flood into the city. Easter festivities include the Pope's Via Crucis at the Colosseum on the evening of Good Friday, and papal masses at St Peter's on both Palm and Easter Sundays.

25 Liberation Day

Late Apr **Mostra delle Azalee**
Piazza di Spagna (see p89)
Spring arrives early in Rome, bringing masses of blooms. Some 3,000 vases of vividly hued azaleas decorate the Spanish Steps.

Mid/late Apr **Settimana della Cultura**
www.beniculturali.it
For one week only in April, all state-owned museums are free to visit, and many otherwise closed sites are open. Dates vary from year to year.

May

1 Primo Maggio
Piazza San Giovanni
www.primomaggio.com
Trade unions organise a huge, free rock concert for May Day.

May-July **Cosmophonies**
www.cosmophonies.com
Roman Theatre, Ostia Antica
(see p156)
World music, light entertainment and opera amid the ruins: the 2010 edition included Patti Smith and Jethro Tull.

Mid May-June **Rome Literature Festival**
Basilica di Massenzio, Roman Forum (see p63)
www.festivaldelleletterature.it
Book launches and readings from Italian and international names.

Mid May-late June **Roseto Comunale**
Via Valle Murcia/clivo dei Pubblici
The annual opening of Rome's municipal rose garden on the Aventine hill.

Late May **Piazza di Siena**
Piazza di Siena, Villa Borghese
(see p91)
www.piazzadisiena.com
The city's ultra-smart four-day show-jumping event.

June

Ongoing Cosmophonies (see May); Rome Literature Festival (see May); Roseto Comunale (see May).

Early June-end Sept **Estate Romana**
Various locations
www.estateromana.comune.roma.it
Piazze, palazzi and parks come alive with music, and films are shown on outdoor screens. Many events are free.

Early June-Aug **Villa Celimontana Jazz Festival**
Villa Celimontana (see p108)
www.villacelimontanajazz.com

A series of summer jazz concerts takes place beneath the trees of this lovely park; check online for concert times and ticket prices.

Mid June-early Aug **Roma Incontra il Mondo**
Villa Ada, via di Ponte Salario
www.villaada.org
World music is performed by the lake in this park in the northern suburbs; in 2010, Devendra Banhart, Mulatu Astatke, and Toots and the Maytals were among the truly global line-up.

Mid June-mid Aug **Fiesta!**
Via Appia Nuova 1245
www.fiesta.it
A vibrant Latin American music festival, held at the Capanelle racecourse near Ciampino.

Late June-early Sept **Gay Village**
Venue varies
www.gayvillage.it
A ten-week open-air bonanza with bars, restaurants, live acts, discos and cinema, for boys and girls. The venue moves from year to year: check the website or Facebook page.

Late June-mid Aug **Teatro dell'Opera Summer Season**
Baths of Caracalla (see p117)
www.operaroma.it
Rome's opera company stages grand performances in these Roman ruins.

29 Santi Pietro e Paolo
Basilica di San Paolo fuori le Mura (see p122)
Street fair outside St Paul's basilica and mass at St Peter's for the feast day of Rome's patron saints.

July

Ongoing Cosmophonies (see May); Estate Romana (see June); Villa Celimontana Jazz Festival (see June); Roma Incontra il Mondo (see June); Gay Village (see June); Fiesta! (see June); Teatro dell'Opera Summer Season (see June).

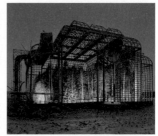

FotoGrafia p40

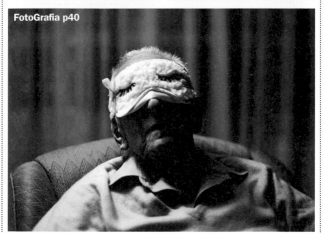

Mid July **Festa di Noantri**
Piazza Santa Maria in Trastevere,
piazza Mastai
Two weeks of arts events, street performances and fairground attractions.

August

Ongoing Estate Romana (see June);
Villa Celimontana Jazz Festival
(see June); Roma Incontra il Mondo
(see June); Gay Village (see June);
Fiesta! (see June); Teatro dell'Opera
Summer Season (see June).

1 **Festa delle Catene**
San Pietro in Vincoli (see p104)
The chains that bound St Peter are dis-
played in a special mass.

5 **Festa della Madonna della Neve**
Santa Maria Maggiore (see p104)
A blizzard of rose petals flutters down
on festive mass-goers to commemorate
a miraculous snowfall on this day in
AD 358.

10 **Notte di San Lorenzo**
San Lorenzo in Panisperna,
via Panisperna 90
Nuns distribute bread and candles on
this, the night of shooting stars.

15 **Ferragosto**
Rome closes down for the feast of the
Assumption. Many locals head to the
coast for the long weekend.

September

Ongoing Estate Romana (see June);
Gay Village (see June).

Sept-Oct **FotoGrafia**
Various locations
www.fotografiafestival.it
Rome's international festival of photography was threatened by funding cuts
in 2009, but struggles on nonetheless.

Sept-Dec **RomaEuropa Festival**
Various locations
www.romaeuropa.net
Rome's most prestigious performing
arts festival.

October

Ongoing FotoGrafia (see Sept);
RomaEuropa Festival (see Sept).

Late Oct **Mostra dell'Antiquariato**
Via de' Coronari
This busy antiques fair is always
packed with dealers.

Oct-Nov **Rome International Film Festival**
Auditorium – Parco della Musica
(see p99) and other venues
www.romacinemafest.org
Ten days of screenings and movie-
related happenings at Rome's international film festival.

November

Ongoing RomaEuropa Festival
(see Sept); Rome International
Film Festival (see Oct).

1-2 **All Saints/All Souls**
Cimitero del Verano
Romans visit family graves at this
cemetery behind the basilica of San
Lorenzo fuori le Mura (see p114).

December

Ongoing RomaEuropa Festival
(see Sept).

8 **Immacolata Concezione**
Piazza di Spagna (see p89)
The pope blesses a wreath and sends a
fireman up his ladder to hang it on the
statue of Mary for the feast of the
Immaculate Conception. At the base of
the statue, the locals deposit their own
elaborate floral tributes.

25-26 **Natale & Santo Stefano**
Nativity scenes in churches; Christmas
fair in piazza Navona (see p79).

31 **San Silvestro**
Free concert in piazza del Popolo and
other free events – check local press
for details; much street partying,
and fireworks and *spumante* corks
shooting off roofs at midnight.

Itineraries

Villa Borghese p45

Rome on Film

In the heady, glamorous *dolce vita* days of the 1950s and '60s, Rome was known as 'Hollywood on the Tiber'. So down by the river, on the **Ponte Sant'Angelo** (see p141), is where we shall start our four-hour walk. From what is arguably the city's most stunning bridge, you get views of Castel Sant' Angelo – the great papal castle built atop Emperor Hadrian's circular mausoleum, while in the distance the dome of St Peter's rises above the medieval Borgo.

Peer over the stone balustrade of the bridge, between Bernini's teams of stone angels, and you'll see a surprisingly rural scene: people fishing, cormorants, ducks, rowers and the odd pleasure boat. Until the 1960s Romans swam from a popular bathing station beneath the ancient bridge. In *Accattone* (1961) Pier Paolo Pasolini's juvenile delinquent makes the sign of the cross before diving off the bridge for a dare.

With real-life drama going on around them in the street, neo-realist directors saw no reason to film in gloomy studios. As a result, almost every corner of this cinematic city has served as a backdrop to one masterpiece or another. When the American studios piled into post-war Rome to make escapist romantic comedies or huge historical sword-and-sandal epics, the city turned into one gigantic cinema lot.

Even today, you are likely to stumble across film-set paraphernalia on Rome's streets: racks of costumes, coils of cables, banks of lights and a generator or two, and a tightly curtained star's trailer. Admittedly, there are more commercials filmed here these days than blockbusters, but big-name stars are also enticed into spending the odd seductive week here.

Cross the busy embankment as you head south off Ponte Sant' Angelo and take via del Panico.

At the far end of this short cobbled street stands the massive bulk of the forbidding **Palazzo Taverna**, chosen by director Jane Campion as the Roman home of heiress Isabel Archer (Nicole Kidman) in *Portrait of a Lady* (1996). If you can, smile sweetly at the porter who guards the main gateway on the corner of via dei Monte Giordano and via degli Orsini, and take a peek at the pretty garden in the courtyard.

Turn right down via degli Orsini towards little piazza dell'Orologio ('clock square', and there is, indeed, a clock on the *palazzo*), and left into via del Governo Vecchio with its wine bars and chic boutiques. At the piazza Pasquino end of the street is the excellent cinema bookshop, **Libreria Altroquando** (via del Governo Vecchio 80, www.altroquando.com), where you can stock up on movie memorabilia and screenplays.

Go left into via Santa Maria dell'Anima, then right beneath the medieval tower on the corner with via Tor Millina, which leads into spectacular **piazza Navona** (see p79). Behind one of the windows on the square here, Vittorio De Sica shot a crucial part of his box-office hit *Ieri, Oggi e Domani* (1963). No red-blooded Italian male could resist this famous scene in which Sophia Loren performs a light-hearted striptease for Marcello Mastroianni in an apartment on the piazza. One of the balconies overlooking the piazza was also used in the film, though it's not easy to decide which.

Cut across piazza Navona and negotiate the traffic on corso Rinascimento. Then, keeping the Italian Senate building Palazzo Madama to your left, duck down via dei Staderari.

Through piazza Sant'Eustachio, the street of the same name leads into piazza della Rotonda, home to the **Pantheon** (see p79). It was in front of this splendid bit of antiquity that a banquet was laid out in Peter Greenaway's film *Belly of an Architect* (1987).

Walk past the Pantheon and head down via dei Pastini to **piazza di Pietra**. Michelangelo Antonioni's movie *L'Eclisse* (*The Eclipse*, 1962), starring Monica Vitti and Alain Delon, has

Ponte Sant'Angelo

Trevi Fountain

memorable scenes set in what used to be Rome's stock exchange, spectacularly inserted into the colonnaded ruins of the Roman temple to the deified Emperor Hadrian in this very attractive pedestrianised square. On piazza di Pietra, the cinema-themed **Café Fandango** – owned by an Italian producer-distributor – is a good coffee or lunch stop.

Cut down via dei Bergamaschi into piazza Colonna, the political heart of Rome, and from here cross via del Corso to admire the elegant shops of the Galleria

Alberto Sordi, renamed in honour of the great Roman comic actor who died in 2003.

Walk through to the rear of the gallery, turn right into via Santa Maria in Vita and then left into via dei Crociferi. Brace yourself for the staggeringly theatrical scene before you as you emerge from this crowded alleyway and come face to face with the **Trevi Fountain** (see p98), where a key scene from *La Dolce Vita* (1959) was shot. You will be no less amazed by the spectacle than Marcello Mastroianni was, but chances are that no one will be dancing in its waters, as Anita Ekberg so memorably did in Federico Fellini's masterpiece. Resist the temptation to emulate the buxom Swede: wading, swimming, and dancing in the Trevi fountain are strictly forbidden. The fountain also appeared as a backdrop in the princess-on-the-lam classic, William Wyler's *Roman Holiday* (1953).

We shall draw a veil over the august monument's brief appearance in the Julia Roberts stinker *Eat, Pray, Love* (2010). One of Roberts' good calls in that movie, however, was nipping around the corner to **Il Gelato di San Crispino** (see p98) in via della Panetteria. Follow her example, and set yourself up for the last part of the walk. You might also like to duck into the **Cinema Trevi** (vicolo del Puttarello 25) and pick up the programme for their screenings of Italian classics. Generally speaking, Italy is a dubbers' paradise; foreign films screened in the original language are marked with the letters 'VO' (*versione originale*).

To your right off busy, polluted via del Tritone is the cavernous, thunderous tunnel where the all-important bicycle was stolen in Vittorio de Sica's much-loved

neo-realist Oscar winner *Ladri di Biciclette* (*Bicycle Thieves*, 1948).

Continue up via del Tritone and into piazza Barberini to admire the fine Bernini fountain of the sea god before embarking on a gentle stroll through the very heart of *dolce vita* Rome. The hotels lining broad via Veneto still charge film-star prices, and wannabe movie stars still sit in dark glasses at pavement cafés. But these days you're more likely to find tour groups than A-listers hanging out here.

So try to imagine the boulevard at the height of its fame, when the paparazzi were snapping at Sophia Loren and Frank Sinatra, Gary Cooper and Ava Gardner – Ava's favourite beauty salon, **Femme Sistina** (via Sistina 75), is still going strong nearby if you feel like breaking your walk with a little old-style pampering. Famous watering holes such as Doney's, Café de Paris and Harry's Bar continue to ply their trade. During the **Rome Film Festival** (www.romacinemafest.org), via Veneto buzzes (a little) like the old days when Business Street is held here.

When the glitz palls, walk under the Porta Pinciana arches at the top of the street and cross the busy intersection, making for the entrance to the Villa Borghese park, marked by a pair of enormous stone eagles. A handy park map here points you in the direction of various attractions including the superb **Galleria Borghese** (see p92) with its world-famous art collection, as well as places to rent bikes and rollerskates, and the zoo. Alternatively, you may wish to stop just inside the park and reward yourself with a delicious open-air drink and/or lunch (brunch at the weekend) under the umbrella pines at the Casa del Cinema's **Cinecaffè** (see p94) while you mull over your evening's cinema-going plans.

Piazza del Campidoglio

Magnificent Seven

Millennia of attrition and landscaping have taken their topographical toll, and Rome just isn't as hilly as it used to be. But despite the general levelling, the magnificent seven are still there. And today, as in antiquity, each retains its own particular flavour.

In ancient times, when wheeled vehicles were banned in the city during daylight hours, Romans used to think nothing of covering all seven hills in a day. We would suggest making the route a little easier by hopping on a bus every now and then.

The route given below is just about feasible in a day if you set off early and stop for nothing more than cursory glimpses at churches en route. But unless you take a marathon-runner approach to your sightseeing, you'll want to linger over the Capitoline Museums and other attractions. We recommend taking two days, particularly if there's a show that interests you

at the Scuderie del Quirinale. End your first day by dedicating a fitting amount of time to the Capitoline Museums, then pick up next morning in the Roman Forum.

There's something decidedly stately – even awe-inspiring – about the airy Quirinal (Quirinale) Hill, where important Roman temples gave way to what began as a papal summer palace but later became the pontiff's main residence when the low-lying Vatican proved a little too unsalubrious and indefensible.

Today, Italy's head of state resides in the **Palazzo del Quirinale** (see p96), which overlooks a square graced by Imperial-era statues of the heavenly twins Castor and Pollux. The view over Rome's rooftops, especially at sunset, is quite stunning.

Its centuries-long role as a seat of decision-making and power-broking has given the Quirinale such an imposing aura that it is generally referred to simply as *il colle* (the hill). If a prime minister is reported to be 'going up the hill', his days in office are probably numbered. If 'the hill' issues a pronouncement, the president is bound to be saying something momentous.

You'll need to visit on a Sunday morning if you want a glimpse inside the presidential palace. But the two glorious churches on via del Quirinale – Bernini's **Sant'Andrea al Quirinale** (see p98) and Borromini's **San Carlino alle Quattro Fontane** (see p96) – make the hike up here worthwhile at any time, as do the excellent exhibitions staged in the **Scuderie al Quirinale** (see p98), the palace's magnificent former stables.

Equally important in ancient times, and still the seat of a city council that stamps SPQR (*senatus populusque romanus*) on the rubbish bins and drain covers, the Capitoline (Campidoglio) Hill is a 20-minute walk to the south (or take bus 40, 60, 64, 70 or 170 from nearby via Nazionale to piazza Venezia).

There were temples here to Jupiter Capitolinus and Juno Moneta. The latter stood where the church of **Santa Maria in Aracoeli** (see p65) stands today, at the head of a daunting flight of steps. The former was nearer piazza del Campidoglio itself, which still looks much as Michelangelo designed it in the 1530s. On the south-east side is the Palazzo del Senatorio, Rome's city hall. Flanking this are the stately piles that house the **Capitoline Museums** (see p58).

If you're gasping for a coffee, the cafés in the museum (you can reach the café without going into the museum) and those half-way up the **Vittoriano** monument (see p65) in piazza Venezia are overpriced but have marvellous views. Even more heart-stopping is the panorama from the top of the Vittoriano.

It's a glorious hike from here through the **Roman Forum** (see p64) to the Palatine (Palatino) Hill, where the movers and shakers of ancient Rome partied and schemed in their grand Hollywood-style spreads. It's a green and pleasant spot these days, offering yet more extraordinary views, plus a collection of ruins and a museum –

Santa Maria Maggiore p49

ITINERARIES

Palazzo del Quirinale p46

the **Museo Palatino** (see p64) – that charts Rome's birth pangs, from the time that Remus and Romulus set up camp here. (Keep your ticket to the Forum and Palatine: it is valid for the Colosseum too, and will allow you to bypass the interminable queues there.) Picnicking isn't strictly allowed, but if you're discreet and take your rubbish home with you, this is a wonderful place to break for lunch.

As the crow flies, it's no distance at all from here to the Aventine (Aventino) and Caelian (Celio) Hills. On the ground, it's slightly more complicated. Exit from the Palatine on the via di San Gregorio (east) side. In ten minutes, you can walk to the **Circus Maximus** (see p58) and the Aventine rises beyond. (Buses 75 and 271 do the same route.)

A flash district of wealthy plebs in Roman times, the green, exclusive Aventine still has some of the Eternal City's highest-priced real estate. It also has a spectacular church (**Santa Sabina**, see p120), a lovely park with a great view (Parco Savello) and a keyhole, at the HQ of the Knights of Malta in piazza dei Cavalieri di Malta, through which you can see three sovereign territories: the Knights', Italy and the Vatican.

In the second century BC, a brave group of plebs holed up on the Aventine in an attempt to get parliamentary government restored to Rome. In 1924, 150 politicians stormed out of Mussolini's lower house and 'withdrew to the Aventine', in protest over the assassination of an opposition MP. Italian MPs with their hackles up still threaten to head Aventino-wards from time to time.

The Caelian lies across via di San Gregorio from the Palatine, and straight up the other side.

It's every bit as green as it was in ancient and medieval times, when it was filled with vegetable gardens and orchards, although now it's rather unkempt. You may even have some misgivings about venturing though the wilderness here, but you'll soon hit the Clivio Scauro, which leads past the towering church of **San Gregorio** (see p109) and **Santi Giovanni e Paolo** (see p110), with its Roman street and homes excavated beneath, and on to the welcome cool of the Villa Celimontana park.

Backtrack to via di San Gregorio and pick up the 75 bus to reach the highest point of the Esquiline (Esquilino) Hill, with the basilica of **Santa Maria Maggiore** (see p104) at its apex. This spot has long been dominated by women: before Mary unseated her, it was the goddess Juno who was worshipped here. The rather seedy Esquilino district has been earmarked for a renaissance for many years; it still has some way to go. But the area around Santa Maria Maggiore definitely has its hidden charms, especially in the shape of the sister churches of **Santa Prassede** (see p104) and **Santa Pudenziana** (see p105), hidden in the backstreets.

Tired of all those hills? Well, take comfort from the fact that you'll miss nothing if you skip out the Viminal (Viminale) Hill. For Italians, *il Viminale* is synonymous with the Interior Ministry, with all the various implications of chaos and graft that have accrued to the term over the years. The dreary 1920s *palazzo* that houses the ministry stands out from the streets of similar dreary *palazzi* from the late 19th and early 20th centuries around it only by virtue of its immense size. And here, there's not even a view to redeem it.

ITINERARIES

Galleria Borghese p52

Baroque's Bad Boy

Michelangelo Merisi da Caravaggio (1571-1610), the iconic Bad Boy of the Baroque, burned through the Roman art world like a dangerous, dazzling meteor. A hard-drinking rebel with an uncontrollable temper and, reputedly, a penchant both for women and boys, Rome's greatest painter ended up on the run after murdering a man during a tennis match in campo de' Fiori in 1606. For the next four years he hid out in Naples, Sicily and Malta, only to die of malaria on a beach in Tuscany while waiting for a pardon from the pope. He was 39.

Of the 50 or so paintings by the master to have survived, 22 of the very best hang in Roman churches and galleries. Why not spend a day or two Caravaggio-spotting in hidden corners, glorious Baroque churches and the city's finest galleries? You should start reasonably early in the morning, since Roman churches tend to close their doors on the stroke of noon. Don't forget to phone ahead or go online to secure your ticket to the Galleria Borghese.

We call him Caravaggio after the small town in northern Italy where it was long believed Michelangelo Merisi was born, on 29 September – the feast day of St Michael Archangel. (In fact, it was dicovered not long ago that he was born in Milan.)

The moment it became clear he had talent, Caravaggio set out for Rome – the city of the popes, the papal court and the juiciest commissions. In this boom time for the Eternal City, the best architects were summoned to build palaces and churches, the best painters to decorate them. There were fortunes, and reputations, to be made.

Set yourself up with a *gran caffè* at the **Bar Sant'Eustachio** (see p81) then stroll around the corner into via Dogana Vecchia, where sentry boxes hold smart-uniformed *carabinieri* protecting the rear of the Italian Senate in Palazzo Madama. On corso Rinascimento, examine the Renaissance façade of this magnificent palace, built in 1503 for Giovanni de' Medici, who would later become Pope Leo X. In 1595, this was the residence of Cardinal Francesco del Monte, a cultivated, art-loving millionaire career cardinal, whose live-in staff included Rome's most talented young painters and musicians; Caravaggio lived in a small room on an upper floor.

It was here that he painted his series of paintings featuring musicians with their lutes, and singers – portraits of fellow palazzo interns. In one composition, a well-known book of madrigals by Francesco de Layolle lies open on the table, painted so meticulously that you could play every note of this 16th-century hit tune. In another version of the painting, the madrigal depicted is by French composer Jacques Arcadelt (1515-68), the lyrics 'Vous savez que je vous aime et vous adore… je fus votre' still clearly visible.

It was through Cardinal del Monte that Caravaggio won his first church commission: to decorate a chapel in memory of a cardinal in Rome's French church. Pop back into via Dogana Vecchia, turn left past the magnificent Palazzo Giustiniani (residence of Vincenzo Giustiniani – another patron of the young artist) and into the ornate **San Luigi dei Francesi** (see p79), which contains three of Caravaggio's finest paintings.

Cardinal Matthieu Cointrel (aka Matteo Contarelli) left detailed instructions that the paintings should illustrate particular scenes from the life of St Matthew: *The Calling* (c.1602), where rich tax collector Matthew, shown counting money (note the coin in the brim of his smart black hat), is called by Jesus; and *The Martyrdom* (c.1600) where the saint collapses, watched by a horrified crowd as an angel flies over the executioner's sword. In the central altarpiece (c.1602), another angel of extraordinary elegance hovers above the head of the pensive saint.

Outside the church, turn left past the French bookshop and left again on to via delle Coppelle. The beautiful church of **Sant' Agostino** (see p80), begun in 1420, had recently been modernised when Caravaggio, flush with his success in the French church, was asked to paint a large altarpiece. His shockingly realistic portrayal of the *Madonna of the Pilgrims* (c.1604) unleashed a storm of controversy, not least because of the dirty feet of the impoverished pilgrims seen kneeling before the infant Jesus.

Caravaggio left the Del Monte household in 1601 to live in the grand *palazzo* of the Mattei family (now Palazzo Caetani, set on via delle Botteghe Oscure), near campo de' Fiori. It was here that the painter famously lost his temper during a tennis match and killed his opponent.

It might be tempting to cut across piazza Navona to try to work out the dynamics of the crime while you sit in the campo over an early lunch; but instead, set off north along via della Scrofa (which becomes via Ripetta) towards piazza del Popolo. It's a pleasant ten-minute stroll, past the **mausoleum of Augustus** and **Ara Pacis Museum** (for both, see p85) to the church of **Santa Maria del Popolo** (see p89).

Sit in the sun for a moment at **Rosati** (see p90) with a restorative cappuccino, but don't linger for too long or you'll miss

ITINERARIES

two of Caravaggio's most dramatic canvases: the upside-down *Crucifixion of St Peter* (1601) and the blinding light of the *Conversion of St Paul* (1601) in the Cerasi chapel to the left of the main altar.

If the weather's fine, you could cut down via del Babuino and pick up that picnic basket you cleverly ordered ahead from **GiNa** (see p89), then stroll up the Spanish Steps into the glorious Villa Borghese park. (If you didn't pre-plan, try the **Cinecaffè**; see p94.)

On the far side of the park, Cardinal Scipione Borghese's jewel-like summer house, now the **Galleria Borghese** (see p92), boasts no less than six Caravaggio masterpieces: the dazzling *Boy with a Basket of Fruit* (c.1593), bursting with good health; the greenish *Sick Bacchus* (c.1593); a shocking *David with the Head of Goliath* (c.1610; the blood-spattered head of Goliath is a self-portrait; in fact, some art historians argue that the two figures are portraits of a younger and an older Caravaggio); two devotional studies – an aged, wrinkled *St Jerome in his Study* (1605) and a youthful, naked *St John the Baptist* (1606); and the positively breathtaking *Madonna with Child and St Anne* (1606), painted for St Peter's but rejected by the church authorities.

It's a downhill stroll back through the Porta Pinciana and along café-lined via Veneto.

Unless you're a close personal friend of the aristocratic Ludovisi family (or it's one of those once in a blue moon openings), there is absolutely no chance whatsoever of getting to inspect the weird frescoes (c.1597) Caravaggio painted in the Casino Ludovisi, in via Lombardia off via Veneto. These depict Jupiter, Neptune and Pluto, the sons of Kronos, in startling perspective.

At the far end of the street, in the gloomy church of **Santa Maria della Concezione** (see p94), is a kneeling, brown-robed *St Francis in Meditation* (c.1606), staring intently at a skull very like the ones piled in designs of grotesque artistic fantasy in the monks' crypt beneath the church. The monks would like us to believe that this is a work by *il maestro*; if so, it was the artist on a bad day, and most experts believe it to be a poor copy.

By now, you may be flagging, but if you can summon up the energy, round out your first day of Caravaggio-gazing with a visit to the **Palazzo Barberini** (see p96), which towers over piazza Barberini at the bottom of via Veneto. Inspect the hauntingly introspective *Narcissus* (c.1599) and the *Decapitation of Holofernes* (c.1599), in which a prim, white-smocked Judith calmly saws off her rapist's head with a kitchen knife.

Alternatively (or as part of Day Two), hop on any of the many buses going from piazza Barberini to via del Corso, and make your way to the **Galleria Doria Pamphilj** (see p77). Here, you can see a variant on the young *St John the Baptist* (c.1602), but also a tender *Penitent Magdalene* (c.1597), and one of the finest of all the Rome paintings, *The Rest on the Flight into Egypt* (c.1595). This work features another musical score – a 1519 motet, *Quam pulchra es et quam decora* by Flemish composer Noel Bauldwin – played to lull an exhausted Madonna and her baby; Joseph holds up the music for the fiddle-playing angel.

The morning of a second Caravaggio day could be pleasantly passed at the Pinacoteca in the **Vatican Museums** (see p146), which has a fine *Deposition of Christ* (c.1604). From there, proceed to the **Capitoline Museums** (see p58), which have two Caravaggios: the splendidly sly *Gypsy Fortune Tellers* (c.1594), plus another simpering *St John the Baptist* (c.1602). Enjoy an alfresco lunch on the museum's roof terrace – not a cheap experience, certainly, but one with a view; or join the office-worker crowds at the **Enoteca Provincia Romana** (see p67) by Trajan's column. Then, if you didn't include the Galleria Doria Pamphilj in Day One, this is the time to visit it.

Sant'Agostino p51

Bags packed, milk cancelled, house raised on stilts.

You've packed the suntan lotion, the snorkel set, the stay-pressed shirts. Just one more thing left to do – your bit for climate change. In some of the world's poorest countries, changing weather patterns are destroying lives.

You can help people to deal with the extreme effects of climate change. Raising houses in flood-prone regions is just one life-saving solution.

**Climate change costs lives.
Give £5 and let's sort it *Here & Now***

www.oxfam.org.uk/climate-change

Be Humankind Oxfam

Rome by Area

Il Centro

Il centro archeologico

Rome took a few centuries to transform itself from a huddle of huts on a hill overlooking the River Tiber into the ancient world's most powerful city.

But by the fifth century BC, magnificent palaces had replaced the ninth-century settlement on the **Palatine** hill. The glorious frescoes on display in the **House of Augustus** show the beauty with which wealthy ancients surrounded themselves.

The Palatine overlooked the bustling **Roman Forum** below. It was from here that the Republic – and later the Empire – was run and justice administered, in grandiose buildings around richly decorated public squares. The facing hill – the **Capitoline** – was Rome's most sacred, with imposing temples. Flanking the Roman Forum, successive emperors strove to assert

their own particular importance and munificence in the **Imperial Fora**. Also in this history-packed area, emperors kept public discontent at bay with gory diversions and heart-stopping sports at the **Colosseum** and the **Circus Maximus**.

The Capitoline (Campidoglio) was the site of two major temples; to Jupiter Capitolinus – chunks of which are visible inside the **Capitoline Museums** – and Juno Moneta, 'giver of advice', where the church of **Santa Maria in Aracoeli** now stands.

The splendid piazza that now tops the Capitoline was designed in the 1530s by Michelangelo; the best approach is via the steps called the *cordonata*, also by Michelangelo, with two giant Roman statues of the mythical twins Castor and Pollux at the top. The building directly opposite is Rome's city hall; on either side are the *palazzi* housing the Capitoline Museums.

ROME BY AREA

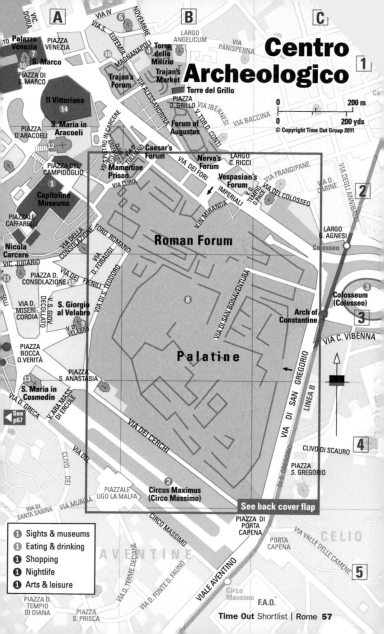

equestrian statue of Marcus ...ius that stands in the centre ...computer-generated replica; the second-century gilded bronze original is inside the museum.

At the bottom of the *cordonata* is piazza Venezia. Dominating this dizzying roundabout is the **Vittoriano**, a vast piece of nationalistic kitsch. Across the piazza, the high-tech display on genteel ancient living in a Roman house excavated below the provincial government HQ, the **Palazzo Valentini**, is excellent.

South of the Capitoline, on low ground by the river, was the *velabrum*, the marshy area where Remus and Romulus were, according to myth, found floating in a basket and then suckled by a she-wolf. Two Republican-age temples still stand here, and the area is dotted with remains of the *forum boarium* and *forum holitorium* (cattle and vegetable markets) that occupied this space.

Sights & museums

Capitoline Museums

Piazza del Campidoglio 1 (06 0608, 06 679 8708, www.museicapitolini.org). **Open** 9am-8pm Tue-Sun. **Admission** €6.50; €4.50 reductions; extra charge during exhibitions. See also p11. **Map** p57 A2 ❶

Housed in two *palazzi* opposite each other on Michelangelo's piazza del Campidoglio, the Capitoline Museums (*Musei capitolini*) are the oldest museums in the world, opened to the public in 1734, though the collection was begun in 1471 by Pope Sixtus IV. His successors continued to add ancient sculptures and, later, paintings.

Entry is through the Palazzo dei Conservatori (to the right at the top of the steps). The courtyard contains parts of a colossal statue of Constantine that originally stood in the Basilica of Maxentius in the Roman Forum. Inside, ancient works are mixed with statues by the Baroque genius Gian Lorenzo Bernini. In room 7 (Sala della Lupa) is a fourth-century BC Etruscan she-wolf and suckling twins (added during the Renaissance).

In a smart modern section on the first floor, the second-century statue of Marcus Aurelius has been given a suitably grand space. Also here are chunks of the Temple of Jupiter.

The second-floor gallery contains paintings by greats such as Titian, Tintoretto and Caravaggio. Across the piazza (or through the underground *Tabularium*, the ancient Capitoline archive building), the Palazzo Nuovo houses one of Europe's greatest collections of ancient sculpture, including the coy *Capitoline Venus*, the *Dying Gaul* and countless portrait busts of emperors and their families.

A top-floor café and restaurant (which are accessible without paying the museum entrance fee) are rather overpriced, but offer a magnificent view over the city.

Circus Maximus

Via del Circo Massimo. **Map** p57 B4 ❷
Little of the actual structure remains at the Circus Maximus, ancient Rome's major chariot-racing venue, but it's still possible to visualise the flat base of this long grassy basin as the racetrack, and the sloping sides as the stands. At the southern end are some brick remains of the original seating (the tower is medieval). The oldest and largest of Rome's ancient arenas, the Circus Maximus hosted chariot races from around the fourth century BC. It was rebuilt by Julius Caesar to hold as many as 300,000 people. Races involved up to 12 rigs of four horses each; the circus was also flooded for mock sea battles.

Colosseum

Piazza del Colosseo (06 700 5469).
Open 8.30am-sunset daily. **Admission** (includes Roman Forum & Palatine)

Capitoline Museums

1000s of things to do...

**TIME OUT GUIDES
WRITTEN BY
LOCAL EXPERTS**
visit timeout.com/shop

€9; €4.50 reductions; extra charge for exhibitions. No credit cards.
Map p57 C3 ❸
Built in AD 72 by Emperor Vespasian, *il Colosseo* hosted gory battles between combinations of gladiators, slaves, prisoners and wild animals of all descriptions. Properly called the *Amphitheatrum flavium*, the building was later known as the Colosseum because of a colossal gold-plated statue, now lost, that stood alongside. The arena was about 500m (a third of a mile) in circumference and could seat over 50,000 people. In the 100 days of carnage held to inaugurate the amphitheatre in AD 80, some 5,000 beasts perished. Sometimes, animals got to kill people: a common sentence in the Roman criminal justice system was *damnatio ad bestias*, where miscreants were turned loose, unarmed, into the arena. After the fall of the Roman Empire, authorities banned games here and the Colosseum became a quarry for stone and marble to build Roman *palazzi*. The pockmarks on the Colosseum's masonry date from the ninth century, when the lead clamps holding the stones together were pillaged. This didn't stop until the mid 18th century, when the Colosseum was consecrated as a church.

Standing beside the Colosseum, Constantine's imposing triumphal arch was erected in AD 315, shortly before the emperor abandoned the city for Byzantium.

If the queue at the Colosseum is huge, get your ticket from the Palatine entrance at via di San Gregorio 30 and bypass the line.

Imperial Fora Museum

Via IV Novembre 94 (06 6992 3521, www.mercatiditraiano.it). **Open** 9am-7pm Tue-Sun. **Admission** €7.50; €5.50 reductions; extra charge during exhibitions. **Map** p57 B1 ❹
When the Roman Forum (*see p63*) became too small to cope with the ever-growing city, emperors combined philanthropy with propaganda and created new fora of their own in what is now known collectively as the *Fori imperiali* (Imperial Fora). Along the via dei Fori Imperiali (sliced cavalierly through the ruins in the early 20th century) are five separate fora – each one built by a different emperor.

Excavations in the 1990s unearthed great swathes of this archaeological space. It's not easy to interpret the ruins, most of which are visible from street level. A pre-emptive visit to the scale model of the *fori* at the visitors' centre (via dei Fori Imperiali, open 9.30am-6.30pm daily) will help.

The best-preserved and unquestionably most impressive part of the complex is Trajan's forum and the towering remains of Trajan's markets behind. Two years of restoration work came to an end in October 2007, giving Trajan's markets a gloriously cleaned-up interior, a beautifully lit collection of marble artefacts and a new name: *il Museo dei fori imperiali*. Moreover, it opened up atmospheric stretches of the ancient streets and medieval buildings surrounding the market itself.

Entering Trajan's markets from via IV Novembre, the first room is the Great Hall, a large space possibly used for the corn dole in antiquity and often hosting exhibitions today. To the south of the Great Hall are the open-air terraces at the top of the spectacular Great Hemicycle, built in AD 107. To the east of the Great Hall, stairs lead down to the so-called via Biberatica, an ancient street flanked by remarkably well-preserved shops; these were probably *tabernae* (bars), hence the name (*bibere* is Latin for 'to drink'). More stairs lead down through the various layers of the Great Hemicycle, where most of the 150 shops or offices are still in perfect condition, many with door jambs still showing the grooves where shutters would have slid into place when the working day was over.

Below the markets, at the piazza Venezia end of via dei Fori Imperiali, is

ROME BY AREA

Colosseum p58

Trajan's forum, laid out in the early second century AD. It's dominated by Trajan's column (AD 113), with detailed spiralling reliefs showing victories over Dacia (modern-day Romania). The rectangular foundation to the south of Trajan's column, where several imposing granite columns still stand, was the basilica Ulpia, an administrative building.

Across the road from Trajan's forum, **Caesar's forum** was the earliest of the *Fori imperiali*, built in 51 BC by Julius Caesar. Three columns of the *Venus generatrix* temple have been rebuilt. Back on the same side as Trajan's forum, **Augustus' forum** was inaugurated in 2 BC. Three columns from the Temple of Mars Ultor still stand, as does the towering wall separating the forum from what was the sprawling Suburra slum. **Nerva's forum** (AD 97) lies mainly beneath via dei Fori Imperiali. On the south side of the road, **Vespasian's forum** (AD 75) was home to the Temple of Pax (Peace), part of which is now incorporated into the church of Santi Cosma e Damiano. Maps put up on a wall here by Mussolini show how Rome ruled the world.

Mamertine Prison

Via del Tulliano (06 68 961). **Open** 9am-7pm daily. **Admission** €7-€10. **Map** p57 A2 ❺

After a makeover, this minor site has become a 'spiritual-archeological experience' with the emphasis on the spiritual and almost nothing in the way of explanation of the archeology: a pity. Into this dank prison went anyone thought to pose a threat to the security of the ancient Roman state. A dark underground dungeon, its lower level (built in the fourth century BC) was once only accessible through a hole in the floor. The most famous of the prison's residents, legend has it, were Saints Peter and Paul. Peter caused a miraculous well to bubble up downstairs in order to baptise his prison

guards, whom he converted. You can pay €7 if you're prepared to do without the spiritual element/audioguide.

Palazzo Valentini – Domus Romane

NEW *Via Quattro Novembre 19A (06 32 810, www.provincia.roma.it).* **Open** 9am-5pm Mon, Wed-Sun. **Admission** €6; €4 reductions. No credit cards. **Map** p57 A1 ❻

Excavated beneath the offices of the Province of Rome, this new-for-2010 attraction not only allows a glimpse into the richly decorated houses of well-heeled citizens of the Roman Empire, but uses ultra-modern technology to reconstruct the surroundings and lifestyles of the ancients. The hour-long visit is the best that central Rome offers for putting the ancient world in context. Visits in English leave at 1.30pm but numbers are very limited: book well ahead.

Palazzo Venezia

Via del Plebiscito 118 (06 678 0131). **Open** 8.30am-7.30pm Tue-Sun. **Admission** €4; €2 reductions; extra charge during exhibitions. No credit cards. **Map** p57 A1 ❼

This collection contains a hotchpotch of anything from terracotta models by Baroque sculptor Gian Lorenzo Bernini (for the angels that now grace Ponte Sant'Angelo), to medieval decorative art. Major exhibitions are staged regularly; they often give access to the huge Sala del Mappamondo, which was used by Mussolini as his office.

On the upper level of the cloister of Pope Paul II's 'secret garden', a lapidarium houses ancient, medieval and Renaissance sarcophagi, coats of arms, funerary monuments and assorted fragments.

Roman Forum & Palatine

Via di San Gregorio 30/largo della Salaria Vecchia 5/6 (06 3996 7700). **Open** 8.30am-1hr before sunset daily. **Admission** (includes Colosseum)

ROME BY AREA

€9; €5.50 reductions; extra charge for exhibitions. No credit cards.

Map p57 B3 **8**

Note: Letters **9** in the text refer to the Roman Forum and Palatine map on the back cover flap of this guide.

The Forum and Palatine, separate but adjoining sites, are visited on the same ticket, which also allows entrance to the Colosseum. We recommend that you enter from the quieter via di San Gregorio entrance, visiting the Palatine first, then making your way down to the Forum.

However, guided tours (€3, in Italian) of parts of the Forum that are generally off-limits depart from the largo della Salaria Vecchia ticket office (off via dei Fori Imperiali); to join these, book your tour and enter from there. If you want to arrange a visit (free of charge) to Augustus' house on the Palatine, you will need to organise a time at this entrance too.

Palatine

Legend relates that a basket holding twin babes Romulus and Remus was found in the swampy area near the Tiber to the west of here, and that the twins had been suckled by a she-wolf in a cave. In 753 BC, having murdered his brother, Romulus scaled the Palatine hill and founded Rome. Archaeological evidence shows that proto-Romans had settled on *il Palatino* a century or more before that.

Later, the Palatine became the Beverly Hills of the ancient city, where movers and shakers built palaces. On the southern side of the Palatine are the remains of vast Imperial dwellings, including Emperor Domitian's *Domus augustana* **9**, with what may have been a private stadium in the garden. Next door, the Museo Palatino **9** charts the history of the Palatine from the eighth century BC.

Immediately west of here is the House of Augustus (*Domus augusti*, **9**; four of its spectacularly frescoed rooms were opened to the public in 2008.

With Rome's decline, the Palatine became a rural backwater; in the 1540s, much of the hill was bought by Cardinal Alessandro Farnese, who created a pleasure villa. His gardens, the *Horti farnesiani* **9**, are still a lovely, leafy – if unkempt – place to wander on a hot day. Beneath the gardens, the *cryptoporticus* **9** is a semi-subterranean tunnel built by Nero.

Roman Forum

During the early years of the Republic, this was an open space with shops and a few temples, and it sufficed; but by the second century BC, ever-conquering Rome needed to convey authority and wealth. Out went the food stalls; in came law courts, offices and immense public buildings with grandiose decorations. The *Foro romano* was the symbolic heart of the Empire.

Seen descending from the Palatine, the Forum is framed by the Arch of Titus (AD 81; **9**), built to celebrate the sack of Jerusalem. To the right are the towering ruins of the Basilica of Maxentius **9**, completed in AD 312.

Beyond this, towards the Colosseum, the massive second-century Temple of Venus and Roma was opened to visitors for the first time in May 2010.

Backtracking, on the left is the house of the Vestal Virgins **9**. Along the via Sacra **9**, the Forum's high street, are (right) the great columns of the Temple of Antoninus and Faustina **9**; the giant Basilica Emilia (right; **9**) – once a bustling place for administration, courts and business; the Curia **9**, the home of the Senate, begun in 45 BC by Julius Caesar; and the Arch of Septimius Severus **9**, built in AD 203. Beside the arch are the remains of an Imperial rostrum **9**, from where Mark Antony supposedly asked Romans to lend him their ears.

San Giorgio in Velabro

Via del Velabro 19 (06 6979 7536, www.sangiorgioinvelabro.org). **Open** 8am-6.30pm daily. **Map** p57 A3 **9**

This austere little church of the seventh century has 16 Roman columns pilfered from the Palatine and the Aventine hills in its nave, and pieces of an eighth- or ninth-century choir incorporated into the walls. In the apse is a much-restored 13th-century fresco of St George. Outside to the left is the Arco degli Argentari, built in AD 204; it was a gate on the road between the main Forum and the *forum boarium* (cattle market), along which money-changers plied their trade.

San Marco

Piazza San Marco 48 (06 679 5205, www.sanmarcoevangelista.it). **Open** 4-7pm Mon; 8.30am-noon, 4-7pm Tue-Sun. **Map** p57 A1 ⑩

Founded, tradition says, in 336 on the site of the house where St Mark the Evangelist stayed, this church was rebuilt by Pope Paul II in the 15th century when the neighbouring Palazzo Venezia was constructed, and was given its Baroque look in the mid 18th century. Remaining from its earlier manifestations are the 12th-century bell tower, and the ninth-century mosaic of Christ in the apse. In the portico is the gravestone of Vanozza Catanei, mother of the notorious Cesare and Lucrezia Borgia.

San Nicola in Carcere

Via del Teatro di Marcello 46 (06 6830 7198). **Open** 7am-7pm Mon-Sat; 9am-7pm Sun. **Map** off p57 A3 ⑪

The 12th-century San Nicola was built over three Roman temples, dating from the second and third centuries BC; a guide (donation appreciated) takes you down to these. On the outside of the church, six columns from the Temple of Janus can be seen on the left; the ones on the right are from the Temple of Spes (Hope).

Santa Maria in Aracoeli

Piazza del Campidoglio 4 (06 679 8155). **Open** 9.30am-12.30pm, 2.30-5.30pm daily. **Map** p57 A2 ⑫

Up a daunting flight of steps, the Romanesque Aracoeli ('altar of heaven') stands on the site of an ancient temple to Juno Moneta. The current basilica-form church was designed in the late 13th century. The first chapel on the right has scenes by Pinturicchio from the life of St Francis of Assisi's helpmate St Bernardino (1486). To the left of the altar, a round chapel contains relics of St Helena, mother of the Emperor Constantine. At the back of the transept, the Chapel of the Holy Child contains a much-venerated, disease-healing *bambinello*, which is often whisked to the bedside of moribund Romans.

Santa Maria in Cosmedin & the Mouth of Truth

Piazza della Bocca della Verità 18 (06 678 1419). **Open** 9.30am-5pm daily. **Map** p57 A3 ⑬

Built in the sixth century and enlarged in the eighth, Santa Maria was embellished with a glorious Cosmati-work floor, throne and choir in the 11th-13th centuries. In the sacristy is a fragment of an eighth-century mosaic of the Holy Family, brought here from the original St Peter's. The church is better known as the *bocca della verità* (the mouth of truth), after the great stone mask of a man with a gaping mouth on the portico wall – probably an ancient drain cover. Anyone who lies while their hand is in the mouth will have that hand bitten off, according to legend. On the little green opposite are the first-century BC Temples of Hercules (round) and Portunus (square).

Vittoriano

Piazza Venezia (06 699 1718). **Open** *Monument* 9.30am-4.30pm daily. *Museo Centrale del Risorgimento* 9.30am-6pm daily. *Complesso del Vittoriano (06 678 0664)* 9.30am-6.30pm Mon-Thur, Sun; 9.30am-11pm Fri, Sat. **Admission** varies. **Map** p57 A1 ⑭

Variously known as 'the wedding cake' and 'the typewriter', this eyesore is a monument to united Italy, built

between 1885 and 1911. You can climb the steps (free) for a good view over the city, or explore the exhibitions – mainly of 19th- and 20th-century art – held in the gallery on the left side of the monument. Along the right side, a door leads to a space that hosts exhibits on Italian history, and memorabilia from the Unification struggle.

Also through this entrance is a new lift (€7.50, €3.50 reductions) to the very top of the monument for a breathtaking 360-degree panorama across the whole of Rome and beyond… from the only spot where the spectacle isn't marred by the Vittoriano itself. There's a (rather pricey) café on one of the lower terraces.

Eating & drinking

San Teodoro
Via dei Fienili 49-51 (06 678 0933, www.st-teodoro.it). **Meals served** 12.45-3.15pm, 8-11.30pm Mon-Sat. Closed 3wks Dec-Jan; 1wk Aug. €€€€. **Creative Italian**. **Map** p57 A3 ⓯
Of a summer's evening, there are few more pleasant places in Rome for an alfresco meal than this seafood-oriented restaurant around the back of the Forum, in a pretty residential piazza. Come prepared to splash out, though. Some dishes are pure *cucina romana*; others, like the *tonnarelli San Teodoro* (with shrimps, courgettes and cherry tomatoes) are lighter and more creative. It opens on Sundays during the summer. San Teodoro's light lunches (€€) are also available in its *caffè-tavola calda* next door.

Enoteca Provincia Romana
NEW *Largo del Foro Traiano 84 (06 6766 2424, www.provincia.roma.it).* **Meals served** 12.30-3pm, 7.30-11pm Mon-Sat. €€. **Roman**. **Map** p57 A1 ⓰
Overlooking Trajan's column, this new wine bar serves wines and produce exclusively from the area around the capital. The atmosphere is cordial; the

food is original and very good; and the wine menu (with a large by-the-glass choice) is full of pleasant surprises. The place is packed at lunch (office workers) and dinner (everyone). There's an *aperitivo* hour with buffet from 5.30pm to 7.30pm. Book ahead.

The Ghetto & Campo de' Fiori

From the earliest of ancient times, the area in the great loop of the River Tiber was the *campus martius* (field of war), where Roman males did physical jerks to stay fighting fit. As time went on, it became packed with theatres providing lowbrow fun. After barbarian hordes rampaged through Rome in the fifth and sixth centuries, the area fell into ruin. By the late Middle Ages, it was densely populated and insalubrious.

That part of the *campus martius* that today stretches south from busy corso Vittorio Emanuele (aka corso Vittorio) to the Tiber saw its fortunes improve when the pope made the Vatican – across the river – his main residence in the mid 15th century. Nowadays, its tightly wedged buildings, cobbled alleys, graceful Renaissance columns and chunky blocks of ancient travertine form the perfect backdrop to Roman streetlife.

The area is one of contrasts: **campo de' Fiori** – with its lively morning market and livelier partying crowds at night – stands next to solemn, dignified **piazza Farnese**, with its grand Palazzo Farnese, partly designed by Michelangelo. Top-end antique dealers in via Giulia rub along with craftsmen plying their trades in streets with names – via dei Leutari (lutemakers), via dei Cappellari (hatmakers) – that recall the jobs of their medieval ancestors.

ROME BY AREA

In the south-east, **largo Argentina** is a polluted transport hub with a chunk of ancient Rome at its heart: visible when you peer over the railings are columns, altars and foundations from four temples, dating from the mid third century BC to c100 BC. South of the square lies the **Ghetto**: its picture-postcard winding alleys mask a sorrowful history. Rome's Jews have maintained a presence in the city for over 2,000 years. The Ghetto was walled off from the rest of the city in 1556, and remained that way until the 1870s. In piazza Mattei stands the beautiful, delicate Turtle Fountain, erected overnight in the 1580s, though the turtles may have been an afterthought.

Sights & museums

Crypta Balbi
Via delle Botteghe Oscure 31 (06 678 0167). **Open** 9am-7pm Tue-Sun. **Admission** €7; €3.50 reductions; extra charge during exhibitions; see also p9 Museo Nazionale Romano. No credit cards. **Map** p71 E4 **⑰**
The Crypta Balbi – the foyer of the ancient Theatre of Balbus – is packed with displays, maps and models that explain (in English) Rome's evolution from a bellicose pre-Imperial era, to early Christian times and on through the dim Middle Ages. Frequent tours take visitors down to the digs beneath the museum; a special guided tour at 3pm on Sundays allows a glimpse of newly excavated sections beyond the museum. Tours (in Italian) are free.

Galleria Spada
Piazza Capo di Ferro 13 (06 683 2409, www.galleriaborghese.it). **Open** 8.30am-7.30pm Tue-Sun. **Admission** €5; €2 reductions. No credit cards. **Map** p70 C4 **⑱**
This gem of a palace – alas, showing signs of neglect – was acquired by art collector Cardinal Bernardino Spada

in 1632; the walls are crammed with paintings. There are some impressive names here: Domenichino, Guercino, Guido Reni plus the father-daughter Gentileschi duo, Orazio and Artemisia. The main attraction of the museum, however, is the Borromini Perspective, where perspective trickery makes a 9m-long (30ft) colonnade look much longer.

Il Gesù
Piazza del Gesù (06 697 001, www.chiesadelgesu.org). **Open** *Church* 7.30am-12.30pm, 4-7.30pm daily. *Loyola's rooms (06 6920 5800)* 4-6pm Mon-Sat; 10am-noon Sun. **Map** p71 E3 **⑲**
The Gesù, built in 1568-84, is the flagship church of the Jesuits, and was designed to involve the congregation as closely as possible in services, with a nave unobstructed by aisles. One of Rome's great Baroque masterpieces – *Triumph in the Name of Jesus* by Il Baciccia (1676-79) – decorates the ceiling of the nave. On the left is the ornate chapel of Sant'Ignazio (1696). Outside the church, at piazza del Gesù 45, you can visit St Ignatius' rooms.

Jewish Museum of Rome
Lungotevere Cenci (06 6840 0661, www.museoebraico.roma.it). **Open** 10am-5pm Mon-Thur, Sun; 9am-2pm Fri. **Admission** €7.50; €4 reductions. **Map** p71 E5 **⑳**
As well as luxurious crowns, mantles and silverware, the *Museo ebraico di Roma* presents vivid reminders of the persecution suffered by Rome's Jews at various times through history, with copies of the 16th-century papal edicts that banned Jews from many activities, and heart-rending relics from World War II concentration camps. Refurbished in 2005, the museum now displays exquisite carvings from long-gone Roman synagogues.

Museo Barracco
Corso Vittorio 166A (06 6821 4105, www.museobarracco.it).

Open 9am-7pm Tue-Sun. **Admission** €4.50; €3.50 reductions; extra charge during exhibitions. No credit cards. **Map** p70 C3 ㉑

This small collection of mainly pre-Roman art was amassed in the first half of the 20th century. Don't miss the copy of the *Wounded Bitch* by the fourth-century BC sculptor Lysippus.

Portico d'Ottavia

Via Portico d'Ottavia. **Map** p71 E5 ㉒

Great ancient columns and a marble frontispiece, held together with rusting iron braces, now form part of the church of Sant'Angelo in Pescheria, but they were originally the entrance of a massive colonnaded square (portico) containing temples and libraries, built in the first century AD by Emperor Augustus and dedicated to his sister Octavia. A walkway (open 9am-6pm daily) has been opened through the *forum piscarium* – the ancient fish market; it continues past ancient masonry to the Teatro di Marcello, passing three towering columns that were once part of the Temple of Apollo (433 BC).

Sant'Andrea della Valle

Piazza Vidoni 6 (06 686 1339).
Open 7.30am-12.30pm, 4.30-7.30pm daily. **Map** p70 C3 ㉓

Perhaps from an original design by Giacomo della Porta, this church was taken in hand in the mid 17th century by Carlo Maderno, who created a dome that is the highest in Rome after St Peter's. Puccini set the opening act of *Tosca* in the chapel on the left.

Theatre of Marcellus

Via Teatro di Marcello. **Map** p71 E5 ㉔

The *Teatro di Marcello* is one of Rome's strangest sights – a Renaissance palace grafted on to an ancient theatre. Julius Caesar began building the theatre, but it was finished in 11 BC by Augustus, who named it after his favourite nephew. It originally had three vast tiers, and seated up to 20,000 people. Abandoned in the fourth century AD,

it was turned into a fortress in the 12th century and then into a palazzo in the 16th by the Savelli family.

Tiber Island & Ponte Rotto

Map p71 D5 ㉕

When the last Etruscan king was driven from Rome, the Romans uprooted the wheat from his fields and threw it in baskets into the river. Silt accumulated and formed an island where Aesculapius, the god of medicine, founded a sanctuary in the third century BC. That's what the legend says, and the island has always had a vocation for public health. Today, a hospital occupies the north end. The church of San Bartolomeo is built over the original sanctuary; the columns in the nave are from that earlier building. Remains can also be seen from the riverside footpath, from where there's also a fine view over the *ponte rotto* (broken bridge). This stands on the site of the *Pons aemilius*, built in 142 BC. It was rebuilt many times before 1598, when they gave up trying. To the east of the bridge is a tunnel in the embankment: the gaping mouth of the city's great *cloaca maxima* sewer, built in the sixth century BC.

Eating & drinking

Alberto Pica

Via della Seggiola 12 (06 686 8405).
Open 8.30am-2am Mon-Sat. Closed 2wks Aug. No credit cards. **Bar/ice-cream**. **Map** p71 D4 ㉖

Horrendous neon lighting, surly staff and some very good ice-cream are the hallmarks of this long-running bar: *riso alla cannella* (cinnamon rice) is particularly delicious. It's also open Sunday evenings in summer and December.

Antica Vineria

Via Monte della Farina 37 (06 6880 6989). **Open** 10.30am-3pm, 6.30-10.30pm Mon-Sat. No credit cards. **Wine bar**. **Map** p71 D4 ㉗

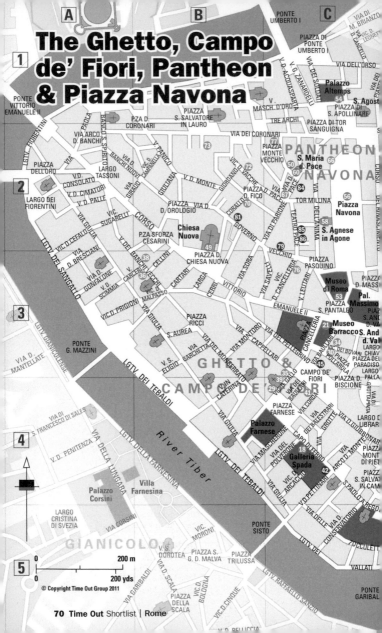

The Ghetto, Campo de' Fiori, Pantheon & Piazza Navona

© Copyright Time Out Group 2011

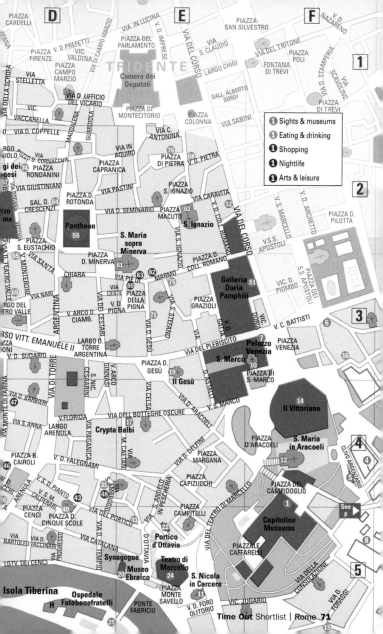

D

PIAZZA CARDELLI

PIAZZA FIRENZE

VIA D. PREFETTI

VIC. VALDINA

PIAZZA CAMPO MARZIO

VIA DELLA SCROFA

VIA D. STELLETTA

VIA D. UFFICIO DEL VICARIO

VIC. VACCARELLA

VIA D. COPPELLE

RGO PIZZO DI POZZO

NIOLO

gi dei cesi

74

PIAZZA RONDANINI

VIA GIUSTINIANI

SAL. D. CRESCENZI 64

zo ma

VIA SANTA

65

PIAZZA S. EUSTACHIO

VIA D. TEATRO VALLE

69

VIA NARI

RGO DEL TRO VALLE

E

VIA IN LUCINA

VIC. D. IMPRESE

VIA DEL CORSO

PIAZZA DEL PARLAMENTO

PIAZZA DI CAMPO MARZIO

VIA DI CAMPO MARZIO

TRIDENTE

Camera dei Deputati

PIAZZA DI MONTECITORIO

MADDALENA

VIA D. CORNACCHIE

VIA IN AQUIRO

GUARDIOLA

PIAZZA CAPRANICA

VIA PASTINI

VIA D. SEMINARIO

PIAZZA D. ROTONDA

Pantheon 55

S. Maria sopra Minerva

CHIARA

PIAZZA D. MINERVA 61

VIA PIE' 83

VIA CESTE

VIA D. PIGNA

80

82

MARMO

PIAZZA DELLA PIGNA

71

VIA ARCO D. CIAMB.

VIA S. STEFANO

PIAZZA GRAZIOLI

F

PIAZZA SAN SILVESTRO

VIA S. CLAUDIO

VIA DEL TRITONE

PIAZZA POLI

FONTANA DI TREVI

LARGO CHIGI

GALL. ALBERTO SORDI

VIA SABINI

VIA D. STAMPERIA

V. D. NAZARENO

V. D. SCAVOLINO

PIAZZA DI TREVI

PIAZZA COLONNA

VIA C. ANTONINA

76 58

PIAZZA DI PIETRA

V. D. PIETRA

PIAZZA S. IGNAZIO

VIA CARAVITA

S. Ignazio

62

52

PIAZZA MACUTO

V. D. COLL. ROMANO

VIA DEL CORSO

V. S. MARCELLO

V.S.S. APOSTOLI

V. D. ARCHETTO

PIAZZA D. PILOTTA

PIAZZA D. COLL. ROMANO

VIC. D. S.S. APOSTOLI

VIA D. GATTA

V. D. DORIA

Galleria Doria Pamphili 51

PIAZZA DEI S.S. APOSTOLI

VIA D. PLEBISCITO

7

Palazzo Venezia

S. Marco

10

V.S. MARCO

VIA D. GESU'

PIAZZA D. GESU'

19

Il Gesù

VIA CELSA

VIA D'ARACOELI

PIAZZA DI S. MARCO

14

Il Vittoriano

PIAZZA VENEZIA

V. C. BATTISTI

6

16

V. D. SUDARIO

ONI

VIA DI TORRE

LARGO D. TORRE ARGENTINA

ARGENTINA

VIA DI TORRE ARGENTINA

VIA D. BARBIERI

47

V.FLORIDA

V. NIC. CESARINI

V. ARCO GINNASI

LARGO ARENULA

VIA DELLE BOTTEGHE OSCURE

Crypta Balbi

17

M. CAETANI

S. Maria in Aracoeli

PIAZZA D'ARACOELI

12

PIAZZA DEL CAMPIDOGLIO

VIA DEL TEATRO DI MARCELLO

VIA DELLA CONSOLAZIONE

VIA MONTE DI FARINA

VIA S. ANNA

PIAZZA B. CAIROLI

46

ARENULA

V.S. D. PIANTO

V.S.M. CALDERARI

V. D. FALEGNAMI

PIAZZA D. CINQUE SCOLE

VIA PAGANICA

VIA D. PORTICO

40

43

31

43

33

VIA PROGRESSO

LGT. DEI CENCI

PIAZZA CENCI

VIA CATALANA

VIA BARTOLOMEO VACCINARI

D'OTTAVIA

S. ANGELO IN PESCHERIA

Portico d'Ottavia

22

Synagogue

Museo Ebraico

20

Teatro di Marcello

24

S. Nicola in Carcere

11

PIAZZA MONTE SAVELLO

PIAZZA CAPIZUCCHI

PIAZZA CAMPITELLI

PIAZZA MARGANA

PIAZZA D. DELFINI

1

Capitoline Museums

PIAZZALE CAFFARELLI

See p ▶

CLIVO ARGENTARIO

4

4

5

8

Isola Tiberina

Ospedale Fatebenefratelli

H

PONTE FABRICIO

VIA D. TEMPIO

25

V. D. FORO OLITORIO

VIC. JUGARIO

V.D. FORAGGI

15

- **1** Sights & museums
- **1** Eating & drinking
- **1** Shopping
- **1** Nightlife
- **1** Arts & leisure

1

2

3

4

5

Bedazzling Baroque

Music and lights at the Gesù.

Gesù

Piped heavenly choirs herald an eye-popping performance of religious theatricality at the **Gesù** (see p68), Rome's most exuberant Baroque church.

A bizarre daily *son et lumière* on the life, but mostly the death, of the Jesuits' founder, Spaniard Ignatius Loyola, offers 15 minutes' respite from the dizzying frescoes on the vast church's ceiling and the sheer opulence of the gold, silver and precious marbles of the Gesù's fixtures and fittings. Proceedings start with mechanical precision at 5.30pm.

The Jesuits were the richest Catholic order, and the most energetic, sending teams of fired-up missionaries to the four corners of the (then) known world. This church is their showcase, and Loyola's final resting place.

After the recent discovery of the original 30ft altarpiece painted by Jesuit brother Andrea Pozzo, depicting the saint's apotheosis, a full-scale restoration began of the complex Baroque mechanics once used to raise and lower the giant altarpiece. These were designed as a saintly spectacle to inspire reverence in awed onlookers. In the 16th century, manpower turned the levers; now, the priest likens the motor harnessed to the antique wooden framework to the sort of thing 'which opens a garage door.'

After a bit of Baroque sacred music and lights dancing over Pozzo's massive canvas while excerpts are read (in Italian) from St Ignatius' *Spiritual Exercises*, the altarpiece begins to disappear, winched down into the bowels of the church. Revealed in its place on the lapis lazuli and gold altar is a huge silver-plated statue of the Spanish mystic.

Baroque art is all about magic, trickery, delight and astonishment. Pozzo showed himself to be a master. For more examples of Baroque playfulness, take a day trip to the **Villa d'Este** (p160) at Tivoli to see Baroque pranks at the service of nature: hidden jets that spray unwary visitors, and a fantastic musical fountain.

This is a laid-back boho-chic stop with standing-only customers spilling out into the picturesque street to sip wine by the glass at very reasonable prices.

Antico Forno Roscioli
Via dei Chiavari 34 (06 686 4045, www.anticofornoroscioli.com).
Open 6am-8pm Mon-Sat. **Bakery**.
Map p70 C4 ㉘
The pizza base at this bakery makes a good snack in itself, but the crowded lunch counter (serves food 11am-2.30pm) provides a greater choice. Roscioli's smarter restaurant, at via dei Giubbonari 21, is good, but it's not a cheap option and staff could definitely be cheerier.

Ar Galletto
Piazza Farnese 102 (06 686 1714).
Meals served 12.15-3pm, 7.15-11pm Mon-Sat. Closed 2wks Dec-Jan, 2wks Aug. €€€. **Roman**. **Map** p70 C4 ㉙
With a ringside view of stately piazza Farnese, Ar Galletto serves unpretentious Roman dishes without the horribly inflated prices charged by other restaurants around here. Dishes such as *penne all'arrabbiata* or *spaghetti alle vongole* are appetising, and there are tables on the square in summer.

Baffetto 2
Piazza del Teatro di Pompeo 18 (06 6821 0807, www.pizzeriabaffetto.it).
Meals served 6.30pm-1am Mon, Wed-Fri; 12.30-3.30pm, 6.30pm-1am Sat, Sun. €. **Pizzeria**. **Map** p70 C3 ㉚
Both branches of the legendary Baffetto serve good pizzas and decent pasta. This newest outpost has tables outside on a bustling square near campo de' Fiori. The original Baffetto can be found at via del Governo Vecchio 114 (evenings only).

Bartaruga
Piazza Mattei 9 (06 689 2299). **Open** 6pm-midnight Tue-Thur; 6pm-2am Fri, Sat; 6pm-1am Sun. No credit cards. **Bar**. **Map** p71 D4 ㉛

This baroque venue, in peach and midnight blue with divans and candelabra, is the haunt of the beautiful, the eccentric and those too entranced by the lovely square outside to move on elsewhere. Staff can be surly.

Bernasconi
Piazza Cairoli 16 (06 8880 6264).
Open 7am-8.30pm Tue-Sun. Closed Aug. No credit cards. **Café/bar**. **Map** p71 D4 ㉜
It's worth fighting your way inside this cramped, inconspicuous bar for unbeatable chewy, yeasty *cornetti* (croissants).

Da Giggetto
Via Portico d'Ottavia 21A-22 (06 686 1105, www.giggettoalportico.it). **Meals served** 12.30-3pm, 7.30-11pm Tue-Sun. Closed 2wks July. €€€. **Roman Jewish**. **Map** p71 E5 ㉝
This old standby in the Ghetto may cater mostly to the tourist trade but it serves decent versions of Roman-Jewish classics such as *carciofi alla giudia* (fried artichokes) and fried *baccalà* (salt cod). The ambience is warm and bustling, and the helpings plentiful.

Ditirambo
Piazza della Cancelleria 75 (06 687 1626, www.ristoranteditirambo.it).
Meals served 7.30-11.30pm Mon; 1-3pm, 7.30-11.30pm Tue-Sun. Closed 2wks Aug. €€. **Creative Italian**. **Map** p70 C3 ㉞
This funky trattoria provides good-value pan-Italian dishes based on fresh, mainly organic ingredients. The chef specialises in traditional fare with a creative kick, as in the excellent baby squid with a purée of *cicerchie* beans or the veal silverside braised in coffee.

Forno Campo de' Fiori
Campo de' Fiori 22/vicolo del Gallo 14 (06 8880 6662, www.fornocampode fiori.com). **Open** 7.30am-2.30pm, 5-8pm Mon-Sat. Closed 2wks Aug. No credit cards. €. **Takeaway pizza**. **Map** p70 C3 ㉟

ROME BY AREA

Spread over two premises, this bakery does excellent takeaway sliced pizza. Its plain *pizza bianca* base is delicious in itself, but check out the one with *fiori di zucca* (courgette flowers) too.

Il Goccetto

Via dei Banchi Vecchi 14 (06 686 4268). **Open** 6.30pm-midnight Tue-Sun. Closed 1wk Jan, 3wks Aug. **Wine bar.** Map p70 B3 **36**

One of the more serious *centro storico* wine bars, with dark wood-clad walls and a cosy, private-club feel. Wine is the main point here, with a satisfying range by the glass from €2.50.

Open Baladin

NEW *Via degli Specchi 6 (06 683 8989, www.openbaladin.com).* **Open** noon-midnight daily. **Birreria.** Map p71 D4 **37**

This new venture from a northern Italian brewery offers 40 beers on tap and over 100 in bottles, all but a handful of them produced in Italy's myriad micro-breweries. To soak it up, there's top-notch snack food such as chicken wings and gourmet hamburgers.

Il Pagliaccio

Via dei Banchi Vecchi 129A (06 6880 9595, www.ristoranteilpagliaccio.com). **Meals served** 8-10pm Tue; 1-2.30pm, 8-10pm Wed-Sat. Closed 1wk Jan, 2wks Aug. €€€€. **Creative Italian.** Map p70 B3 **38**

Chef Anthony Genovese's two Michelin-starred restaurant offers a seasonally changing menu that encompasses Far Eastern influences and fresh approaches to Mediterranean classics. The desserts are excellent.

Le Piramidi

Vicolo del Gallo 11 (06 687 9061, www.cucinaraba.com). **Open** 10am-midnight Tue Sun. Closed Aug. €. No credit cards. **Middle Eastern takeaway.** Map p70 C4 **39**

Le Piramidi makes for a welcome change from takeaway pizza, if you're just in the mood for a quick snack. The range of Middle Eastern take-away fare is fresh, cheap and tasty.

Sora Margherita

Piazza delle Cinque Scole 30 (06 687 4216). **Meals served** 12.45-2.45pm Mon, Wed; 12.45-2.45pm Tue, Thur; 12.45-2.45pm, 8-11.30pm Fri, Sat. Closed Aug. €€. No credit cards. **Roman Jewish.** Map p71 D5 **40**

This hole-in-the-wall trattoria is not for health freaks, but no one argues with serious Roman Jewish cooking at these prices. The classic pasta and meat dishes on offer here include a superlative *pasta e fagioli* (pasta with beans), *tonnarelli cacio e pepe* (pasta with cheese and pepper) and *ossobuco* washed down with rough-and-ready house wine. On Friday and Saturday evenings, you have to book for one of two sittings.

La Vineria

Campo de' Fiori 15 (06 6880 3268). **Open** 8.30am-2am Mon-Sat. Closed 2wks Aug. **Wine bar.** Map p70 C4 **41**

Known variously as Vineria Reggio or just plain La Vineria, this is the longest-running wine bar on the campo, and where locals flock to plan the evening ahead over a glass of wine. (Very small) glasses start from a mere €2.

Shopping

See also **Forno Campo de' Fiori** (p73).

Borini

Via dei Pettinari 86 (06 687 5670). **Open** 3.30-7.30pm Mon; 9.30am-1pm, 3.30-7.30pm Tue-Sat. Closed 3wks Aug. Map p70 C4 **42**

Franco Borini's busily chaotic shop is piled to the rafters with durable footwear, ranging from classical to outrageous, in rainbow colours. Shoes come at prices that won't make you gasp – too much.

Da Giggetto p73

Forno del Ghetto

Via Portico d'Ottavia 1 (06 687 8637). **Open** 7am-2pm, 3.30-7.30pm Mon-Thur; 7am-2pm Fri; 7.30am-5pm Sun. Closed 3wks Aug & Jewish holidays. No credit cards. **Map** p71 D4 ❸

This tiny bakery staffed by a gaggle of tight-lipped women has no sign, but is immediately recognisable by the line of slavering regulars outside. The damson and ricotta tart is memorable.

Ibiz

Via dei Chiavari 39 (06 6830 7297). **Open** 9.30am-7.30pm Mon-Sat. Closed 2wks Aug. **Map** p70 C4 ❹

Elisa Nepi's leather bags are fast becoming classics: you can decide which suits you as you watch them being made in the on-site workshop. There are briefcases, belts and even chairs too.

Loco

Via dei Baullari 22 (06 6880 8216). **Open** 3.30-8pm Mon; 10.30am-8.30pm Tue-Sat. **Map** p70 C3 ❺

If you like your shoes avant-garde, this small copper and wood decorated store is the place for you. From classy to wild and eccentric, its pieces are always one step ahead of the flock.

Momento

Piazza Cairoli 9 (06 6880 8157). **Open** 10am-7.30pm Mon-Fri; 10am-1.30pm, 3.30-7.30pm Sat. **Map** p71 D4 ❻

The poshest of princesses and her boho cousin will be equally awed by the collection of clothes and accessories at Momento. There's something here for the fearless and the flamboyant, all at very approachable prices.

Spazio Sette

Via dei Barbieri 7 (06 686 9747). **Open** 3.30-7.30pm Mon; 9.30am-1pm, 3.30-7.30pm Tue-Sat. Closed 3wks Aug. **Map** p71 D4 ❼

A stalwart of the Roman design circuit since it opened in the 1970s, Spazio Sette is a chic treasure trove of kitchen-ware, table decorations, rugs, furniture and lights, occupying three floors of a delightful 17th-century palazzo.

Arts & leisure

Acquamadre

Via di Sant'Ambrogio 17 (06 686 4272, www.acquamadre.it). **Open** 2-9pm Tue; 11am-9pm Wed-Sun. Closed Aug. **Map** p71 D4 ❽

What better way to remove the grime of Roman traffic than to sweat it out in this modern take on an ancient bath house: calm, steamy and offering an array of massages and beauty treatments. Wednesday and Friday are women-only days.

The Pantheon & Piazza Navona

Like its counterpart to the south (The Ghetto & Campo de' Fiori, pp67-76), this area of picturesque alleys in the loop of the river north of corso Vittorio Emanuele was part of the ancient *campus martius*.

After the Empire fell, the *campus* was prime construction territory, and every medieval wall tells a tale of primitive recycling: grand *palazzi* were constructed from stolen marble, while humbler souls built little houses among the ruins. It's still a democratic area, where mink-clad contessas mingle with pensioners, craftsmen and tradesmen. After dark, hip bars, smart restaurants and, increasingly, tourist-trap rip-offs, fill to bursting, especially around Santa Maria della Pace.

Two squares – both living links to ancient Rome – dominate the district: **piazza della Rotonda** – home to the **Pantheon** – and magnificent **piazza Navona**.

West of piazza Navona, piazza Pasquino is home to a truncated classical statue; for centuries, Romans have pinned satirical verse (*pasquinades*) to this sculpture. Further north, the elegant, antiques shop-lined via dei Coronari was once the haunt of pilgrim-fleecing rosary-makers (*coronari*).

When the corso Vittorio was hacked through the medieval fabric in the 1870s, only the most grandiose of homes were spared: Palazzo Massimo at no.141, with its curved façade following the stands in Domitian's *odeon* (small theatre), is one.

To the east of the Pantheon, **Galleria Doria Pamphili** contains one of Rome's finest art collections, while the charmingly rococo **piazza Sant'Ignazio** looks like a stage set. In neighbouring piazza di Pietra, the columns of the Temple of Hadrian can be seen embedded in the walls of Rome's former stock exchange.

Sights & museums

Chiesa Nuova/ Santa Maria in Vallicella

Piazza della Chiesa Nuova (06 687 5289, www.vallicella.org). **Open** 7.30am-noon, 4.30-7.30pm daily. **Map** p70 B2 ➍➒

Filippo Neri (1515-95) was a wealthy Florentine who abandoned commerce to live among the poor in Rome. He founded the Oratorian order in 1544. In 1575, work began on the order's headquarters, the Chiesa Nuova. Neri wanted a large, simple building; the walls were covered with the exuberant frescoes and multicoloured marbles only after his death. Pietro da Cortona painted the *Assumption of the Virgin* (1650) in the apse, Rubens the *Virgin and Child* (1608) over the altar.

Chiostro del Bramante

Via della Pace 5 (06 6880 9036, www.chiostrodelbramante.it). **Open** 10am-8pm Tue-Fri, Sun; 10am-9pm Sat. **Admission** €10; €7.50 reductions. No credit cards. **Map** p70 C2 ➎➌

Attached to the church of Santa Maria della Pace (see p80) is this beautifully harmonious cloister, designed by Donato Bramante – his first work after arriving in Rome in the early 16th century. The space hosts one-off exhibitions that are usually of high quality. The café-restaurant upstairs (no need to buy a ticket to get in; credit cards accepted) is a delightful place at which to rest and refuel.

Doria Pamphilj Gallery

Via del Corso 305 (06 679 7323, www. doriapamphilj.it). **Open** 10am-5pm daily. **Admission** €10; €7 reductions. No credit cards. **Map** p71 F3 ➎➊

While the most impressive exhibition spaces of this treasure-filled, privately owned gallery are situated around the central courtyard, it is in the rooms off the long Galleria degli Specchi that the highlights of the collection are to be found; the tiny Gabinetto di Velázquez contains that artist's dramatic portrait of the Pamphilj Pope Innocent X; there's also a splendid bust by Bernini of the same pontiff next to it; off the other end of the *galleria* are four smaller rooms ordered by century.

In the 17th-century room, Caravaggio (for more on the artist, see pp50-53) is represented by the *Rest on the Flight into Egypt* and the *Penitent Magdalene*; the 16th-century room includes Titian's shameless *Salome* and a *Portrait of Two Men* by Raphael. There's a sequence of plush state apartments to admire.

Museo del Corso

Via del Corso 320/via Marco Minghetti 22 (06 678 6209, www.museodel corso.it). **Open** 10am-6pm days vary. **Admission** €10; €8 reductions. **Map** p71 E2 ➎➋

In these two spaces owned by the Banca di Roma there are displays of the bank's private collection of works from the 16th to the 20th centuries, as well as one-off exhibitions. The latter can be interesting, but don't always live up to their blockbuster presentation.

Virtual Rome

A 21st-century tour of the ancient city.

For those who prefer their culture digitally packaged, Rome has an array of attractions: the flight-simulator **Time Elevator** (via dei SS Apostoli 20, www.time elevator.it) offers a 20-minute ride through two millennia of history – best not experienced on a full stomach. **Rewind Rome** (see p108) uses 3D-imaging wizardry and mixes video game technology and rather cheesy virtual guides for a romp through *Caput mundi*.

On a more erudite note, computers in the **Crypta Balbi** (see p68) offer an interactive guide to how rubbish raised Rome's street levels, while the **Baths of Diocletian** (see p101) has an animated explanation (in Italian only) of how the via Flaminia would have looked when ancient Romans tramped along it, en route to the Adriatic sea port of Ariminum (modern Rimini).

Impressive technical wizardry is to be found in the basement of **Palazzo Valentini** (see p63), HQ of the Rome provincial government. During a guided tour of the remains of a late Roman *domus*, computer-generated reconstructions show what this gracious dwelling, probably of a wealthy senator, would have looked like in its heyday. The effect is quite startlingly realistic.

One plan to sell a 'repackaged' Rome has – thankfully – been allowed to slip into obscurity with the onset of belt-tightening: in 2008, the city council was cock-a-hoop over plans to cover 300 hectares of countryside outside the city with an Imperial Roman theme park. More likely to materialise – though not by its 2011 deadline – is **Cinecittà World** (www.cinecittaworld.it), a theme park south of Rome charting the city's contribution to the movie industry.

In the meantime, skeptics point out that the Appian Way is unkempt and label-less, museums complain of serious underfunding, a handful of gardeners struggle to keep parks presentable and little has been done to render the Roman Forum more 'legible'.

ROME BY AREA

Museo di Roma

Palazzo Braschi, via di San Pantaleo 10 (06 0608, www.museodiroma.it). **Open** 9am-7pm Tue-Sun. **Admission** €6.50; €4.50 reductions; extra charge during exhibitions. **Map** p70 C3 🄧

A moderately interesting rotating collection recounts the evolution of the city from the Middle Ages to the early 20th century. Sculpture, clothing, furniture and photographs help to put the city's monuments in a human context. One-off exhibitions on Roman themes can be enlightening.

Palazzo Altemps

Piazza Sant'Apollinare 46 (06 3996 7700). **Open** 9am-7.45pm Tue-Sun. **Admission** €7; €3.50 reductions; extra charge during exhibitions; see also p9 Museo Nazionale Romano. No credit cards. **Map** p70 C1 🄴

The 15th-century Palazzo Altemps houses part of the state-owned stock of Roman treasures: gems of classical statuary purchased from the Boncompagni-Ludovisi, Altemps and Mattei families. The Ludovisis liked 'fixing' statues: an *Athena with Serpent* was revamped in the 17th century by Alessandro Algardi, who also 'improved' the *Hermes Loghios*. The museum's finest treasure is the Ludovisi Throne, a fifth-century BC work from Magna Grecia… though some believe it to be a fake.

Pantheon

Piazza della Rotonda (06 6830 0230). **Open** 8.30am-7.30pm Mon-Sat; 9am-6pm Sun; 9am-1pm public holidays. **Map** p71 D2 🄵

The Pantheon was built by Hadrian in AD 119-125 as a temple to the most important deities; the inscription on the pediment records a Pantheon built 100 years before by General Marcus Agrippa (which confused historians for centuries). Its fine state of preservation is due to the building's conversion to a church in AD 608, though its bronze cladding was stolen over the centuries: part is now in Bernini's

baldacchino in St Peter's. The bronze doors are the original Roman ones. Inside, the Pantheon's glory lies in its dimensions. The diameter of the hemispherical dome is exactly equal to the height of the building. At the centre of the dome is the oculus, a circular hole 9m (30ft) in diameter, a symbolic link between the temple and the heavens. Until the 18th century, the portico was used as a marketplace: supports for the stalls were inserted into the notches that today are still visible in the columns.

Piazza Navona

Map p70 C2 🄶

This tremendous theatrical space owes its shape to an ancient athletics stadium, built in AD 86 by Emperor Domitian. Just north of the piazza, in piazza di Tor Sanguigna, remains of the original arena are visible from the street. Piazza Navona acquired its current form in the mid 17th century. The central fountain of the Four Rivers, finished in 1651, is one of the most extravagant masterpieces designed by Bernini. Its main figures represent the longest rivers of the four continents known at the time; the Ganges of Asia, the Nile of Africa, the Danube of Europe and the Plata of the Americas, all with appropriate flora. The figure of the Nile is veiled, because its source was unknown.

San Luigi dei Francesi

Piazza San Luigi dei Francesi 5 (06 688 271). **Open** 10am-12.30pm, 4-7pm Mon-Wed, Fri-Sun; 10am-12.30pm Thur. **Map** p71 D2 🄷

Completed in 1589, San Luigi (St Louis) is the church of Rome's French community. In the fifth chapel on the left are Caravaggio's spectacular scenes from the life of St Matthew (1600-02; see also pp50-53). But equally, make sure that you don't overlook the lovely frescoes of St Cecilia by Domenichino (1615-17), which can be found in the second chapel on the right.

ROME BY AREA

Sant'Agnese in Agone

Piazza Navona (06 6819 2134, www. santagneseinagone.org). **Open** 9.30am-12.30pm, 4-7pm Tue-Sat; 9am-1pm, 4-7pm Sun. **Map** p70 C2 **⑤⑧**

Legend has it that the teenage St Agnes was cast naked into the stadium of Domitian around AD 304, when she refused to renounce Christ and marry a powerful local. Her pagan persecutors chopped her head off (the implausibly small skull is still here), supposedly on the exact spot where the church now stands. Begun in 1652, the church was given its splendidly fluid concave façade by Borromini. Concerts are held in the sacristy at 6pm most Friday evenings during winter.

Sant'Agostino

Piazza Sant'Agostino 80 (06 6880 1962). **Open** 7.30am-noon, 4-7.30pm daily. **Map** p70 C1 **⑤⑨**

This 15th-century church has one of the earliest Renaissance façades in Rome, made of travertine filched from the Colosseum. Inside, the third column on the left bears a fresco of Isaiah by Raphael (1512). In the first chapel on the left is Caravaggio's depiction of the grubbiest pilgrims ever to present themselves at the feet of the startlingly beautiful *Madonna of the Pilgrims* (1604).

Santa Maria della Pace

Arco della Pace 5 (06 686 1156). **Open** 10am-noon Mon, Wed, Sat. **Map** p70 C2 **⑥⓪**

Built in 1482, Santa Maria della Pace was given its theatrical Baroque façade by Pietro da Cortona in 1656. Just inside the door is Raphael's *Sybils* (1514). See also p77 Chiostro del Bramante.

Santa Maria sopra Minerva

Piazza della Minerva 42 (06 679 3926, www.basilicaminerva.it). **Open** 7am-1pm, 3-7pm daily. **Map** p71 E3 **⑥①**

Rome's only Gothic church was built in 1280 on the site of an ancient temple of Minerva. Its best works of art are

Renaissance: on the right of the transept is the Carafa chapel, with frescoes by Filippino Lippi (1457-1504). Also here is the tomb of the Carafa Pope Paul IV (1555-59), famous for enclosing the Jewish Ghetto and having loincloths painted on the nudes of Michelangelo's *Last Judgment* in the Sistine Chapel. A bronze loincloth was also ordered to cover Christ's genitals on a work here by Michelangelo, a Christ holding up a cross. The *Madonna and Child*, an earlier work by either Fra Angelico or Benozzo Gozzoli, is in the chapel to the left of the altar, close to Fra Angelico's tomb. The father of modern astronomy, Galileo Galilei, who dared suggest that the earth revolved around the sun, was tried for heresy in the adjoining monastery in 1633. In the square in front of the church is a charming marble elephant bearing an obelisk on its back, by Bernini.

Sant'Ignazio di Loyola

Piazza Sant'Ignazio (06 679 4406). **Open** 7.30am-7pm Mon-Sat; 9am-7pm Sun. **Map** p71 E2 **⑥②**

Work on Sant'Ignazio began in 1626, to commemorate the canonisation of St Ignatius, founder of the Jesuits. Trompe l'oeil columns soar above the nave, and architraves by Andrea Pozzo open to a cloudy heaven. When the monks next door claimed that a dome would rob them of light, Pozzo simply painted a dome on the ceiling. The illusion is fairly convincing if you stand on the disc set in the floor of the nave. Walk away, however, and it quickly collapses.

Sant'Ivo alla Sapienza

Corso Rinascimento 40 (06 361 2562). **Open** 9am-noon Sun. **Map** p71 D3 **⑥③**

In this crowning glory of Borromini's tortured imagination, completed in 1660, the concave façade is countered by the convex bulk of the dome, which terminates in a bizarre corkscrew spire.

Inside, the convex and concave surfaces on the walls and up into the dome leave you feeling like someone spiked your cappuccino.

Eating & drinking

See also **Baffetto 2** (p73), **Chiostro del Bramante** (p77) and **Friends Art Café** (p135).

Armando al Pantheon

Salita de' Crescenzi 31 (06 6880 3034, www.armandoalpantheon.it). **Meals served** 12.30-3pm, 7.15-11pm Mon-Fri; 12.30-3pm Sat. Closed Aug. €€. **Roman**. Map p71 D2 ⑥④
Armando's charming sons continue to serve the kind of simple no-frills Roman fare at honest prices that has been on offer here since 1961: a miracle in this neighbourhood of postmodern makeovers and tourist rip-offs. The menu's only concessions to changing times are a range of vegetarian and gluten-free dishes.

Bar Sant'Eustachio

Piazza Sant'Eustachio 82 (06 6880 2048, www.santeustachioilcaffe.it). **Open** 8.30am-1am Mon-Thur, Sun; 8.30am-1.20am Fri, Sat. No credit cards. **Café**. Map p71 D3 ⑥⑤
This is one of the city's most famous coffee bars and its walls are plastered with celebrity testimonials. The coffee is quite extraordinary, if expensive. Try the *gran caffè*: the *schiuma* (froth) can be slurped out afterwards with spoon or fingers.

Caffè Bernini

Piazza Navona 44 (06 6819 2998, www.caffebernini.it). **Open** 9am-12.30am daily. *Meals served* 10am-11.30pm daily. Closed 4wks Jan-Feb. **Café/Creative Italian**. Map p70 C2 ⑥⑥
A plethora of tourist rip-off eateries can make a visit to glorious piazza Navona a trial. But at Caffè Bernini the pan-Med food is good and fairly priced for

the area (€€€), and sitting outside for a coffee or *aperitivo* is a pleasure.

Caffè della Pace

Via della Pace 3/7 (06 686 1216, www.caffedellapace.it). **Open** 4pm-3am Mon; 8.30am-2am Tue-Sun. **Café/bar**. Map p70 C2 ⑥⑦
Eternally à la mode, Caffè della Pace has warm, antiques- and flower-filled rooms for the colder months, and (comparatively pricey) pavement tables, beneath the trademark ivy-clad façade, for sunny weather.

La Caffettiera

Piazza di Pietra 65 (06 679 8147, www.grancaffelacaffettiera.com). **Open** 7am-10pm daily. Closed Sun in summer. **Café**. Map p71 E2 ⑥⑨
Politicians from the nearby parliament buildings lounge in the sumptuous tea room of this temple to Neapolitan goodies, while lesser mortals bolt coffees at the bar. The rum babà reigns supreme, but ricotta-lovers rave over the crunchy *sfogliatella*.

Casa Bleve

Via del Teatro Valle 48-49 (06 686 5970, www.casableve.it). **Meals served** 12.30-2.30pm, 7.30-10pm Tue, Sat; 1-3pm, 7-10pm Wed-Fri. Closed 3wks Aug. €€€. **Wine bar/Italian**. Map p71 D3 ⑦⓪
The main room of this elegant wine bar occupies a huge, colonnaded roofed-in courtyard in a palazzo near the Pantheon. Bleve's signature buffet has been replaced by an à la carte menu, but there's still the same impressive selection of wines to choose from. The original Bleve off-licence/eaterie, located in the Ghetto (La Vecchia Bottega del Vino, via Santa Maria del Pianto 9-11) now focuses on fine cheeses, which can be sampled on the spot.

Da Francesco

Piazza del Fico 29 (06 686 4009). **Meals served** 11.50-3pm, 7pm-

12.30am Mon, Wed-Sun. €€.
Pizzeria. Map p70 B2 ⑩
Da Francesco serves tasty pizzas and a range of competent, classic dishes in a warm, traditional ambience. Service is brisk but friendly.

Enoteca Corsi

Via del Gesù 87-88 (06 679 0821, www.enotecacorsi.com). **Meals served** noon-3.30pm Mon-Sat. Closed Aug. €€. **Roman**. Map p71 E3 ⑪
The menu changes daily at this 1940s wine shop – you'll find it written up on the board at the entrance. Dishes at Enoteca Corsi follow the traditional Roman culinary calendar – potato *gnocchi* on Thursday and stewed salt cod on Friday.

Etabli

Vicolo delle Vacche 9 (06 9761 6694, www.etabli.it). **Open** 12.30-3pm, 6pm-2am daily. Closed 2wks Aug. **Bar**. Map p70 B2 ⑫
This venue in the super-chic *triangolo della pace* area attracts Rome's bright young things with its minimalist decor, twiddly chandeliers and deep armchairs around the fireplace. The welcome is warm, the vibe intimate. In one room, light meals are served at appropriate times; there's a restaurant (€€€) upstairs.

Gelateria del Teatro

Via di San Simone 70 (06 4547 4880). **Open** noon-10.30pm daily. **Ice-cream**. Map p70 B2 ⑬
See box p97.

Grano

Piazza Rondanini 53 (06 6819 2096, www.ristorantegrano.it). **Open** 12.30-3pm, 7.30pm-midnight daily. €€€. **Creative Southern Italian**. Map p71 D2 ⑭
The name means wheat in Italian, and pasta and delicious own-made bread make their presence felt in this country-chic restaurant with southern Italian influences.

Green T

Via Pie' di Marmo 28 (06 679 8628, www.green-tea.it). **Meals served** 12.15-3pm, 6pm-midnight Mon-Sat. Closed 2wks Aug. €€€. **Chinese**. Map p71 E3 ⑮
Stylishly pared back in its decor, this Chinese restaurant has a coolly hushed air that comes as a welcome break after a hot morning's sightseeing and when you just can't take another plate of pasta. The set-lunch menus are a good deal, and it reopens at 6pm for a wide and excellent choice of teas and snacks.

Salotto 42

Piazza di Pietra 42 (06 678 5804, www.salotto42.it). **Open** 10am-2am Tue-Sat; 10am-midnight Mon, Sun. Closed Aug. **Bar**. Map p71 E2 ⑯
Incredibly comfortable chairs and sofas give a cosy feel to Salotto 42 during the day, when a smörgåsbord of nibbles is available. By night, the sleek room becomes a gorgeous cocktail bar with a great soundtrack and excellent cocktails. There's also a selection of books and magazines on fashion, art and design.

Société Lutèce

Piazza di Montevecchio 17 (06 6830 1472, www.societe-lutece.it). **Open** 6.30pm-2am Tue-Sun. Closed 2wks Aug. No credit cards. **Bar**. Map p70 C2 ⑰
Popular with eclectic Roman hipsters, the Société Lutèce's cramped quarters often cause a spill-over into the small piazza. The *aperitivo* buffet (from 6.30pm) is plentiful, and the vibe is decidedly laid-back.

Shopping

Ai Monasteri

Corso Rinascimento 72 (06 6880 2783, www.aimonasteri.it). **Open** 10am-1pm, 5-7.30pm Mon-Wed, Fri, Sat; 9am-1pm Thur. Closed 2wks Aug. Map p70 C2 ⑱

This richly perfumed shop, founded in 1894, sells jams, chocolates, cosmetics and cure-all potions produced by religious orders around Italy.

Arsenale

Via del Governo Vecchio 64 (06 686 1380, www.patriziapieroni.it). **Open** 3.30-7.30pm Mon; 10am-7.30pm Tue-Sat. Closed 2wks Aug. **Map** p70 C2 ❼❾
Patrizia Pieroni's wonderful garments make for great window displays – not to mention successful party conversation pieces – and have been going down well with the Roman boho-chic luvvy crowd for years.

Ditta G Poggi

Via del Gesù 74-75 (06 679 3674, www.poggi1825.it). **Open** 9am-1pm, 4-7.30pm Mon-Sat (closed Sat in Aug). **Map** p71 E3 ❽⓪
This wonderfully old-fashioned shop has been selling paints, brushes, canvases and artists' supplies of every description since 1825.

Maga Morgana

Via del Governo Vecchio 27 (06 687 9995). **Open** 10am-8pm Mon-Sat. **Map** p70 B2 ❽❶
Designer Luciana Iannace's quirky women's clothes include hand-knitted sweaters, skirts and dresses. More knitted and woollen items are sold at the sister shop down the road at no.98.

Moriondo & Gariglio

Via del Piè di Marmo 21 (06 699 0856). **Open** 9am-7.30pm Mon-Sat. Closed Aug. **Map** p71 E3 ❽❷
This fairytale chocolate shop with beautiful gift boxes is especially lovely close to Christmas, when you will have to fight to get your hands on the excellent *marrons glacés*. At Easter, they'll seal your gift to that special someone inside delicious eggs.

Le Tartarughe

Via Pie' di Marmo 17 (06 679 2240, www.susannalisoperletartarughe.it).

Open noon-7.30pm Mon; 10am-7.30pm Tue-Sat. Closed 2wks Aug.
Map p71 E3 ❽❸
Designer Susanna Liso's sumptuous classic-with-a-twist creations range from cocktail dresses to elegant workwear, in eye-catching colours. Gorgeous accessories can be found across the road at no.33. And there's a new branch at via Mastrogiorgio 70, in Testaccio.

Nightlife

See also **Friends Art Café** (p135), **Salotto 42** and **Société Lutèce** (for both, p82).

Anima

Via Santa Maria dell'Anima 57 (347 850 9256). **Open** 7pm-4am daily. **Map** p70 C2 ❽❹
With improbably baroque gilded mouldings, this small venue has a buzzing atmosphere and serves great drinks. It caters for a mixed crowd of all ages and nationalities. Expect to hear hip hop, R&B, funk, soul and reggae.

Bloom

Via Santa Maria dell'Anima 57 (347 850 9256). **Open** 7pm-4am daily. **Map** p70 C2 ❽❺
A bar and disco (generally on Friday and Saturday), Bloom is cooler than ice: eat sushi, sip a cocktail, have a dance or simply relax and join your fashionable fellow guests checking out each others' outfits.

La Maison

Vicolo dei Granari 3 (06 683 3312, www.lamaisonroma.it). **Open** 11pm-4am Wed-Sat. Closed June-Sept. **Map** p70 C2 ❽❻
One of the clubs of choice of Rome's fashion victims, La Maison is dressed to impress. Huge chandeliers, dark red walls and curvy sofas give it an opulent, courtly feeling. Surprisingly, the music on offer is not banal and the atmosphere is buzzing. The doormen are picky, however.

Tridente, Trevi & Borghese

Il Tridente

With its English banks and English bookshops, the wedge-shaped Tridente was a home-from-home for the Grand Tourists of the 18th and 19th centuries. English '*milords*' took lodgings in and around piazza di Spagna. When venturing beyond the familiar streets, they resorted to guides to help them avoid pitfalls.

Even today, there are visitors who never make it further than the Tridente's plethora of glorious fashion retailers: from Armani to Zegna, there's hardly a big name in *moda* that hasn't staked a claim in the narrow, thronging streets of the Tridente.

The whole area was built as a showpiece. At the head of the wedge is **piazza del Popolo**, given its oval form by architect Giuseppe Valadier during the early 19th century.

Leading out centrally from the square is the Tridente's principal thoroughfare, via del Corso, which passes high-street clothing retailers en route to the towering column of Marcus Aurelius (piazza Colonna) – which was built between AD 180 and 196 to commemorate the victories on the battlefield of that most intellectual of Roman emperors – and piazza Venezia.

Via Ripetta veers off down the riverside, leading to Augustus' mausoleum and the **Ara Pacis**.

The third street, chic via del Babuino, runs past a series of tempting antique and designer stores to the **Spanish Steps**.

Parallel to via del Babuino, tucked right below the Pincio hill, is via Margutta, fondly remembered as the focus of the 1960s art scene and 'home' to Gregory Peck in the 1953 classic *Roman Holiday*. Fellini also lived on this artsy alley.

Criss-crossing the three main arteries are boutique-lined streets such as via Condotti, which have given Rome its reputation as a major fashion centre.

Sights & museums

Ara Pacis Museum

Via Ripetta/lungotevere in Augusta (06 0608, www.arapacis.it). **Open** 9am-7pm Tue-Sun. **Admission** €8; €6 reductions; extra charge during exhibitions. **Map** p86 A2 **1**

The *Ara pacis augustae* ('Augustan Altar of Peace') was inaugurated in 9 BC to celebrate the security that the Emperor Augustus's victories had brought. The altar was rebuilt in the early 20th century from fragments amassed through a long dig and a trawl through the world's museums. The altar itself sits inside an enclosure carved with exquisitely realistic reliefs. The upper band shows the ceremonies surrounding the dedication of the altar. The carved faces of Augustus and his family have all been identified. The monument resides in a container designed by US architect Richard Meier, with an exhibition space below. Meier agreed in 2010 to demolish an exterior wall of his structure which obscured the view of neighbouring churches.

The brick cylinder next door in piazza Augusto Imperatore was originally a mausoleum covered with marble pillars and statues, begun in 28 BC. Augustus was laid to rest in the central chamber on his death in AD 14. The square is currently being refurbished.

Explora – Museo dei Bambini di Roma

Via Flaminia 82 (06 361 3776, www.mdbr.it). **Open** sessions at 10am, noon, 3pm, 5pm Tue-Sun. **Admission** €7; €6 Thur afternoon; under-3s free. **Map** p93 A2 **2**

This children's museum provides educational fun for under-12s. Booking is essential at weekends.

Keats-Shelley Memorial House

Piazza di Spagna 26 (06 678 4235, www.keats-shelley-house.org). **Open** 10am-1pm, 2-6pm Mon-Fri; 11am-2pm, 3-6pm Sat. Closed 1wk Dec. **Admission** €4; €3 reductions. **Map** p86 C3 **3**

The house at the bottom of the Spanish Steps where the 25-year-old John Keats died of tuberculosis in 1821 is crammed with mementos: a lock of Keats's hair and his death mask, an urn holding tiny pieces of Shelley's charred skeleton, and copies of documents and letters.

Palazzo Ruspoli – Fondazione Memmo

Via del Corso 418 (06 687 4704, www.fondazionememmo.com). **Open** times vary. **Admission** varies. No credit cards. **Map** p86 B3 **4**

The palace of one of Rome's old noble families is used for touring exhibitions of art, archaeology and history. The basement rooms often host photo exhibitions; admission is sometimes free.

Propaganda Fide Museum

NEW *Via di Propaganda 1C (06 6988 0266, www.museopropagandafide.it).* **Open** 2.30-6pm Mon, Wed, Fri or mornings by appt. **Admission** €8. **Map** p86 C3 **5**

Bernini and Borromini had a hand in designing this Vatican-owned pile facing piazza di Spagna. Long the HQ of the Inquisition, it now displays its art collection, which includes a Canova and much plunder from missions.

San Lorenzo in Lucina

Piazza San Lorenzo in Lucina 16A (06 687 1494). **Open** 8am-8pm daily. **Map** p86 B3 **6**

This 12th-century church – built on the site of an early Christian place of worship – incorporates Roman columns into its exterior. The 17th-century interior has Bernini portrait busts, a 17th-century *Crucifixion* by Guido Reni and a monument to French artist Nicolas

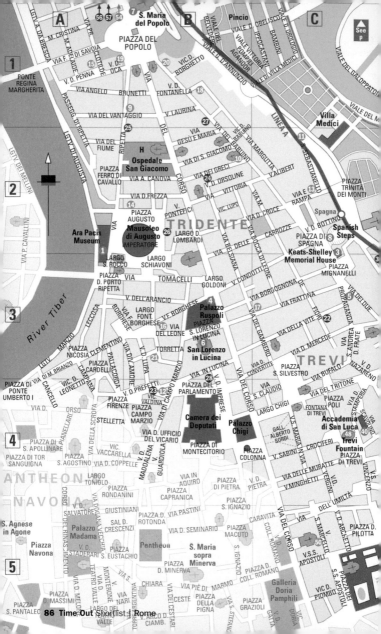

Ara Pacis Museum p85

Poussin, who died in Rome in 1665. In the first chapel on the right is a grill, reputed to be the one on which St Lawrence was roasted to death.

Santa Maria del Popolo

Piazza del Popolo 12 (06 361 0836).
Open 7.30am-noon, 4-7pm Mon-Sat; 7.30am-1.30pm, 4.30-7.30pm Sun.
Map p86 B1 **7**

According to legend, Santa Maria del Popolo occupies the site where the hated Emperor Nero was buried. In 1099, Pope Paschal II built a chapel here to dispel demons still believed to haunt the spot. In 1472, Pope Sixtus IV rebuilt the chapel as a church. In the apse, which was designed by Bramante, are Rome's first stained-glass windows (1509). The choir ceiling and first and third chapels in the right aisle were frescoed by Pinturicchio, while the Chigi Chapel was designed by Raphael for wealthy banker Agostino Chigi, and features Chigi's horoscope. The biggest draw, though, are the two masterpieces by Caravaggio to the left of the main altar, showing the stories of Peter and Paul.

Spanish Steps & Piazza di Spagna

Map p86 C2 **8**

Piazza di Spagna has been considered a compulsory stop for visitors to Rome since the 18th century. The square takes its name from the Spanish Embassy, but is most famous for the Spanish Steps (Scalinata di Trinità dei Monti), an elegant cascade down from the church of Trinità dei Monti. The steps (completed in 1725) were, in fact, funded by a French diplomat. At the foot of the stairs is a boat-shaped fountain designed in 1627 by either Gian Lorenzo Bernini or his father Pietro.

Eating & drinking

Buccone

Via Ripetta 19-20 (06 361 2154, www.enotecabuccone.com). **Open** *Shop* 9am-8.30pm Mon-Thur; 9am-11.30pm

Fri, Sat. **Meals served** 12.30-3pm Mon-Thur; 12.30-3pm, 7.30-10.30pm Fri, Sat. Closed 2wks Aug. €€.
Enoteca. **Map** p86 B1 **9**

Originally – and still – a bottle shop, Buccone has tables squeezed between its high wooden shelves. The fare – a few pasta dishes, meaty seconds and creative salads – is simple but good, the prices very reasonable.

Caffè Canova-Tadolini

Via del Babuino 150A (06 3211 0702, www.canovatadolini.com). **Open** 8am-midnight daily. Closed 2wks Aug.
Café. **Map** p86 B2 **10**

Once the studio of 19th-century sculptor Antonio Canova, this café has tables among its sculpture models and a refined and elegant old-world feel.

Ciampini – Café du Jardin

Piazza Trinità dei Monti (06 678 5678, www.caffeciampini.com). **Open** 8am-1am daily. Closed mid Oct-Mar.
Café. **Map** p86 C2 **11**

This open-air café and restaurant near the top of the Spanish Steps is surrounded by creeper-curtained trellises and has a pond in the centre. There's a spectacular view, especially at sunset.

Da Gino

Vicolo Rosini 4 (06 687 3434). **Meals served** 1-2.45pm, 8-10.30pm Mon-Sat. Closed Aug. €€. No credit cards.
Roman. **Map** p86 B4 **12**

In a hard-to-find lane just off piazza del Parlamento, this old-style *osteria* champions the lighter side of the local tradition in dishes like *tonnarelli alla ciociara* (pasta with mushrooms and tomatoes), and pasta and chickpeas in ray sauce; desserts include an excellent tiramisù.

GiNa

Via San Sebastianello 7A (06 678 0251, www.ginaroma.com). **Open** 11am-8pm daily. Closed 2wks Aug. €€. **Italian/bar**. **Map** p86 C2 **13**

This bright and artsy light-lunch and dinner bar is a rather good option for snacking by the Spanish Steps. The menu is homely: a couple of soups, four or five daily pasta dishes, a range of creative and gourmet salads, and wine by the glass or bottle. You can also order a gourmet picnic hamper.

'Gusto

Piazza Augusto Imperatore 9 (06 322 6273, www.gusto.it). **Open** *Wine bar* noon-1am daily. **Meals served** *Pizzeria* 12.30-3pm, 7.30pm-1am daily. *Restaurant* 12.30-3pm, 7.45pm-midnight daily. €€-€€€. **Pizzeria/Italian/Wine bar**. Map p86 B2 ⑭
'Gusto is a multi-purpose, split-level pizzeria, restaurant and wine bar, with a kitchen shop and bookshop next door. The ground-floor pizza and salad bar is always packed; the buffet lunch is good value. Upstairs, the more expensive restaurant applies oriental techniques to Italian models, not always convincingly. The stylish wine bar at the back is buzzing, with a good choice of wines by the glass and nibbles. Around the corner at via della Frezza 16, the mod L'Osteria is part of the same outfit. 'Gusto's newest out-post – Tati al 28 – is a minimal-chic fish restaurant and wine bar at piazza Augusto Imperatore 28.

Hotel Locarno Bar

Via della Penna 22 (06 361 0841, www.hotellocarno.com). **Open** 7am-1am daily. €€. **Café/bar**. Map p86 A1 ⑮
The art-nouveau ground-floor café in this historic hotel has become one of *the* places to rub shoulders with Rome's bright young things at *aperitivo* hour (from 6.30pm). The acting crowd in particular lounge at its fire-side tables or in the delightful courtyard.

Matricianella

Via del Leone 4 (06 683 2100, www.matricianella.it). **Meals served** 12.30-3pm, 7.30-11pm Mon-Sat. €€€. **Roman**. Map p86 B3 ⑯
A friendly, bustling place with good prices. The Roman imprint is most

evident in classics such as the *bucatini all'amatriciana* (pasta with a spicy sausage sauce) or the *abbacchio a scottadito* (thin strips of lamb), but there are lots of creative options. The well-chosen wine list is a model of honest pricing. Book ahead.

Palatium

Via Frattina 94 (06 6920 2132, www.enotecapalatium.it). **Open** 11am-11pm Mon-Sat. Closed 2wks Aug. €€. **Wine bar/Italian**. Map p86 C3 ⑰
Although it's backed by the Lazio regional government, this wine bar and eaterie is more than a PR exercise, offering the chance to go beyond the Castelli romani clichés to explore lesser-known local vintages such as Cesanese or Aleatico. After *aperitivi* (6.30-8pm), Palatium switches into restaurant mode, offering light, innovative dishes.

RistorArte Il Margutta

Via Margutta 118 (06 3265 0577, www.ilmarguttavegetariano.it). **Meals served** 10.30am-3.30pm, 7.30-11.30pm daily. €€. **Vegetarian**. Map p86 B1 ⑱
Located in Rome's gallery alley, this long-running vegetarian eaterie offers a good pile-your-plate buffet lunch (€12-€15) all week, and even more choice plus live music on Sunday (€25). Lunch is a livelier, better-value bet than the *à la carte* evenings.

Rosati

Piazza del Popolo 4/5A (06 322 5859, www.rosatibar.it). **Open** 7am-11pm daily. **Café/bar**. Map p86 A1 ⑲
Once frequented by Calvino and Pasolini, this bar's elegant interior has remained unchanged since 1922. Try the *Sogni romani* cocktail: orange juice with liqueurs in red and yellow – the colours of the city.

Stravinskij Bar

Via del Babuino 9 (06 328 881, 06 689 1694, www.hotelderussie.it). **Open** 9am-1am daily. **Café/bar**. Map p86 B1 ⑳

Inside the swanky De Russie hotel, this chic bar has an inside area with comfy armchairs and a fabulous patio where tables are surrounded by orange trees.

Vic's

Vicolo della Torretta 60 (06 687 1445). **Meals served** 12.30-3pm, 7.30-11pm Mon-Sat. **€.** No credit cards. **Italian. Map** p86 B3 **㉑**

This wine and salad bar offers imaginative salads such as radicchio, pine nuts, sultanas and parmesan. Pared-back decor, charming service and a fairly priced wine list complete the picture.

Shopping

The Tridente is Rome's chic shopping area *per eccellenza*. In this wedge you'll find all the big names of Italian fashion: Prada, Fendi, Gucci, Dolce & Gabbana, et al.

Anglo-American Book Co

Via della Vite 102 (06 679 5222, www.aab.it). **Open** 3.30-7.30pm Mon; 10.30am-7.30pm Tue-Sat. Closed 2wks Aug. **Map** p86 C3 **㉒**

A good selection of books in English.

Bottega dei sapori della legalità

Via dei Prefetti 23 (06 6992 5262, www.liberaterra.it). **Open** 10am-1pm, 3-6.30pm Mon-Fri. Closed Aug. **Map** p86 B4 **㉓**

This shop may look like any other upmarket food emporium, with delicious olive oil, wine and organic foodstuffs. What sets it apart is that everything is produced by co-operatives of young people on land confiscated from organised crime outfits. See box p123.

Lion Bookshop

Via dei Greci 36 (06 3265 4007, www.thelionbookshop.com). **Open** 3.30-7.30pm Mon; 10am-7pm Tue-Sun. **Map** p86 B2 **㉔**

This friendly shop is a great place for modern fiction and children's books.

L'Olfattorio – Bar à Parfums

Via Ripetta 34 (06 361 2325, www.olfattorio.it). **Open** 11am-7.30pm Mon-Sat. Closed 1wk Aug. **Map** p86 B1 **㉕**

One of the resident scent-mixing experts will awaken your olfactory organs, and guide you towards your perfect perfume.

La Soffitta Sotto i Portici

Piazza Augusto Imperatore (06 3600 5345). **Open** 9am-sunset 1st & 3rd Sun of mth. Closed Aug. **Map** p86 B2 **㉖**

A street market with collectibles of all kinds, ranging from magazines to jewellery, at non-bargain prices. There's a multilingual information desk.

WeTAD

Via del Babuino 155A (06 3269 5131, www.wetad.it). **Open** noon-7.30pm Mon, Sun; 10.30am-7.30pm Tue-Fri; 10.30am-8pm Sat. **Map** p86 B1 **㉗**

The idea behind this 'concept store' is that you can shop for clothes, shoes, flowers, household goods, magazines, CDs and perfumes, get your hair done, eat fusion Thai-Italian and drink – all in one place.

Arts & leisure

Nuovo Olimpia

Via in Lucina 16G (06 686 1068). **Map** p86 B3 **㉘**

High-(ish) profile arthouse movies are likely to turn up on this cinema's screens in the original language.

Villa Borghese & Via Veneto

Until the 1870s, when Rome became the capital of newly united Italy and speculators set to work to house the soaring population, the the city was dotted with splendid private estates. An act of unusual foresight by the state in 1901 saved Villa Borghese from the carve-up, and left us with this delightful green space.

The area has always been green. Ancient aristocrats built sprawling villas here, and noble families and monastic orders continued the tradition right up until the 1800s. Now the city's most central public park, it offers a great art repository – the superb **Galleria Borghese** – plus one of Rome's greatest views: from the Pincio, over piazza del Popolo to the dome of St Peter's.

Descending south from the park, via Vittorio Veneto (known simply as via Veneto) was the haunt of the famous and glamorous in the *dolce vita* years of the 1950s and '60s. These days, it's home to insurance companies, luxury hotels and visitors wondering where the stars and paparazzi went.

At the southern end of via Veneto is piazza Barberini. In ancient times, erotic dances were performed here to mark the coming of spring. The square's magnificent centrepiece, Bernini's Triton fountain, was once in open countryside. Now he sits – his two fish-tail legs tucked beneath him on a shell supported by four dolphins – amid thundering traffic. The bees around him are the Barberini family emblem.

Sights & museums

Bioparco-Zoo

Piazzale del Giardino Zoologico 20 (06 360 8211, www.bioparco.it). **Open** 9.30am-5pm daily. **Admission** €12.50; €10.50 reductions. **Map** p93 D1/D2 ㉙
Slightly more sprightly since its makeover from 'zoo' to 'biopark', this place will easily keep your kids happy for an afternoon. Next door – and accessible through the zoo – is the Museo Civico di Zoologia di Roma, with sections on biodiversity and extreme habitats.

Galleria Borghese

Piazzale del Museo Borghese 5 (06 32 810, www.galleriaborghese.it). **Open** 9am-7pm Tue-Sun. **Admission** €8.50; €5.25 reductions; extra charge during exhibitions. **Map** p93 E2 ㉚
Note: booking (€2) is obligatory.
Begun in 1608, the Casinò Borghese was designed to house the art collection of Cardinal Scipione Borghese, Bernini's greatest patron. The interior decoration (1775-90) was restored in the 1990s. A double staircase leads to the entrance salon, with fourth-century AD mosaics showing gladiators fighting wild animals.

In room 1 is Antonio Canova's 1808 marble figure of Pauline, sister of Napoleon and wife of Prince Camillo Borghese, as a topless *Venus*; the Prince thought the work so provocative that he forbade even the artist from seeing it after completion. Rooms 2-4 contain some wonderful sculptures by Gian Lorenzo Bernini: the *David* (1624) in room 2 is a self-portrait of the artist; room 3 houses his *Apollo and Daphne* (1625); room 4 his *Rape of Proserpine* (1622).

Room 5's important pieces of classical sculpture include a Roman copy of a Greek dancing faun and a sleeping hermaphrodite. Bernini's *Aeneas and Anchises* (1620) dominates room 6. The six Caravaggios in room 8 include the *Boy with a Basket of Fruit* (c1594) and the *Sick Bacchus* (c1593), believed to be a self-portrait.

Upstairs, the picture gallery holds a surfeit of masterpieces. Look out for: Raphael's *Deposition* and Pinturicchio's *Crucifixion with Saints Jerome and Christopher* (room 9); Lucas Cranach's *Venus and Cupid with Honeycomb* (room 10); and Rubens' spectacular *Pietà* and *Susanna and the Elders* (room 18). Titian's *Venus Blindfolding Cupid* and *Sacred and Profane Love*, recently restored but still difficult to interpret, are the stars of room 20, which also contains a stunning *Portrait of a Man* by Antonello da Messina.

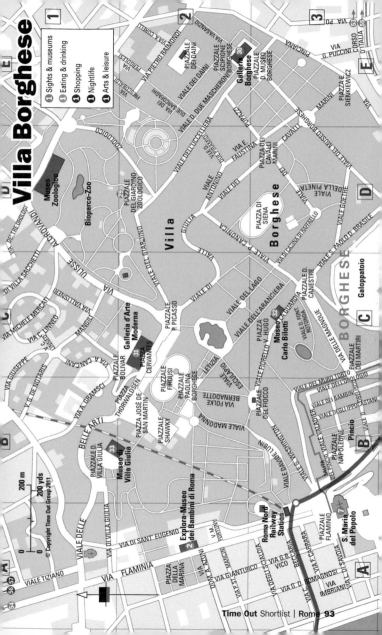

Villa Borghese

Legend:
- ① Sights & museums
- ① Eating & drinking
- ② Shopping
- ① Nightlife
- ① Arts & leisure

Key locations

Museo Zoologico
Bioparco-Zoo
Galleria Borghese 30
Galleria d'Arte Moderna 31
Museo Carlo Bilotti 32
Museo di Villa Giulia 33
Explora-Museo dei Bambini di Roma 2
Roma Nord Railway Station
S. Maria del Popolo
Galoppatoio

Map roads and piazzas

VIA PO
CORSO D'ITALIA
VIA G. PUCCINI
VIA PETROSELLI
VIA PIETRO RAIMONDI
VIA VASANZIO
VIA CORELLI
PIAZZALE SCIPIONE BORGHESE
VIA DEI DAINI
PIAZZALE D. MUSEO BORGHESE
VIALE DEL MUSEO BORGHESE
PIAZZA E. SIENKIEWICZ
VIA DEL SAMBUCOGRAMI
VIA D. DUE MASCHERONI
VIA DEI
VIALE DELL'UCCELLIERA
VIA F. FAUSTINA
PIAZZA DEI CAVALLI MARINI
VIALE ANTONINO
ZOOLOGICO
PIAZZALE DEL GIARDINO ZOOLOGICO
VIA DELL'URANIO
VIALE DELL'ORTOBOTANICO
VIALE DELLA PINETA
VIA DEL GIARDINO
VIALE GOETHE
PIAZZA DI SIENA
Villa Borghese
VIALE P. CANONICA
VIALE DI
VIA DI PORTA PINCIANA
VIA DI CASINA DI RAFFAELLO
VIALE DEL LAGO
VIALE S. PAOLO DEL BRASILE
BORGHESE
PIAZZALE D. CANESTRE
VIALE DELLE MAGNOLIE
VIALE DELL'ARANCIERA
PIAZZALE DELL'OROLOGIO
PIAZZA FIORELLO V. HUGO
PIAZZALE D. MARTIRI
VIA MICHELE MERCATI
VIA C. LINNEO
VIA CANCANI
VIALE TASSO
VIA G. DE NOTARIS
VIA GIUSEPPE
VIA A. GRAMSCI
PIAZZALE BOLIVAR
PIAZZA CERVANTES
PIAZZA THORWALDSEN
PIAZZA JOSÉ DE SAN MARTIN
PIAZZALE FIRDUSI
PIAZZALE PAOLINA BORGHESE
PIAZZALE SHAWKY
VIALE FIORELLO V. HUGO
VIA FOLKE BERNADOTTE
VIA GIULIA
VIALE ESQUILINO
PIAZZALE DEL FIOCCO
VIALE DELL'OROLOGIO
VIALE DEI BAMBINI
VIALE DEGLI IPPOCASTANI
PIAZZALE NAPOLEONE
PIAZZA MADONNA
VIALE DANTE
VIALE LUBIN
SALITA DEL PINCIO
VIALE VALADIER
PIAZZALE DEL PINCIO
Pincio
VIA DELL'ORSO
VIA DI VILLA SACCHETTI
VIA ULISSE ALDROVANDI
VIA DEI MONTI PARIOLI
VIA DI VILLA GIULIA
BELLE ARTI
PIAZZALE D. VILLA GIULIA
VIALE DELLE BELLE ARTI
VIALE TIZIANO
VIA FLAMINIA
VIA DI SANT'EUGENIO
VIA V. M. FORTUNY
PIAZZA DELLA MARINA
VIA DEGLI SCIALOJA
VIA DELLE
VIA G.B. VICO
VIA G.A. SARTORIO
VIA GIANTURCO
VIA ST. MANCINI
VIA G.B. BODONI
PIAZZALE FLAMINIO
VIA BECCARIA
VIA LUISA DI SAVOIA
VIA CARRARA
VIA G.D. ROMAGNOSI
VIA IMBRIANI
VIA GALVANI

200 m
200 yds
0
© Copyright Time Out Group 2011

Galleria Nazionale d'Arte Moderna e Contemporanea

Viale delle Belle Arti 131 (06 3229 8221, www.gnam.beniculturali.it). **Open** 8.30am-7.15pm Tue-Sun. **Admission** €8; €4 reductions; extra charge during exhibitions. No credit cards. **Map** p93 C2 ③

This collection begins with the 19th century: an enormous statue of *Hercules* by Canova dominates the central hall of the left wing; elsewhere are charming views of the 19th-century Italian landscape. The 20th-century component includes works by de Chirico, Modigliani, Morandi and Marini. International stars include *The Three Ages* by Klimt and *The Gardener* and *Madame Ginoux* by Van Gogh. Cézanne, Braque, Rodin and Henry Moore are also represented.

Museo Carlo Bilotti

Viale Fiorello La Guardia (06 0608, www.museocarlobilotti.it). **Open** 9am-7pm Tue-Sun. **Admission** €4.50; €2.50 reductions; extra charge for exhibitions. No credit cards. **Map** p93 C3 ③

This museum houses the collection of billionaire art tycoon Carlo Bilotti: Giorgio de Chirico, Larry Rivers, Jean Dubuffet and Andy Warhol all feature.

Museo di Villa Giulia

Piazzale di Villa Giulia 9 (06 322 6571, www.villaborghese.it). **Open** 8.30am-7.30pm Tue-Sun. **Admission** €8; €4 reductions. No credit cards. **Map** p93 B1 ③

In a villa designed by Michelangelo and Vignola in the mid 1500s, the museum records the pre-Roman peoples of central Italy, including the sophisticated Etruscans. The latter went to their graves well prepared, and most of the collection comes from excavated tombs: hundreds of vases, pieces of furniture and models of buildings made to accompany the dead. In the courtyard, stairs descend to the nymphaeum; in an adjacent room is the sixth-century BC *Apollo of Veio*. In the garden is a reconstruction of an Etruscan temple, and a café.

Santa Maria della Concezione

Via V Veneto 27 (06 487 1185, www.cappucciniviaveneto.it). **Open** *Church* 7.30am-noon, 3-7pm daily. *Crypt* 9am-noon, 3-6pm Mon-Wed, Fri-Sun. **Admission** *Crypt* donation expected. **Map** p87 E3 ③

Commonly known as *i cappuccini* (the Capuchins) after the long-bearded, brown-clad Franciscan sub-order to which it belongs, this Baroque church's attraction lies in the crypt: the skeletons of over 4,000 monks have been dismantled and arranged in swirls and curlicues through four chapels. Ribs hang from the ceiling in the form of chandeliers, and inverted pelvic bones make the shape of hour-glasses – a reminder (as a notice states) that 'you will be what we now are'.

Eating & drinking

Cantina Cantarini

Piazza Sallustio 12 (06 485 528). **Meals served** 12.30-3pm, 7.30-10.30pm Mon-Sat. Closed 3wks Aug, 2wks Dec-Jan. **€€€**. **Roman**. **Map** off p87 F2 ③

This good-value, high-quality trattoria is meat-based for the first part of the week, then turns fishy thereafter. The atmosphere is as *allegro* as seating is tight – though outside tables take off some of the pressure during the summer months.

Cinecaffè – Casina delle Rose

Largo M Mastroianni 1 (06 4201 6224, www.cinecaffe.it). **Open** *Café* 9am-8pm daily. *Restaurant* 12.30-3pm Mon-Fri; 12.30-4pm Sat, Sun. **Café/Italian**. **Map** p87 D1 ③

This ultra-civilised café at the via Veneto end of Villa Borghese serves excellent coffee, drinks and wallet-friendly light lunches to office workers, tourists and cinema aficionados. The restaurant, serving mod-Med fare, is pricier.

Filippo La Mantia

NEW *Hotel Majestic, via Veneto 50 (06 4214 4715, www.filippolamantia.com).* **Meals served** 12.30-2.30pm, 8.30-11.30pm Mon-Fri; 8.30-11.30pm Sat; 12.30-3.30pm Sun. €€€€. **Sicilian**. **Map** p87 E2 ㊲
See box p177.

Time Seafood Café

NEW *Via Veneto 155 (06 487 881, www.ghvv.it).* **Open** 7.30am-2am daily. €€. **Seafood/wine bar**. **Map** p87 E2 ㊳
This street-level bar of the recently opened Grand Hotel Via Veneto has swiftly become a chic meeting place for Rome's see-and-be-seen set. From power breakfast through great snacky lunches – seafood is the main act but there are good filled rolls and club sandwiches too – to a buzzing *aperitivo* scene and late into the evening, Time provides ample opportunities for people-watching.

Nightlife

Gregory's

Via Gregoriana 54A (06 679 6386, www.gregorysjazz.com). **Open** 7pm-2am Thur-Sun. Closed Aug. **Map** p86 C3 ㊴
This cosy live venue oozes jazz culture from every pore; it has top live acts and a jam session on Wednesdays. Book ahead for the restaurant.

Trevi Fountain & Quirinale

Water is the dominant theme in the area nestling beneath the immense **Quirinal palace**, once home to popes and kings and now the official residence of Italy's president. The water that cascades into the **Trevi Fountain** is *acqua vergine,* said to be Rome's best, and used by Grand Tourists to make their tea. (Don't try drinking straight from the fountain: it's full of coins and chlorine.)

The surrounding medieval streets conceal many other testimonies to the importance of water: from the 'miraculous' well in the church of **Santa Maria in Via** (via Mortaro 24), from where cupfuls of healing liquid are still dispensed, to the **Città d'Acqua** (vicolo del Puttarello 25), where the *acqua vergine* can be heard rushing below a recently excavated ancient Roman street.

The Trevi district was a service area for the palace, home to the printing presses, bureaucratic departments and service industries that oiled the machinery of state. Aristocratic families, such as the Barberinis and Colonnas, built their palaces close by; their art collections are now on view. Another fine collection lurks inside the Accademia di San Luca

For an altogether more 21st-century take on the Eternal City, catch the 45-minute flight-simulator projection on Rome's history at **Time Elevator** (via dei SS Apostoli 20, www.timeelevator.it, from €11, from €8 reductions; see box p78).

Sharing the Quirinal hill with the president's palace are two of Rome's finest small Baroque churches, **San Carlino** and **Sant'Andrea**, and a crossroads with four fountains (1593) representing river gods.

Sights & museums

Accademia di San Luca

Piazza dell'Accademia 77 (06 679 8850, www.accademiasanluca.it). **Open** 9am-2pm Mon-Sat. **Admission** free. **Map** p86 C4 ㊵
Admire Borromini's glorious spiral staircase in the courtyard, then make your way upstairs to the collection put together over the centuries by this artists' academy. Recently reopened after a lengthy restoration, the gallery

ROME BY AREA

includes plaster casts – 'sketches' for sculptures by Antonio Canova, et al – and a wonderful collection of charming scenes of 17th- and 18th-century Rome. Note how frequently the river Tiber flooded the city.

Galleria Colonna

Piazza SS Apostoli 66 (06 678 4350, www.galleriacolonna.it). **Open** 9am-1pm Sat. Closed Aug. **Admission** €10; €8 reductions. No credit cards. **Map** p87 D5 ④

This splendid six-room gallery was completed in 1703 for the Colonna family, whose descendants still live in the palace. The immense frescoed ceiling of the mirrored Great Hall pays tribute to family hero Marcantonio Colonna, who led the papal fleet to victory against the Turks in the Battle of Lepanto in 1571. The gallery's most famous picture is Annibale Caracci's earthy peasant *Bean Eater*, but don't miss Bronzino's wonderfully sensuous *Venus and Cupid*. Private visits can be arranged on other days.

Palazzo Barberini – Galleria Nazionale d'Arte Antica

Via delle Quattro Fontane 13 (06 481 4591, 06 32 810 bookings, www.galleriaborghese.it). **Open** 9am-7pm Tue-Sun. **Admission** €5; €2.50 reductions. No credit cards. **Map** p87 E3 ④

This vast Baroque palace, built by the Barberini Pope Urban VIII, houses one of Rome's most important art collections. Top architects such as Maderno, Borromini and Bernini worked on this pile, which was completed in just five years (1627-33). Entrance is via Borromini's graceful oval staircase and through the grand reception room, whose ceiling is adorned with Pietro da Cortona's *Allegory of Divine Providence* (1639) – reputedly Europe's largest painting. The collection includes Filippo Lippi's *Madonna*; an enigmatic portrait by Raphael of a courtesan believed to be

his mistress; a *Nativity* and *Baptism of Christ* by El Greco; Titian's *Venus and Adonis*; Tintoretto's *Christ and the Woman taken in Adultery*; Caravaggio's *Judith beheading Holofernes* and the beautiful *Narcissus*; a Holbein portrait, *Henry VIII Dressed for his Wedding to Anne of Cleves*; and a bust by Bernini of Pope Urban VIII.

Palazzo del Quirinale

Piazza del Quirinale (06 46 991, www.quirinale.it). **Open** 8.30am-noon Sun. Closed late June-early Sept. **Admission** €5. No credit cards. **Map** p87 D4 ④

The popes still hadn't finished the new St Peter's when (in 1574) they started building a summer palace on the Quirinal hill. In case an elderly pope died on his hols and had to be replaced, the Cappella Paolina was built as a replica of the Vatican's Sistine Chapel minus the Michelangelos. On Sunday mornings, when parts of the presidential palace open to the public, you may be fortunate enough to catch one of the noon concerts held in this chapel.

San Carlino alle Quattro Fontane

Via del Quirinale 23 (06 488 3261, www.sancarlino-borromini.it). **Open** 10am-1pm, 3-6pm Mon-Fri; 10am-1pm Sat; noon-1pm Sun. **Map** p87 E4 ④

This was Borromini's first solo piece (built in 1638-42), and the one he was proudest of. The oval dome is remarkable: its geometrical coffers decrease in size towards the lantern to give the illusion of added height; hidden windows make the dome seem to float in mid air.

Santa Maria della Vittoria

Via XX Settembre 17 (06 4274 0571). **Open** 8.30am-noon, 3.30-6pm Mon-Sat; 3.30-6pm Sun. **Map** p87 F3 ④

This early Baroque church holds one of Bernini's most famous works. *The Ecstasy of St Teresa*, in the Cornaro chapel, shows the Spanish mystic floating on a cloud in a supposedly spiritual

Gelato wizards

The scoop on Rome's finest ice-cream.

Il Gelato di San Crispino

In the beginning was **Il Gelato di San Crispino** (see p98). In 1992, the Alongi brothers – fanatical ice-cream purists – began whipping up something completely new in their first outlet in the southern suburbs: ice-cream made from scratch (even good *gelatai* resort to industrially made ice-cream bases), with flavours provided by the finest pistacchios from Bronte in Sicily, 20-year-old marsala (*zabaione*) and seasonal fruit so fresh it's like tasting the original, whipped up and frozen.

This sudden eruption on to a Roman scene where gelato was good but never truly great forced others to pull themselves up by their bootstraps and unleashed a new wave of copycat gourmet *gelaterie*, some of which were not bad at all but none of which truly rivalled the original.

The past few years, though, have seen more aggressive competitors for the Alongi's unofficial title of manufacturers of some of the best ice-cream, anywhere. Applying the same strict standards to their methods, the new generation has allowed its imagination to run free with all sorts of experimental flavours and textures.

At **Gelateria del Teatro** (see p82), Stefano and his wife Silvia draw from a past as pastry chefs to create surprises such as cannolo- and panettone-flavoured *gelato*. Their chocolate – 80 per cent pure cocoa – is exquisite, as is caramel and pear with sesame.

Claudio Torcè began his ice-cream career with a suburban outlet – called, simply, **Il Gelato** (see p120) – which became a word-of-mouth destination for *gelato* lovers. Nowadays, you can experience his product in the Aventine district. Torcè's flavours are even more outlandish, with cream of capsicum, ricotta cheese with orange peel, and tomato with rice on the menu of around a hundred varieties. His peanut ice-cream is superb, as is the wide range of chocolate flavours: 80 per cent cocoa with ginger is sublime.

ROME BY AREA

trance after an androgynous angel has pierced her with a burning arrow. The result is more than a little ambiguous.

Sant'Andrea al Quirinale

Via del Quirinale 29 (06 474 0807). **Open** 8.30am-noon, 4-7pm Mon-Sat; 9am-noon, 4-7pm Sun. **Map** p87 E4 🔞

Pope Alexander VII (1655-67) was so pleased with Bernini's design for this little church, built out of pale pink marble, that it became in effect the chapel of the Quirinal palace across the road. It is designed to create a sense of grandeur in such a tiny space. The star turn is a plaster St Andrew floating through a broken pediment on his way to heaven.

Scuderie Papali al Quirinale

Via XXIV Maggio 16 (06 696 270, 06 3996 7500 bookings, www.scuderie quirinale.it). **Open** (during exhibitions only) 10am-8pm Mon-Thur, Sun; 10am-10.30pm Fri, Sat. **Admission** €10; €7.50 reductions. **Map** p87 D5 🔞

The old stables of the Quirinal palace were reworked a decade ago by architect Gae Aulenti, preserving the original features; the exhibitions held here are generally excellent. There is a breathtaking view of Rome's skyline from the rear staircase as you leave. Credit cards accepted for phone bookings only.

Event highlights Filippino Lippi (until Jan 2012).

Trevi Fountain

Piazza di Trevi. **Map** p86 C4 🔞

Anita Ekberg plunged into this fountain wearing a strapless black evening dress in Fellini's classic *La dolce vita*. Now, wading is strictly forbidden. Moreover, the sparkling water is full of chlorine (there's a chlorine-free spout hidden at the back of the fountain to the right). The *acqua vergine* was the finest water in the city, brought by Emperor Agrippa's 25km (15.5-mile) aqueduct to the foot of the Quirinal hill. The fountain as we know it was designed by Nicolo Salvi in 1762. It's a rococo extravaganza

of sea horses, conch-blowing tritons, craggy rocks and flimsy trees. Nobody can quite remember when the custom started of tossing coins in to ensure one's return to the Eternal City. The money goes to charity.

Eating & drinking

Al Presidente

Via in Arcione 95 (06 679 7342, www.alpresidente.it). **Meals served** 1-3pm, 8-11pm Tue-Sun. Closed 2wks Jan, 2wks Aug. €€€€. **Italian**. **Map** p87 D4 🔞

This restaurant, under the walls of the Quirinal palace, is one of the few really reliable addresses in this *menu turistico*-dominated area. The creative Italian menu is strong on fish: among the *primi* is a delicious asparagus and squid soup, while one of the highlights of the *secondi* is the fish and vegetable millefeuille. There's a light lunch menu (€€) and outside tables too.

Antica Birreria Peroni

Via San Marcello 19 (06 679 5310, www.anticabirreriaperoni.it). **Meals served** noon-midnight Mon-Sat. Closed 2wks Aug. €-€€. **Bar/ Italian**. **Map** p86 C5 🔞

This long-running *birreria* is the perfect place for a quick lunch or dinner. Service is rough-and-Roman but friendly, and the food is good and relatively cheap. Sausage is the main act, with three types of German-style *wurstel* on offer.

Il Gelato di San Crispino

Via della Panetteria 42 (06 679 3924, www.ilgelatodisancrispino.com). **Open** noon-midnight Mon-Thur, Sun; noon-12.30am Fri, Sat. **Ice-cream**. **Map** p87 D2 🔞

Il Gelato di San Crispino serves some of the best ice-cream to be found in Rome. Flavours change according to what's in season. There's a branch at piazza della Maddelena 3, near the Pantheon. See box p97.

Arts & leisure

Kamispa

Via degli Avignonesi 12 (06 4201 0039, www.kamispa.com). **Open** 10am-10pm daily. **Map** p87 D3 🟢
Massages, scrubs and a wide selection of beauty treatments are available in this gloriously spice-scented haven. There's a small swimming pool and a shop. Booking is recommended.

Heading north

North from Villa Borghese, well-heeled suburbs fill the area that stretches between the **Villa Torlonia** and Villa Ada public parks. By the river, a vibrant sport and arts hub is springing to life: rugby is played in the Stadio Flaminio, and football across the Tiber at the **Stadio Olimpico**; while the new **Auditorium** seethes with music-related activity.

Sights & museums

MACRO

NEW *Via Nizza 138 (06 6710 70400, www.macro.roma.museum).* **Open** 11am-10pm Tue-Sun. **Admission** €11; €9 reductions. No credit cards. **Map** off p87 F1 🟢
Rome's contemporary art scene was given a boost in the 1990s with the opening of this gallery in a converted brewery – now sporting a striking new extension by architect Odile Decq. Shows spill over into MACRO-Future in the Mattatoio in Testaccio.

MAXXI

NEW *Via Guido Reni 2F (06 3996 7350, www.fondazionemaxxi.it).* **Open** 11am-7pm Tue, Wed, Fri, Sun; 11am-10pm Thur, Sat. **Admission** €11; €7 reductions; free under-14s. **Map** off p93 A1 🟢
This extraordinary new gallery of 21st-century art and architecture, designed by Zaha Hadid, was inaugurated in

spring 2010. Whatever's on s worth a visit to see the buildi **Event highlights** Evanescent (until Nov 2011).

Villa Torlonia

Via Nomentana 70 (06 0608, www. museivillatorlonia.it). **Open** *Park* dawn-sunset daily. *Museums* 9am-7pm Tue-Sun. **Admission** €10; €8 reductions; extra charge for exhibitions. No credit cards. **Map** off p87 F1 🟢
With its lush park and scattered attractions, Villa Torlonia is a pleasant place to pass a hot day. Once home to the Torlonia family, and wartime residence of Mussolini, it was bought by the council some 30 years ago and has been *in restauro* since. Open to the public are the art nouveau *Casina della civette* with its collection of stained glass; the *Casino nobile* with its frescoes; the *Casino dei principi,* housing exhibitions; the faux-medieval villa, home to the Technotown centre; and a restaurant/tea room.

Arts & leisure

Auditorium – Parco della Musica

Via P de Coubertin 15 (info 06 8024 1281, bookings 06 808 2058, www. auditorium.com). **Map** off p93 A1 🟢
This huge performing arts facility has an eclectic programme. Guided tours of the complex cost €9 (€5 reductions).

Foro Italico & Stadio Olimpico

Piazza de Bosis/via del Foro Italico. **Map** off p93 A1 🟢
An obelisk 36m (120ft) high, with the words *Mussolini Dux* carved on it, greets visitors to the Foro Italico, a sports complex conceived in the late 1920s. The avenue leading west of the obelisk is paved with mosaics of good Fascists doing sporty Fascist things. The same avenue is now trampled on by the hordes that visit the Stadio Olimpico to watch Roma and Lazio football teams. For information on tickets, see p31.

ROME BY AREA

San Giovanni in Laterano p109

Esquilino, Celio & San Lorenzo

If you've come to Rome on a budget package, there's a fairly good chance that you'll end up in a hotel on the Esquiline hill, around Termini railway station. It may not be quite what you expected.

In ancient times, and right up until the 1870s when the developers moved in and covered the land with apartment blocks for the bureaucrats of newly united Italy, this was where the rich and powerful had their magnificent villas with spreading gardens. Recently, municipal authorities have tried hard to convince us that a 'renaissance' is under way, but there's no escaping the fact that Esquilino's *palazzi* are grimy and its after-dark denizens can be dodgy. Don't despair, though: the area has charms and attractions.

Piazza Vittorio Emanuele II – the city's biggest square, and known simply as piazza Vittorio – was given a new lease of life in the 1980s by a revamp of the central gardens (now in need of a further makeover) and the emergence of a multi-ethnic community; the food market in a nearby ex-barracks (via Lamarmora) bursts with exotic produce and smells. Then there are vast basilicas (**Santa Maria Maggiore**), intimate mosaic-encrusted churches (**Santa Prassede**), Roman artefacts (**Palazzo Massimo**) and a magnificent post-war railway station building at Termini.

Via Nazionale is a traffic artery lined by carbon-copy high street shops; halfway down is the huge **Palazzo delle Esposizioni** gallery; the pretty **Villa Aldobrandini** park, up a flight of steps at the south-western end, has superb views over the city.

Present-day Monti was the giant, thunderous Suburra slum,

where streets ran with effluent and many inhabitants died young.

Nowadays, the alleyways of Monti – north-east of the Forum, between *vie* Nazionale and Cavour – are still noisy and bustling, the difference being that this area is seriously hip.

To the south, on Colle Oppio, Nero fiddled in his **Domus Aurea**, entertaining his guests with his Imperial twanging. These days, this stretch of green is peopled by Roman mums and their offspring during the day, and some very dubious characters after dark.

Sights & museums

Baths of Diocletian

Viale Enrico de Nicola 78 (06 3996 7700). **Open** 9am-7.30pm Tue-Sun. **Admission** €7; €3.50 reductions; extra charge during exhibitions. No credit cards. **Map** p102 C1 ❶

Diocletian's baths were the largest in Rome when they were built in AD 298-306, covering over a hectare and able to accommodate 3,000 people. A convent complex, designed by Michelangelo, was built around the largest surviving chunk of the baths in the 1560s. It now contains a collection of stone inscriptions that is sufficiently low-key to allow you to focus on the massive bath buildings themselves and on Michelangelo's 16th-century restoration, including the fine cloister. (The church of Santa Maria degli Angeli in piazza della Repubblica, and the Aula Ottagona at via Romita 8, were also part of the structure.)

Domus Aurea

Via della Domus Aurea 1 (06 3996 7700). **Open** by appt only. **Map** p102 B3 ❷

In the summer of AD 64, much of central Rome was devastated by fire. Afterwards, anything unsinged east of the Forum was knocked down to make way for Emperor Nero's Domus Aurea (Golden House). Its main façade looked south and was entirely clad in gold;

inside, every inch not inlaid with gems was frescoed by Nero's pet aesthete Fabullus. The moment Nero died in AD 68, however, work was begun to eradicate every vestige of the hated tyrant. So thorough was the cover-up job that for decades after its frescoes were rediscovered in 1480, no one realised it was the Domus Aurea that they had stumbled across.

Crumbling masonry shut the Domus down in 2005 and again in early 2010; we recommend you call to find out whether guided tours of unaffected areas are still going ahead.

Museo Nazionale d'Arte Orientale

Via Merulana 248 (06 4697 4832). **Open** 9am-2pm Tue, Wed, Fri; 9am-7.30pm Thur, Sat, Sun. **Admission** €6; €3 reductions. No credit cards. **Map** p102 C3 ❸

This impressive collection of oriental art includes artefacts from the Near East, such as pottery, gold, votive offerings – some from the third millennium BC – painted fans from Tibet, sacred sculptures, and some Chinese pottery from the 15th century.

Palazzo delle Esposizioni

Via Nazionale 194 (06 696 271, www.palazzoesposizioni.it). **Open** 10am-8pm Tue-Thur, Sun; 10am-10.30pm Fri, Sat. **Admission** from €10.50; €7.50 reductions. **Map** p102 A2 ❹

This imposing, purpose-built 19th-century exhibition space reopened in 2008 after a major restoration. Note that ticket prices can go as high as €12.50, depending on how many shows are on.

Palazzo Massimo alle Terme

Largo di Villa Peretti 1 (06 480 201). **Open** 9am-7.30pm Tue-Sun. **Admission** €7; €3.50 reductions; extra charge during exhibitions. No credit cards. **Map** p102 C1 ❺

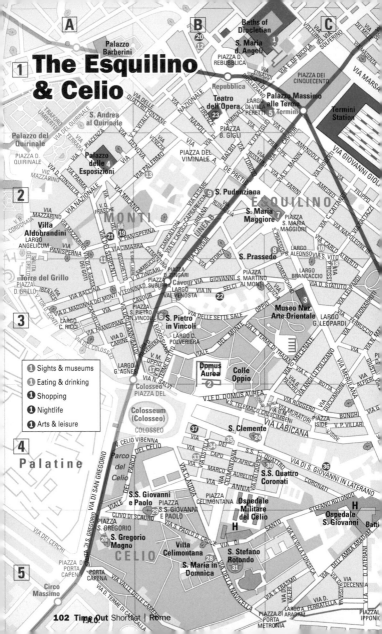

The Esquilino & Celio

A
Palazzo Barberini

B
Baths of Diocletian
S. Maria d. Angeli
PIAZZA DELLA REPUBBLICA
Repubblica
Teatro dell'Opera
Palazzo Massimo alle Terme
Termini

C
PIAZZA DEI CINQUECENTO
Termini Station

S. Andrea al Quirinale
Palazzo del Quirinale
PIAZZA D. QUIRINALE
Palazzo delle Esposizioni

2
Villa Aldobrandini
LARGO ANGELICUM
MONTI
PIAZZA DEL VIMINALE
S. Pudenziana
ESQUILINO
S. Maria Maggiore
Torre del Grillo
PIAZZA D. GRILLO
S. Prassede
LARGO BRANCACCIO

3
S. Pietro in Vincoli
PIAZZA S. PIETRO IN VINCOLI
Cavour
Museo Naz. Arte Orientale
LARGO G. LEOPARDI

- 1 Sights & museums
- 1 Eating & drinking
- 1 Shopping
- 1 Nightlife
- 1 Arts & leisure

Domus Aurea
Colle Oppio
Colosseo PIAZZA DEL
Colosseum (Colosseo)
COLOSSEO

4
Palatine
Parco del Celio
S. Clemente
S. Giovanni e Paolo
PIAZZA SS. GIOVANNI E PAOLO
S.S. Quattro Coronati
Ospedale Militare del Celio
H
Ospedale S. Giovanni
Batti

5
S. Gregorio Magno
Villa Celimontana
S. Stefano Rotondo
S. Maria in Domnica
CELIO
PIAZZA DI PORTA CAPENA
PORTA CAPENA
Circo Massimo

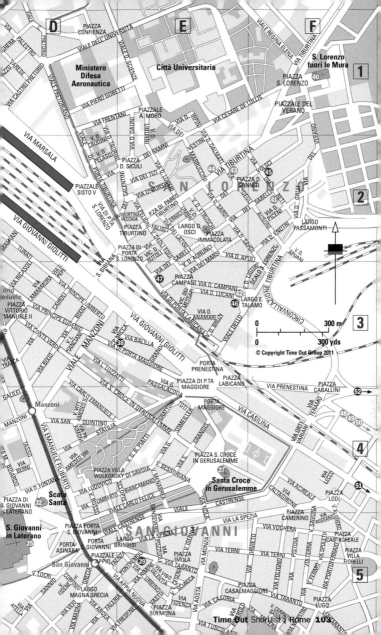

In the basement of Palazzo Massimo – home to a large chunk of the Museo Nazionale Romano collection – is an extensive array of coins and Roman luxuries, along with descriptions of trade routes and audio-visual displays. On the ground and first floors, busts of emperors – including a magnificent Augustus – and lesser mortals provide a fine opportunity to appreciate changing hairstyles through the ages. The first floor begins with the age of Vespasian (AD 69-79): his pugilistic bust is in room 1. Room 5 has a graceful crouching Aphrodite from Hadrian's Villa at Tivoli, while in room 7 is a peacefully sleeping hermaphrodite, a second-century AD copy of a Greek original. On the second floor are rare wall paintings from various villas, including a stunning garden scene from Livia's Villa near Rome. Room 10 contains Botero-like, larger-than-life (megalographic) paintings, and room 11 features some dazzlingly bright marble intarsio works.

San Pietro in Vincoli

Piazza di San Pietro in Vincoli 4A (06 9784 4952). **Open** 8am-12.30pm, 3-7pm daily. **Map** p102 B3 ⑥

Built in the fifth century but reworked many times since, this church is dominated by the monument to Pope Julius II, with Michelangelo's imposing *Moses* (1515). Julius wanted a much grander tomb, but died too soon to oversee it; his successors were less ambitious. As a result, the mighty *Moses* (in a bad translation of the Old Testament, the Hebrew word for 'radiant' was mistaken for 'horned') is wildly out of proportion, and far better than others by Michelangelo's students.

Pilgrims come here for the chains. Eudoxia, the wife of Emperor Valentinian III (425-55), was given a set of chains said to have been used to shackle St Peter in Jerusalem; with others used on the saint in the Mamertine Prison, they are now conserved in a reliquary on the main altar.

Santa Maria Maggiore

Piazza Santa Maria Maggiore (06 6988 6800). **Open** *Church* 7am-7pm daily. *Museum* 9am-6pm daily. *Loggia* (guided tours only; booking obligatory) 9am & 1pm Mon-Sat. **Admission** *Church* free. *Museum* €4; €2 reductions. *Loggia* €5; €3 reductions. No credit cards. **Map** p102 C2 ⑦

Local tradition has it that a church was built on this spot in around AD 366; documents place it almost 100 years later. The church was extended in the 13th and 18th centuries. Inside, above the columns of the nave, restored fifth-century mosaics depict scenes from the Old Testament. In the apse, 13th-century mosaics show Christ crowning Mary Queen of Heaven. The Virgin theme continues in fifth-century mosaics on the triumphal arch.

The ceiling in the main nave, commissioned by Pope Alexander VI – aka Rodrigo Borgia – is said to have been made from the first shipment of gold from the Americas. In the 16th and 17th centuries, two chapels were added: the first was the Cappella Sistina (last on the right of the nave), designed by Domenico Fontana for Sixtus V (1585-90); directly opposite is the Cappella Paolina, a Greek-cross chapel, designed in 1611 by Flaminio Ponzio for Paul V to house a ninth-century icon of the Madonna on its altar. To the right of the main altar, a plaque marks the burial place of Baroque genius Gian Lorenzo Bernini. In the loggia, high up on the front of the church (tours leave from the baptistry), are glorious 13th-century mosaics that decorated the façade of the old basilica, showing the legend of the foundation of Santa Maria Maggiore. A miraculous mid-summer snowfall showed founders where to erect their church, legend relates.

Santa Prassede

Via Santa Prassede 9A (06 488 2456). **Open** 7.30am-12.30pm, 4-7pm daily. **Map** p102 C2 ⑧

This church is a ninth-century scale copy of the original St Peter's. Artists from Byzantium made the rich mosaics; in the apse, Christ is being introduced to St Praxedes by St Paul on the right, while St Peter is doing the honours on the left for her sister St Pudenziana. The mosaic on the triumphal arch shows the heavenly Jerusalem, with palm-toting martyrs. Off the right-hand side of the nave is the chapel of San Zeno, a dazzling swirl of blue and gold mosaics, punctuated with saints, animals and depictions of Christ and his mother. The wall and ceiling mosaics are ninth century; Mary in the niche above the altar is 13th century. In a room to the right is a portion of column said to be the one that Jesus was tied to for scourging. Visitors are asked to avoid disturbing masses on Sunday morning.

Santa Pudenziana
Via Urbana 160 (06 481 4622).
Open 8.30am-noon, 3-6pm daily.
Map p102 B2 **9**
The mosaic in the apse of Santa Pudenziana dates from the fourth century, and is a remarkable example of the continuity between pagan and Christian art. It depicts Christ and the apostles as wealthy Roman citizens wearing togas, against an ancient Roman cityscape.

Eating & drinking

Agata e Romeo
Via Carlo Alberto 45 (06 446 6115, www.agataeromeo.it). **Meals served** 12.30-2.30pm, 7.30-10.30pm Mon-Fri. Closed 2wks Jan, 2wks Aug. €€€€.
Roman. Map p102 C2 **10**
Agata Parisella was the first chef to demonstrate that Roman cuisine could be refined without sacrificing its wholesome essence. Oxtail-stuffed ravioli, for example, is a tribute to the traditional use of less prestigious cuts of meat. Recent visitors have lamented a lack of reliability since Agata got her Michelin star, but on a good night, she's very good, and husband Romeo Caraccio

continues to preside with charm over the dining room and huge wine list.

Al Vino al Vino
Via dei Serpenti 19 (06 485 803).
Open 5.30pm-1am daily. Closed Aug.
Wine bar. Map p102 A3 **11**
This hostelry offers some 500 wines, with more than 25 available by the glass. But its speciality is *distillati*: grappas, whiskeys and other strong spirits, plus Sicilian-inspired food to soak it all up. Service is sometimes brusque. As a bottle shop, Al Vino opens 10.30am-2pm daily too.

Dagnino
Galleria Esedra, via VE Orlando 75 (06 481 8660, www.pasticceriadagnino. com). **Open** 7am-11pm daily.
Bar/café. Map p102 B1 **12**
Genuine 1950s decor sets the scene at this café-*pasticceria*, which is a corner of Sicily in Rome. If it's Sicilian and edible, it's here: ice-cream in buns, crisp *cannoli siciliani* filled with ricotta cheese, and shiny green-iced *cassata*.

Doozo
Via Palermo 51-53 (06 481 5655, www.doozo.it). **Meals served** 12.30-3pm, 7.30-11pm Tue-Sat; 8-11.30pm Sun. €€. **Japanese**. Map p102 B2 **13**
This Japanese restaurant on a quiet street parallel to via Nazionale is spacious and cultured, with tables spilling into a gallery, bookshop and a lovely little Zen garden. There's good sushi, sashimi, tempura and karaage chicken served in bento boxes.

Hang Zhou
Via Principe Eugenio 82 (06 487 2732). **Meals served** noon-3pm, 7pm-midnight daily. Closed Aug. €€. **Chinese**. Map p103 D3 **14**
Hang Zhou rises above most of Rome's dull Chinese eateries, not so much for the food – which is, however, quite acceptable – but because it's colourful, friendly and incredibly good value. Be prepared to queue.

ROME BY AREA

Doozo p105

どうぞ

Kabir Fast Food

Via Mamiani 11 (06 446 0792).
Open 11am-4pm, 5.30-10pm daily.
€. No credit cards. **Indian**. Map
p103 D3 ⓯
This Indian takeaway is just off piazza
Vittorio. You can eat in too, accompa-
nied by Indian music videos.

L'Asino d'Oro

NEW *Via del Boschetto 73 (06 4891
3832, www.lasinodororoma.it).* **Meals
served** 12.30-3pm, 5-7pm, 7.30-11pm
daily. **€€**. **Creative Italian**. Map
p102 A2 ⓰
Lucio Sforza's original Asino d'Oro, in
the town of Orvieto, served excellent
rustic-chic fare in a rustic-chic setting.
Here, the pared-back retro-feel decor
chimes less well with the food but
what's on the plate continues to be fantastic. The daily-changing menu might
include creamed cod on chickpea purée,
a range of offal and game dishes, and
fennel baked with orange. There's an
extensive wine and (strangely) beer
menu, plus a €12 lunch offer, which is
hard to beat, and an *aperitivo* hour.

Oppio Caffè

NEW *Via delle Terme di Tito 72
(06 474 5262, www.oppiocaffe.it).*
Open 7am-2am daily. **Meals served**
noon-3pm, 7.30-11pm daily. **€/€€**.
Café/bar. Map p102 B3 ⓱
From the people behind Micca Club
(see p114), this happening new venture
would be worth frequenting simply for
its view over the Colosseum. But there's
also a €10 drink and *aperitivo* buffet
from 5pm to 10pm, a grill-restaurant,
resident DJs and events galore. As a
bonus, children eat for free.

Trattoria Monti

Via di San Vito 13A (06 446 6573).
Meals served 12.45-2.45pm, 7.45-
11pm Tue-Sat; 12.45-2.45pm Sun.
Closed Aug, 1wk Dec. **€€€**.
Creative Italian. Map p102 C3 ⓲
The cuisine, like the family that runs
this chic, understated eaterie, is from

the Marches region – so meat, fish and
game all feature on an interesting
menu. Vegetarians are well served by
a range of *tortini* (pastry-less pies).
Make sure you book in the evening.
The trattoria is at the lower end of this
price bracket.

Shopping

The Monday-Saturday morning
food market once located right on
piazza Vittorio has moved into
more salubrious premises in via
Lamarmora: stalls stock the usual
Italian fresh produce, cheese and
meats, supplemented by halal meat
and spices, as well as some exotic
fabrics and household goods. It's
worth a visit just to experience
the colour and bustle.

Abito – Le Gallinelle

NEW *Via Panisperna 61 (06 488
1017, http://abito61.blogspot.com).*
Open 3.30-7pm Mon; 10am-1pm,
3.30-7.30pm Tue-Sat. Closed 2wks
Aug. Map p102 A2 ⓳
In this new outlet – formerly a
convent – Wilma Silvestri and her
daughter Giorgia sell the same mix of
gorgeously idiosyncratic reworked
vintage gear and elegant linen creations as they used to stock around
the corner at Le Gallinelle (via del
Boschetto 76, now the preserve of
young designers who have worked
with the Silvestris).

Feltrinelli International

Via VE Orlando 84 (06 482 7878).
Open 9am-8pm Mon-Sat; 10.30am-
1.30pm, 4-8pm Sun. **Map** p102 B1 ⓴
An excellent range of fiction, non-
fiction, magazines and guidebooks in
English and other languages.

Tina Sondergaard

Via del Boschetto 1D (334 385 0799).
Open 3-7.30pm Mon; 10.30am-1pm,
1.30-7.30pm Tue-Sat. Closed 3wks
Aug. **Map** p102 A2 ㉑

ROME BY AREA

This Danish designer and her team whip up delightfully stylish one-off, 1960s-inspired women's clothes on the premises in this tiny, pared-back space situated on trendy via del Boschetto. The fabrics are eye-catching, and Tina will do on-the-spot alterations to make sure your purchases fit perfectly. Space is tight here, so last season's leftovers are sold off at extremely interesting prices.

Nightlife

See also **Oppio Caffè** (p107).

Hangar

Via in Selci 69 (06 488 1397, www.hangaronline.it). **Open** 10.30pm-2.30am Mon, Wed-Sun. No credit cards. **Map** p102 B3 ㉒

American John Moss has been at the helm of Rome's oldest gay bar since it opened in 1984. Hangar maintains its friendly but sexy atmosphere whether half full (occasionally midweek) or packed (at weekends and for porn video Monday and striptease Thursday). The venue also has a small dark area.

Arts & leisure

Teatro dell'Opera di Roma – Teatro Costanzi

Piazza B Gigli 1 (06 4816 0255, www.operaroma.it). **Map** p102 B1 ㉓

The lavish late 19th-century *teatro all' italiana* interior is quite a surprise after the Mussolini-era angular grey façade and its esplanade with tacky potted palms. The acoustics vary considerably: the higher (cheaper) seats aren't great, so splash out on a box.

Celio & San Giovanni

After Emperor Constantine legalised Christianity in the fourth century, he donated the land on which the basilica of **San Giovanni in Laterano** was built. This was a groundbreaking move

in the sense that it brought the new religion out into the open, but was fence-sitting in that the new cult was restricted to this neighbourhood, which was about as far as you could get from the city's centre of power.

If the San Giovanni area fell prey to property developers in the late 19th century, the Celio – a haven for an elite of a bucolic bent in ancient times – remains lush and unkempt. It gives a glimpse of what ancient, early Christian and medieval Rome were like. From the remains of ancient aqueducts near the verdant and lovely **Villa Celimontana** park, to frescoes of martyrs in the church of **Santo Stefano Rotondo**, this area has a bit of everything.

Around Villa Celimontana is a whole slew of ancient churches, including **Santi Giovanni e Paolo**, with its excavated Roman houses beneath.

The tight grid of streets south-east of the Colosseum is home to the fascinating church of **San Clemente**, and **Santi Quattro Coronati**, which is blessed with several extraordinary frescoes.

Also here is **Rewind Rome** (via Capo d'Africa 5, 06 7707 6627, www.3drewind.com), a dramatic 3D representation of fourth-century Rome in which tigers will leap at you when you don your 3D glasses and you'll have to dodge gladiators fighting in the Colosseum (see box p78).

Further east, amid traffic, smog and drab post-Unification apartment buildings, are some of Christianity's most important churches – including Vatican-owned San Giovanni itself – and a host of fascinating minor ancient remains.

To the south of the basilica are the sunken brick remains of the Porta Asinaria, an ancient gate in the third-century AD Aurelian

Wall. A park follows the ancient wall north to **Santa Croce in Gerusalemme**, which is surrounded by a panoply of easily visible Roman ruins: through the opening in the Aurelian Walls to the right of the church is the Amphitheatrum Castrum (now the monks' vegetable garden, currently sadly closed to the public), and part of the Circus Varianus; the Baths of Helena, of which you can see only the cistern; and the monumental travertine archway built by Emperor Claudius in the first century AD to mark the triumphal entrance of the aqueducts into the city.

Sights & museums

San Clemente
Via San Giovanni in Laterano (06 774 0021). **Open** 9am-12.30pm, 3-6pm Mon-Sat; noon-6pm Sun. **Admission** *Church* free. *Excavations* €5; €3.50 reductions. No credit cards. **Map** p102 B4 ㉔
This 12th-century basilica is a 3D timeline. In the main church, the *schola cantorum* (choir), with its exquisite carving and mosaic decorations, survives from the fourth-century structure. The apse mosaic is 12th century: from the drops of Christ's blood springs the vine representing the Church, which swirls around peasants in their daily tasks, Doctors of the Church and a host of animals. In the chapel of St Catherine of Alexandria, frescoes by Masolino (c1430) show the saint praying as her torturers prepare the wheel on which she was stretched to death (later giving her name to a firework).

From the sacristy, steps lead down to the fourth-century basilica. From there, a stairway descends to an ancient Roman alley. On one side is a second-century Roman *insula* (apartment building) containing a site where the Persian god Mithras was worshipped. On the other side are rooms of a Roman house used for meetings by early Christians.

San Giovanni in Laterano
Piazza San Giovanni in Laterano 4 (06 6988 6433). **Open** *Church* 7am-6.30pm daily. *Baptistry* 8am-noon, 4-7pm daily. *Cloister* 9am-6pm daily. *Lateran Museum* (06 6988 6376) 9am-noon Mon-Sat. **Admission** *Church* free. *Cloister* €2. *Museum* €5; €2 reductions. No credit cards. **Map** p103 D5 ㉕
San Giovanni and the Lateran palace were the papal headquarters until they were moved across the river to the Vatican in the 15th century. Constantine gave the plot of land to Pope Melchiades to build the church in 313, but little remains of the original basilica. The interior was revamped by Borromini in 1646; the façade, with its huge statues of Christ, the two Johns (Baptist and Evangelist) and Doctors of the Church, was added in 1735. A few treasures from earlier times survive: a 13th-century mosaic in the apse, a fragment of a fresco attributed to Giotto (behind the first column on the right) showing Pope Boniface VIII announcing the first Holy Year in 1300, and the Gothic *baldacchino* over the main altar. Off the left aisle is the 13th-century cloister; a small museum contains vestments and some original manuscripts of music by Palestrina. The north façade was designed in 1586 by Domenico Fontana, who also placed Rome's tallest Egyptian obelisk outside. Also on this side is the octagonal baptistry that Constantine had built. The four chapels around the font have fifth- and seventh-century mosaics.

San Gregorio Magno
Piazza di San Gregorio 1 (06 700 8227). **Open** 9am-12.30pm, 3-6.30pm Mon-Fri, Sun. **Map** p102 A5 ㉖
This Baroque church stands on the site of the home of one of the most remarkable popes, Gregory I (the

ROME BY AREA

Great; 590-604), who spent his 14-year pontificate vigorously reorganising the Church. In a chapel on the right is a marble chair dating from the first century BC, said to have been used by Gregory as his papal throne. Also here is the tomb of Tudor diplomat Sir Edward Carne, England's wily ambassador to the Holy See in the 16th century (see box p111). Outside stand three small chapels (open 10am-noon Tue, Thur, Sat, Sun; closed 2wks Dec-Jan, 1wk Easter, Aug), behind which are the remains of shops that lined this ancient road, the *clivus scauri*.

Santa Croce in Gerusalemme

Piazza Santa Croce in Gerusalemme 12 (06 7061 3053). **Open** 7am-noon, 3.30-7.30pm daily. **Map** p103 E4 ㉗

Founded in 320 by St Helena, mother of Emperor Constantine (who legalised Christianity in 313), this church was rebuilt in the 12th century, and again in 1743. It was constructed to house relics Helena brought back from the Holy Land: three chunks of Christ's cross, a nail, two thorns from his crown and the finger of St Thomas – allegedly, the very one that the doubting saint stuck into Christ's wound. All of these are displayed in a chapel at the end of a Fascist-era hall at the left side of the nave. The monks' exquisite vegetable garden, once open to visitors, was closed to the public as this guide went to press; its gates were designed by Jannis Kounellis and mounted in 2007.

Santa Maria in Domnica

Via della Navicella 10 (06 7720 2685). **Open** 9am-noon, 4.30-7pm daily. **Map** p102 B5 ㉓

The carved wood ceiling and porticoed façade date from the 16th century, but Santa Maria in Domnica – known as the *navicella* (little ship), after the Roman statue that stands outside – is a ninth-century structure containing one of Rome's most charming apse mosaics. What sets this lovely design in rich colours apart is that Mary and Jesus look cheerful: the cherry-red daubs of blush on their cheeks give them a healthy glow.

Santi Giovanni e Paolo

Piazza Santi Giovanni e Paolo 13 (06 700 5745 church, 06 7045 4544 excavations, www.caseromane.it). **Open** *Church* 8.30am-noon, 3.30-6pm daily. *Excavations* 10am-1pm, 3-6pm Mon, Thur-Sun. **Admission** *Church* free. *Excavations* €6; €4 reductions. No credit cards. **Map** p102 B5 ㉙

Traces of the original fourth-century church can still be seen in the 12th-century façade, which is overlooked by a bell tower. An 18th-century revamp left the church's interior looking like an over-the-top banqueting hall.

Around the corner, in Clivo di Scauro, steps lead down to labyrinthine excavations: dating from the first century AD on, these 20-odd excavated rooms are the remains of four different buildings, including the house of fourth-century martyrs John and Paul. There are also rooms which were evidently used for secret Christian worship. Call ahead to arrange tours in English.

Santi Quattro Coronati

Via dei Santi Quattro 20 (06 7047 5427). **Open** *Church* 7am-12.30pm, 3.30-7.30pm daily. *Cloister* 10-11.30am, 4-5.30pm daily. *Oratory* 9.30am-noon, 3.30-6pm daily. **Map** p102 C4 ㉚

A fourth-century church here was rebuilt as a fortified monastery in the 11th century; the outsized apse is from the original church, which was all but destroyed in the Norman sack of Rome of 1084. The church has an upper-level *matronium*, where women sat during religious functions, and there is a beautiful cloister from the early 13th century. In the oratory next to the church (ring the bell and ask for the key) are frescoes, also painted in the 13th century as a defence of the

Clever Carne

How a Welsh aristocrat became a Roman hero.

San Gregorio Magno

Welsh aristocrat Sir Edward Carne (c1500-61) – whose tomb is in the church of San Gregorio Magno (see p109) – was a scholar, a member of parliament and a wily player on the 16th-century diplomatic circuit.

As illustrious heads rolled in an England torn apart by intolerance, Carne crested the wave, working for monarchs Henry (Protestant... kind of), Mary (Catholic) and Elizabeth (Protestant). Henry VIII and/or the Boleyn family dispatched the diplomat to Rome to plead the king's case for divorcing Catherine of Aragon and marrying Anne Boleyn; Carne obtained a tidy little piece of Church property – Ewenny Abbey in Glamorganshire – after helping Henry dissolve the monasteries when Pope Clement VII refused point blank to annul the marriage; and he remained in Rome as England's ambassador during both Mary's and Elizabeth's rules.

But to keep his hand in with both sides, this staunchly Catholic

manipulator engaged in a cover-up, one which only emerged in papers discovered centuries later.

With Elizabeth's anti-Rome stance making Carne's pretence of loyalty to the 'heretical' Crown ever more difficult, the diplomat had to devise a way to extricate himself from his post without risking the Queen's revenge on his wife and children back in Britain. He petitioned Elizabeth to be able to retire from his post for family reasons, then secretly begged the pope to refuse him permission to leave Rome... effectively making him a hostage.

Elizabeth concurred. The pope concurred. Carne was a hero at home, a hero in Rome and had a nice little sinecure to boot as director of Rome's British hospice.

What he didn't have, however, was his family, making this elderly gentleman an object of pity around Europe for years afterwards and giving break-away England yet another reason to heap derision on the Church of Rome.

ROME BY AREA

Micca Club p114

popes' temporal power. They show a pox-ridden Constantine being healed by Pope Sylvester, crowning him with a tiara and giving him a cap to symbolise the pope's spiritual and earthly authority.

Santo Stefano Rotondo

Via di Santo Stefano Rotondo 7 (06 421 191). **Open** 9.30am-12.30pm, 2-5pm Tue-Sat; 9.30am-12.30pm Sun. **Map** p102 B5 ❸

One of the few round churches in Rome, Santo Stefano dates from the fifth century. The church is exceptionally beautiful, with its Byzantine-inspired simplicity. The 34 horrifically graphic 16th-century frescoes of martyrs being boiled, stretched and slashed disturb the atmosphere somewhat.

Scala Santa & Sancta Sanctorum

Piazza di San Giovanni in Laterano (06 772 6641). **Open** *Scala Santa* 6.30am-noon, 3.30-6.30pm daily. *Sancta Sanctorum* (booking required) 10.30am-noon, 3.30-5pm Mon, Tue, Thur-Sat; 3.30-4.30pm Wed. **Admission** *Scala Santa* free. *Sancta Sanctorum & San Silvestro chapel* €5. No credit cards. **Map** p103 D4 ❸

Tradition has it, these are the stairs that Jesus climbed in Pontius Pilate's house before being sent to his crucifixion. They were brought to Rome in the fourth century by St Helena, mother of the Emperor Constantine. A crawl up the Scala Santa has been a fixture on every serious pilgrim's list ever since. At the top of the Holy Stairs (but also accessible by non-holy stairs to the left) is the pope's private chapel, the Sancta Sanctorum. In a glass case on the left wall is a fragment of the table on which the Last Supper was supposedly served. The truly exquisite 13th-century frescoes in the lunettes and on the ceiling are attributed to Cimabue. Freshly restored, the San Silvestro chapel area of the Sancta Sanctorum is also now on view.

Eating & drinking

Il Bocconcino

Via Ostilia 23 (06 7707 9175, www.ilbocconcino.com). **Meals served** 12.30-3.30pm, 7.30-11.30pm Mon, Tue, Thur-Sun. Closed 2wks Aug. €€. **Roman. Map** p102 B4 ❸

This trattoria near the Colosseum looks as if it has been around for generations, but in fact it's a fairly recent addition. Expect a friendly welcome, good renditions of a small-ish choice of Roman favourites and a short but well-priced wine list. Service can be extremely slow.

Café Café

Via dei Santi Quattro 44 (06 700 8743, www.cafecafebistrot.it). **Open** 11am-1.30am daily. €. **Café/snacks**. **Map** p102 B4 ❸

A café, yes, but also a perfect spot for lunch – with soups, salads and a pasta dish or two – after a stomp around the Colosseum. There's a brunch buffet from 11.30am to 4pm on Sundays.

Luzzi

Via San Giovanni in Laterano 88 (06 709 6332). **Meals served** noon-midnight Mon, Tue, Thur-Sun. Closed 2wks Aug. €€. **Roman**. **Map** p102 B4 ❸

On busy nights (and most are) this neighbourhood trattoria is the loudest and most crowded 40 square metres in Rome. The cooking won't win any prizes but there are perfectly decent pizzas, pasta dishes and *secondi*, all strictly in the Roman tradition. Outside tables operate all year round.

Shopping

Immediately outside the Roman walls by the basilica of San Giovanni, via Sannio is home each weekday morning and all day Saturday to stalls piled high with cheap new and second-hand clothes.

ROME BY AREA

Soul Food

Via San Giovanni in Laterano 192-194 (06 7045 2025, www.haterecords.com). **Open** 10.30am-1.30pm, 3.30-8pm Tue-Sat. Closed 2wks Aug. **Map** p102 C4 **36**

This vintage record shop is a vinyl-collector's heaven, with indie-rock, punk, beat music, exotica, lounge, rockabilly and more.

Nightlife

Coming Out

Via San Giovanni in Laterano 8 (06 700 9871, www.comingout.it). **Open** 10am-2am daily. **Map** p102 B4 **37**

This hugely popular pub offers beers, cocktails and a reasonably wide range of snacks to a predominantly youthful crowd of gay men and women, who spill out of the venue and on to the street most evenings. Things hot up during the 6.30-8.30pm happy hour. There are DJ sets from 11pm on Wed, Thur and Sun.

Micca Club

Via Pietro Micca 7A (06 8744 0079, www.miccaclub.com). **Open** 7-10pm Mon, Tue; 7pm-2am Wed; 10pm-4am Thur-Sat; 6pm-1am Sun. Closed June-Aug. **Map** p103 E3 **38**

A huge spiral staircase leads down to this cavernous underground venue. It offers one of Rome's most eclectic nightlife programmes, ranging from live acts and international DJ sets to serious jazz. There's a music-fuelled Sunday vintage market from 6pm (with *aperitivo* €10). Each evening kicks off at 7pm with *aperitivi* and a generous buffet for €10.

Skyline

Via Pontremoli 36 (06 700 9431, www.skylineclub.it). **Open** 10.30pm-3am Mon-Thur, Sun; 10.30pm-4am Fri, Sat. **Map** p103 E5 **39**

At this ever-popular gay club, the crowd is relaxed and mixed, with constant movement between the bar areas,

the video parlour and the cruisy cubicle and dark areas. It hosts naked parties on Mondays.

San Lorenzo

San Lorenzo has a history of rebellion. It was planned in the 1880s as a working-class ghetto, with few public services or amenities. Unsurprisingly, it soon developed into Rome's most politically radical district.

These days it retains some of its threadbare, jerry-built, working-class character. But it's more radical-chic than just plain radical: a constant influx of artists and students mingles with the few surviving salt-of-the-earth locals.

Along the north-east side is the vast Verano cemetery, with the basilica of **San Lorenzo fuori le Mura** by its entrance.

To the north-west, the **Città universitaria** (the main campus of Europe's biggest university, La Sapienza), with buildings designed in the 1930s by Marcello Piacentini and Arnaldo Foschini, shows the Fascist take on the architecture of higher education.

Sights & museums

San Lorenzo fuori le Mura

Piazzale del Verano 3 (06 491 511). **Open** 8am-noon, 4-6.30pm daily. **Map** p103 F1 **40**

This basilica was donated by the Emperor Constantine to house the remains of St Lawrence after the saint met his fiery end on a griddle. Rebuilt in the sixth century, it was later united with a neighbouring church. Bombs plunged through the roof in 1943, making San Lorenzo the only Roman church to suffer war damage, but it was painstakingly reconstructed by 1949. On the right side of the basilica's 13th-century portico are frescoes showing scenes from the life of St Lawrence.

Inside the triumphal arch are sixth-century mosaics. Behind the church is Rome's major cemetery.

Eating & drinking

Bar à Book

Via dei Piceni 23 (06 9604 3014, www.barabook.it). **Open** 4pm-2am Tue-Sun. Closed Aug. **Café/bar.** Map p103 F2 ㉛
With its long wooden central table and shelves piled high with books, this café in artsy San Lorenzo looks like the design-conscious study of an eccentric 1960s-loving academic. In the bar, *aperitivi* come with a DJ on Thursdays from 7.30pm.

Marcello

Via dei Campani 12 (06 446 3311). **Meals served** 7.30-11.30pm Mon-Fri. Closed 3wks Aug. **€.** No credit cards. **Roman.** Map p103 E3 ㉜
Inside this anonymous-looking trat, hordes of hungry students wolf down piles of food at old wooden tables. Alongside offal specialities like tripe and *pajata* (calf intestines) are light and more creative dishes such as *straccetti ai carciofi* (strips of veal with artichokes).

Pastificio San Lorenzo

NEW *Via Tiburtina 196 (06 9727 3519, www.pastificiocerere.com).* **Meals served** 12.30-3pm, 8pm-1.30am Tue-Fri, Sun; 7pm-2am Sat. Closed 3wks Aug. **€€.** **Creative Italian.** Map p103 E2 ㉝
The Cerere pasta factory stopped production in 1960, after which its loft spaces were transformed into artists' studios: exhibitions here are first-rate. Late 2009 saw the opening of an industrial-chic restaurant inside the building, helmed by up-and-coming chef Stefano Preli. The menu is firmly but creatively rooted in local tradition. Prices are on the high side; try lunchtime for a chattier vibe and lower bill. You can snack until closing.

Said

Via Tiburtina 135 (06 446 9204, www.said.it). **Open** 12.30pm-midnight Mon-Sat. Closed 2wks Aug. **Café/Italian.** Map p103 E2 ㉞
Said has been producing exquisite chocolate in this factory – with its fantastic chocolatey aroma – in San Lorenzo since 1923; you can purchase it in the shop at the same address from 10am to 10pm. But its tea room and restaurant, with a fireplace, comfortable armchairs and glassed-over courtyard, is a recent addition. Chocolate pops up in unexpected places on the lunch menu (€€); dinner is served from 7.30pm.

Nightlife

Dimmidisì

Via dei Volsci 126B (06 446 1855, www.dimmidisiroma.it). **Open** 7pm-2am Thur-Sun. Closed July-Sept. Map p103 F2 ㊺
From its *aperitivo* hour, often accompanied by bands, until into the early hours, this space hosts live acts and top DJs from Italy and abroad.

Locanda Atlantide

Via dei Lucani 22B (06 4470 4540, www.locandatlantide.it). **Open** 9.30pm-3am Mon, Wed-Sun. No credit cards. Map p103 E3 ㊻
An unpretentious venue hosting an array of events that range from concerts and DJ sets to theatrical performances. It pulls an alternative crowd. Extra charge for concerts.

Mads

Via dei Sabelli 2 (328 641 8983, www.mads-project.it). **Open** 10pm-2am Tue-Sat. Closed July & Aug. No credit cards. Map p103 E3 ㊼
The cavernous space of this laid-back venue in San Lorenzo hosts regular concerts, plus themed parties, women-only nights and excellent DJ sets. Some special events are held on Sundays. Check the website for events in outdoor venues during the summer closure.

ROME BY AREA

Heading south

Beyond San Lorenzo and San Giovanni lie the endless, ugly suburbs that sprung up, largely unplanned, to house the influx of workers to the capital in the economic boom of the 1960s and '70s. The average visitor to Rome is unlikely to venture this far. But those who do will find an attraction or two to make the trek worthwhile.

Squeezed between via Casilina and via Prenestina, the Pigneto district has recently achieved that critical mass of bars, restaurants and trendsters that turns a below-the-radar zone hip. Heavily bombed in World War II and rebuilt piecemeal, the anarchic, bohemian feel of the place attracted arty types such as Pier Paolo Pasolini (much of his first film, *Accattone*, was shot here). Today, partly pedestrianised via del Pigneto is home to a morning market (Mon-Sat) and some cool restaurants and bars.

Eating & drinking

Bar Necci dal 1924

Via Fanfulla da Lodi 68 (06 9760 1552, www.necci1924.com). **Meals served** 12.30-3pm, 7.30-11pm Mon-Sat; 7-11pm Sun. **€€. Creative Italian.** **Map** off p103 F4 ㊽

This former old blokes' bar (used by Pasolini as his HQ when filming *Accattone* nearby), is now a shabby-chic brunch/lunch/dinner place with marvellous 1960s-style decor. British co-owner and chef Ben Hirst is responsible for the quality mod-Med cuisine. There are tables outside on a delightful terrace. As a bar, it functions from 8am to 1am daily (closed weekends in Aug).

Primo

Via del Pigneto 46 (06 701 3827, www.primoalpigneto.it). **Meals served** 10am-1.30am daily. Closed 1wk Aug. **€€. Creative Italian.** **Map** off p103 F4 ㊾

Slow Food-inspired Primo is warehouse-cool in design and eclectic in its culinary offerings, which are usually (though not consistently) good. The vibe is relaxed, with staff clad in matching T-shirts, and an endless stream of customers coming for Roman classics or dishes with a creative twist. Doors stay open until 1am or later for drinks and tapas.

Il Tiaso

Via Perugia 20 (333 284 5283, www.iltiaso.com). **Open** 6pm-2am daily. Closed 1wk Aug. **Wine bar.** **Map** off p103 F4 ㊿

This book-lined wine bar in vibrant Pigneto is as unpretentious and laid-back as they come.

Nightlife

Circolo degli Artisti

Via Casilina Vecchia 42 (06 7030 5684, www.circoloartisti.it). **Open** 9.30pm-3.30am Tue-Thur; 9pm-4.30am Fri-Sun. Closed Aug. No credit cards. **Map** off p103 F4 (51)

This is Rome's most popular venue for small- and medium-scale bands, from international alternative music circuits. There's a popular gay night on Fridays. On Saturdays (€5 after midnight), 'Screamadelica' offers concerts by some of Europe's best alternative artists and emerging Italian bands. Check out the website for Monday event listings.

Qube

Via di Portonaccio 212 (06 438 5445, www.qubedisco.com). **Open** 11.30pm-5am Thur-Sat. Closed May-Oct. **Map** off p103 F3 (52)

Thursday means rock and Saturday brings sets by well-known DJs, but it's on Friday that this cavernous space explodes, when it's taken over by the Muccassassina crew for their wildly extravagant gay event.

Centrale Montemartini p122

The Aventine & Testaccio

There's an air of moneyed calm on the leafy Aventine hill, which was first colonised by King Ancius Marcius in the seventh century BC. At first, foreigners and other undesirables drifted up here from the river port below. But they were driven out when the hill was set aside for plebeians in 456 BC. And here the *plebs* remained, building their temples and villas.

It's a lovely place for a stroll. Upkeep of the Parco Savello – surrounded by the crenellated walls of a 12th-century fortress – has been allowed to slide recently, but dozens of orange trees and a spectacular view over the city, especially at sunset, make it worth a visit. In nearby piazza Cavalieri di Malta, peek through the keyhole of the priory of the Knights of Malta to enjoy the surprise designed by Gian Battista Piranesi: a telescopic view of the dome of St Peter's.

Across busy viale Aventino is the similarly well-heeled San Saba district and, beyond the white cuboids of the UN's Food and Agricultural Organisation, the giant **Baths of Caracalla**.

Sights & museums

Baths of Caracalla

Viale delle Terme di Caracalla 52 (06 3996 7700). **Open** 9am-2pm Mon; 9am-1hr before sunset Tue-Sun. **Admission** €6 (includes Tomb of Cecilia Metella & Villa dei Quintili); €3 reductions; extra charge during exhibitions. No credit cards. **Map** p118 D2 ❶
The high-vaulted ruins of the Terme di Caracalla are peaceful today, but were anything but tranquil in their heyday, when up to 1,600 Romans could sweat it out in the baths and gyms. You can get some idea of their original splendour from the fragments of mosaic and statuary that litter the site.

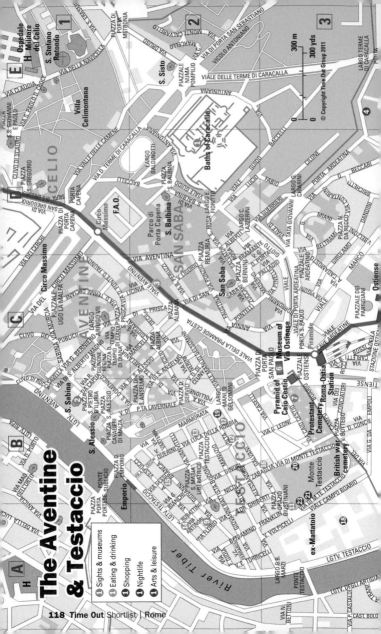

The Aventine & Testaccio

- ① Sights & museums
- ① Eating & drinking
- ① Shopping
- ① Nightlife
- ① Arts & leisure

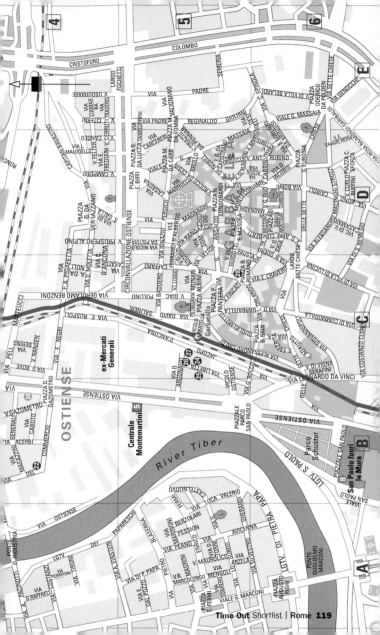

The baths were built between AD 213 and 216. The two cavernous rooms down the sides were the gymnasia, where Romans engaged in such strenuous sports as toss-the-beanbag. There was also a large *natatio* (pool), saunas and baths, as well as a library, a garden, shops and stalls. Underneath it all was a network of tunnels where slaves trod the giant wheels that pumped clean water up to bathers. Caracalla's baths operated until 537, when the Visigoths cut the city's aqueducts.

Santa Sabina

Piazza Pietro d'Illiria 1 (06 574 3573). **Open** 8.30am-12.30pm, 3-7pm daily. **Admission** free. **Map** p118 B1 ❷

Santa Sabina was built in the fifth century over an early Christian place of worship; the mosaic floor visible through a grate at the entrance is from the earlier building. Restoration in the 1930s returned the church to its fifth to ninth-century appearance. The fifth-century cypress doors are carved with biblical scenes. The nave's Corinthian columns support an arcade decorated with ninth-century marble inlay work; the choir dates from the same period. Selenite has been placed in the windows as it would have been in the ninth century. A window in the entrance porch looks on to the place where St Dominic is said to have planted an orange tree brought from Spain in 1220. The lovely cloister dates from the 13th century.

Eating & drinking

See also **Casa del Jazz** (right).

Il Gelato

Viale Aventino 59 (338 446 3434). **Open** 11am-11pm Mon-Sat. Closed 3wks Jan. **Ice-cream**. **Map** p118 C2 ❸

Finally, there's no need to schlep out to the EUR district to experience Claudio Torcè's truly extraordinary ice-cream. The chocolate and ginger, and peanut flavours are sublime.

Nightlife

Casa del Jazz

Viale di Porta Ardeatina 55 (06 704 731, www.casajazz.it). **Open** varies depending on event. Closed 2wks Jan, 2wks Aug. **Map** p118 E3 ❹

In a villa confiscated from a local crime boss, the Casa del Jazz offers great concerts, plus a café/restaurant (open 8-11.15pm Tue-Sat, 11am-3pm, 8-11.15pm Sun) with a shady garden. The €10 weekend brunch with jazz is wonderful.

Testaccio & Ostiense

Testaccio is bustling, noisy, workaday and still populated by brusquely salt-of-the-earth long-term residents. But this close to the *centro storico*, the district couldn't remain exclusively working class for long: an influx of young(ish) professionals has upped property prices and turned Testaccio into a very desirable area.

Locals of all stripes mix contendibly in the gardens of piazza Santa Maria Liberatrice on warm evenings, linked by an almost universal devotion to the AS Roma football team and an indulgent fondness for the elderly ladies who still traipse to the market in their slippers of a morning.

There are no major monuments here, just traces of Testaccio's hard-working past: an ancient river port, a rubbish tip composed of discarded potsherds (Monte Testaccio) and an abandoned abattoir slowly being made over into an arts centre-cum-alternative marketplace, the **Città dell'Altra Economia**. Testaccio is also home to the most vibrant slice of Rome's nightlife scene.

Further south, via Ostiense cuts through once run-down suburbs earmarked for some interesting development: Dutch architectural superstar Rem Koolhaas is turning the former wholesale fruit and

PULITI
NO CORONE

CALAMARI
PULITI
SPEC €14

vegetable market into a complex of youth-oriented exhibition spaces, sports centres and shopping centres – what the authorities describe as 'Rome's Covent Garden'.

However, the signs of change and renewal have been visible for a while – ever since the **Centrale Montemartini** power station was converted into one of the capital's most striking museums, the **Teatro Palladium** reopened (revamped and with a fascinating programme), and Testaccio's vibrant after-hours activity began seeping south.

Sights & museums

Centrale Montemartini

Via Ostiense 106 (06 574 8030, www.centralemontemartini.org).
Open 9am-7pm Tue-Sun. **Admission** €4.50; €3.50 reductions; extra charge during exhibitions. No credit cards.
Map p119 B5 ❺
Centrale Montemartini contains the leftover ancient statuary from the Capitoline Museums – but the dregs are pretty impressive, and the setting itself is well worth a visit. Fauns and Minervas, bacchic revellers and Apollos are starkly white but oddly at home in this decommissioned generating station. Excellent jazz concerts (€8) on Friday nights make the Centrale even more alluring.

Museum of Via Ostiense

Via R Persichetti 3 (06 574 3193).
Open 9.30am-1.30pm, 2.30-4.30pm Tue, Thur; 9.30am-1.30pm Wed, Fri, Sat, 1st & 3rd Sun of mth. **Admission** free.
Map p118 C3 ❻
This third-century AD gatehouse, called Porta Ostiensis in antiquity and Porta San Paolo today, contains a quaint collection of artefacts and prints describing the history of via Ostiense – the Ostian Way, built in the third century BC to join Rome to its port at Ostia. There's a large-scale model of

the ancient port, and you can cross the crenellated walkway for a bird's-eye view of the true finesse of the modern Roman motorist.

Protestant Cemetery

Via Caio Cestio 6 (06 574 1900, www.cemeteryrome.it). **Open** 9am-5pm Mon-Sat; 9am-1pm Sun.
Admission free (donation of €2 requested). **Map** p118 B3 ❼
This heavenly oasis of calm in the midst of a ruckus of traffic has been the resting place for foreigners who have passed on to a better place since 1784. Officially the 'non-Catholic' cemetery, this charmingly old-world corner of the city accommodates Buddhists, Russian Orthodox Christians and atheists. In the older sector you'll find the grave of John Keats, who coughed his last in Rome at the age of 26. Close by is the tomb of Shelley, who died a year after Keats in a boating accident.

San Paolo fuori le Mura

Via Ostiense 184 (06 541 0341, www.basilicasanpaolo.org). **Open**
Basilica 6.45am-6.30pm daily.
Cloister 9am-1pm, 3-6pm daily.
Map p119 B6 ❽
Constantine founded this basilica to commemorate the martyrdom of St Paul nearby. The church has been rebuilt several times; most of the present church is only 150 years old. Features to have survived include 11th-century doors; a strange 12th-century Easter candlestick featuring human-, lion- and goat-headed beasts spewing the vine of life from their mouths; and a 13th-century canopy above the altar, by Arnolfo di Cambio. In the nave are mosaic portraits of all the popes from Peter to the present incumbent. There are seven spaces left; once they're filled, the world, apparently, will end. In the *confessio* beneath the altar is the tomb of St Paul, topped by a stone slab pierced with holes through which devotees stuff bits of cloth to imbue them with the apostle's holiness.

Proceeds of crime

Seized Mafia land is finally being put to good use.

Bottega dei Sapori della Legalità

Your chances of getting caught in the cross-fire of some *Cosa nostra* shoot-out in Rome are remote. But over the years, 10,000 Italians have been victims of gun-toting clan members, according to Roberto Saviano, crusading best-selling author of *Gomorrah*, a devastating exposé of Italy's flourishing organised crime scene.

All is not bleak, though. A change in the law in 1996 allowed organised crime-owned assets – including agricultural properties – to be confiscated. The **Bottega dei Sapori della Legalità** (Via dei Prefetti 23, 06 6992 5262, www.liberaterra.it) is the Rome outlet for organic produce grown on land liberated from the Mafia, under the aegis of an organisation called Libera. Father Luigi Ciotti, a frontier priest, founded Libera in 1995. He now has the satisfaction of seeing over 1,000 acres of ex-Mafia land, in Sicily and the south – but also in the Lazio area around Rome – farmed by volunteer members of local groups, youth organisations and co-operatives.

No distance at all from the parliament building, the Bottega dei Sapori provides an excellent souvenir alternative to plaster casts of the Colosseum and industrially produced *limoncello* liqueur. In this little treasure trove, you'll find wholly legal jars of sun-dried tomatoes and packs of untainted organic *rigatoni* and *tagliatelle* pasta. There's honey, too, from hives once buzzing with bees belonging to the Mob. They'll ship you a case or two of fine green extra virgin olive oil; their wine is good too.

The state's asset-grabbing record is impressive and isn't restricted to farm land. Some 4,500 flats and villas have been confiscated, including Rome's fabulous **Casa del Jazz** (see p118). Once the chic pad of Rome's 'Magliana Gang' mobster Enrico Nicoletti, the palatial villa is now a haven for sophisticated swing sessions and contemporary jazz. Try a weekend jazz brunch in the excellent restaurant, or just turn up for one of the free events.

Monks chant vespers at 6pm weekdays, 5pm weekends.

Eating & drinking

See also **Città dell'Altra Economia** (p125) and **Volpetti** (p125).

00100

Via G Branca (06 4341 9624, www.00100pizza.com). **Open** noon-11pm daily. Closed 3wks Aug.
Takeway pizza. Map p118 A2 **9**
Elbow your way through the crowds in this tiny space for delicious slow-rise pizza with toppings such as stilton cheese with reduction of port. Trademark 'trapizzini' are pizza pockets opened out and filled with anything from tripe to cuttlefish.

Andreotti

Via Ostiense 54B (06 575 0773, www.andreottiroma.com). **Open** 7.30am-9.30pm daily. Closed 1wk Aug. **Café/bar**. Map p119 B4 **10**
The Andreotti family claims to serve 700 cups of its excellent coffee every day – and that was before a recent overhaul doubled the space and lengthened the counter. This has allowed even more scope for sampling this historic bar's excellent breakfast *cornetti*, cakes, light lunchtime snacks and evening *aperitivi* with nibbles.

Checchino dal 1887

Via di Monte Testaccio 30 (06 574 6318, www.checchino-dal-1887.com). **Meals served** 12.30-3pm, 8pm-midnight Tue-Sat. Closed Aug & 1wk Dec. €€€€. **Roman**. Map p118 A3 **11**
Imagine a pie shop becoming a top-class restaurant, and the odd mix of humble decor, elegant service, hearty food, huge cellar – and hefty bill – falls into place. Vegetarians should give the Mariani family's restaurant a wide berth: offal is the speciality. Pasta dishes such as *bucatini all'amatriciana* are delicious.

Da Felice

Via Mastro Giorgio 29 (06 574 6800, www.felicetestaccio.com). **Meals served** 12.30-2.45pm, 8-11.30pm daily. Closed 1wk Aug. €€€. **Roman**. Map p118 B2 **12**
This former spit-and-sawdust trattoria has undergone an industrial-chic makeover, but its high-quality traditional fare – including time-honoured classics such as *tonnarelli cacio e pepe* and *abbacchio al forno con patate* (baked lamb with potatoes) – remains good. The wine list is impressive. Be sure to book.

L'Oasi della Birra

Piazza Testaccio 41 (06 574 6122, www.oasidellabirra.com). **Open** 4.30pm-12.30am daily. Closed 2wks Aug. **Wine bar**. Map p118 B2 **13**
An off-licence and speciality food shop (and open from 8.30am for this purpose), the 'Oasis of Beer' becomes an *aperitivo* haunt in the evening, with hundreds of brews on offer – including beers from many award-winning Italian microbreweries. The selection of wines by the bottle is almost as impressive, and the *aperitivo* buffet (4.30-8pm) delicious. Full-scale meals with a Teutonic slant are also served. There are tables outside.

Piccolo Alpino

Via Orazio Antinori 5 (06 574 1386). **Meals served** 12.30-2.30pm, 7-11pm Tue-Sun. Closed 1wk Aug. €. No credit cards. **Italian/pizzeria**. Map p118 A2 **14**
There are no frills in this very cheap, very cheerful eaterie, where the pizzas are good and some of the pastas – the *spaghetti con le vongole* stands out – are perfectly acceptable too (though these will push the bill into the €€ bracket).

Remo

Piazza Santa Maria Liberatrice 44 (06 574 6270). **Meals served** 7pm-1am Mon-Sat. Closed 3wks Aug. €.
Pizzeria. Map p118 B2 **15**

This pizzeria is a veritable institution. You can choose to sit at one of the wonky tables on the pavement, or in the deafening interior. The thin-crust Roman pizzas are excellent, as are the *bruschette al pomodoro*.

Il Seme e la Foglia

Via Galvani 18 (06 574 3008). **Open** 7.30am-2am Mon-Sat; 6pm-2am Sun. Closed 3wks Aug. No credit cards. **Café/bar**. Map p118 B3 ⑯
This lively daytime snack bar and evening pre-club stop is always packed with students from the music school opposite. At midday, there's a pasta dish, plus generously proportioned salads (€5-€7) and a selection of creative filled rolls.

Tuttifrutti

Via Luca della Robbia 3A (06 575 7902). **Meals served** 7.30-11.30pm Mon-Sat. Closed 2wks Aug. **€€€**. **Italian**. Map p118 B2 ⑰
Behind an anonymous glass door, this trattoria is Testaccio's best-value dining experience, at the lower end of this price bracket. Michele guides you through a changing menu of creative fare. There is usually a veggie option and the wine is excellently priced.

Shopping

The produce market (Mon-Sat, mornings) that sets up in piazza Testaccio is a great place to pick up picnic fare.

Nearby streets, and the north-western aisle of the market itself, have been colonised by vendors of shoes of all descriptions, including bargains on last season's models. For men's shoes, stop by the market on Saturday.

Città dell'Altra Economia

Largo Dino Frisullo (06 5730 0419, www.cittadellaltraeconomia.org). **Open** *Food shop* 10am-1.30pm, 2.30-8pm

Tue-Sat; 10am-1.30pm, 2.30-7pm Sun. *Fair-trade shop* noon-8pm Tue-Fri; 10am-8pm Sat; 10am-7pm Sun. *Bar* 10am-8pm Tue-Thur; 10am-10.30 Fri, Sat; 10am-7pm Sun. *Restaurant* 7.30-11pm Tue-Fri; 1-3pm, 7.30-11pm Sat, Sun. Map p118 A3 ⑱
Difficult to find, this 'city of alternative economy' comprises an organic food shop selling local products, a fair-trade store, plus a bar and a wholesome restaurant (€€). It's all set inside a gloriously restored pavilion of the former municipal slaughterhouse, with a huge open area outside, overlooked by Monte Testaccio, where you can let kids loose for a runabout on sunny days. Be aware that the opening hours change frequently. There's a lively organic farmers' market some Sundays.

Volpetti

Via Marmorata 47 (06 574 2352, www.fooditaly.com). **Open** 8am-2pm, 5-8.15pm Mon-Sat. **Map** p118 B2 ⑲
This is one of the best delis in Rome. It's hard to get away without one of the jolly assistants loading you with samples of their wares, from 25-year-old cheeses to exquisite salted anchovies – pleasant, but painful on the wallet. Around the corner is Volpetti Più (via A Volta 8-10, 06 574 4306, open 10.30am-3.30pm, 5.30-9.30pm Mon-Sat), a self-service restaurant where you can taste the deli's delicious cured meats and cheeses, along with pizza, salads and more.

Nightlife

Akab

Via di Monte Testaccio 68-69 (06 5725 0585, www.akabcave.com). **Open** 11.30pm-4.30am Tue, Thur-Sat. Closed Aug. **Map** p118 B3 ⑳
This long-term fixture of the Testaccio scene has an underground cellar and a street-level room, plus a garden for the warmer months. The Tuesday night L-Ektrica sessions

Teatro Palladium

feature a host of international DJs, and there's house and more on Friday and Saturday nights.

L'Alibi

Via di Monte Testaccio 40-44 (06 574 3448, www.lalibi.it). **Open** 11.30pm-5am Thur-Sun. **Map** p118 B3 ㉑
Rome's original gay club, the Alibi is still, in theory, a great place to dance away, with a well-oiled sound system. But it's showing its age. And a new straight-friendly approach and Friday hetero night have proved something of a turn-off all round.

Alpheus

Via del Commercio 36 (06 574 7826, www.alpheus.it). **Open** 10.30pm-4am Fri-Sun; other days vary. Closed July & Aug. **Map** p119 B4 ㉒
An eclectic club with a varied crowd, the Alpheus has four halls for live gigs, music festivals, theatre and cabaret, all followed by a disco. The music changes nightly and from room to room: rock, R&B and Latin alongside world music, retro and happy trash. Watch out for the regular *Gorgeous I Am* gay events.

Caruso-Café de Oriente

Via di Monte Testaccio 36 (06 574 5019, www.carusocafe.com). **Open** 10.30pm-3.30am Tue-Thur; 11pm-4.30am Fri, Sat; 10.30pm-4am Sun. Closed end June-mid Sept. **Map** p118 B3 ㉓
A must for lovers of salsa, this club offers Latin American tunes every night apart from Saturday (anything from reggae to hip hop), and live acts almost daily. The roof terrace is great for summer-evening lounging.

Classico Village

Via Libetta 3 (06 5728 8857, www.classico.it). **Open** 9pm-1.30am Mon-Thur; 9pm-4am Fri, Sat. **Map** p119 C5 ㉔
This former factory in the trendy Ostiense neighbourhood is able to offer up to three (mainly rock-based) events simultaneously in its large

spaces, all of which face on to a courtyard – a heavenly spot in which to chill out on warm evenings. DJ sets often follow the shows.

Goa

Via Libetta 13 (06 574 8277). **Open** 11.30pm-4am Thur-Sat. Closed mid May-mid Sept. **Map** p119 C5 ㉕
One of the longest-running and best of Rome's fashionable clubs, Goa is a techno-ethno fantasy of iron and steel with oriental-style statues and colours. Thursday's Ultrabeat night brings in Europe's top electronic music DJs. Goa opens some Sundays (6pm-4.30am); there's a women-only event on the last Sunday of the month.

Rashomon

Via degli Argonauti 16 (347 340 5710). **Open** 11pm-4am Fri, Sat. Closed June-Sept. **Map** p119 C5 ㉖
Run by afficionados of alternative clubs in London and Berlin, Rashomon offers an eclectic mix of electro-rock, indie, electronica and new wave. There are often live acts, including appearances from emerging locals.

La Saponeria

Via degli Argonauti 20 (06 574 6999, www.saponeriaclub.it). **Open** midnight-4.30am Fri, Sat. **Map** p119 C5 ㉗
One of the liveliest clubs in Ostiense, this stylish, curvy, white space gets hopelessly packed at weekends. Friday is techno and electronic, Saturday is hip hop and R&B. It's open Saturday only from mid June to mid Sept.

Arts & leisure

Teatro Palladium

Piazza Bartolomeo Romano 8 (06 5733 2768, www.teatro-palladium.it). **Map** p119 C5 ㉘
This beautiful 1920s theatre in Garbatella offers a mix of top-quality electronic music acts, cutting-edge theatre and art performances.

Santa Maria in Trastevere

Trastevere
& the Gianicolo

Trastevere

Trastevere is the Rome of your romantic dreams. It's quaint but buzzing, historical but without the imposing ruins and galleries you feel you have to 'do' on the other side of the river. Here – across the Tiber – your main tasks will include rambling through narrow cobbled streets, soaking up the rustic charm, basking in the laid-back feel of the place and selecting the likeliest-looking of the over-abundant bars for *aperitivi*.

Trasteverini claim descent from slave stock. Through the Imperial period, much of the *trans Tiberim* area was agricultural, with farms, vineyards, country villas and gardens laid out for the pleasure of the Caesars. Trastevere was a working-class district in papal Rome, and remained so until well after Unification.

Viale Trastevere slices the district in two. At the hub of the much-visited western part is piazza **Santa Maria in Trastevere**, with its eponymous church. Fewer tourists make it to the warren of cobbled alleys in the eastern half, where craftsmen still ply their trades around the lovely church of **Santa Cecilia in Trastevere**.

Ponte Sisto provides pedestrian access back to the *centro storico*.

Sights & museums

Museo di Roma in Trastevere

Piazza Sant'Egidio 1B (06 589 7123, www.museodiromaintrastevere.it).
Open 10am-8pm Tue-Sun. **Admission** €3, €1.50 reductions. No credit cards.
Map p130 C3 ❶
This dusty folklore museum, housed in a 17th-century convent, showcases a series of watercolours of 19th-century

Rome and some whiskery waxwork tableaux evoking the life of 18th- and 19th-century *trasteverini*.

Orto botanico (Botanical Garden)

Largo Cristina di Svezia 24 (06 4991 7107). **Open** 9am-6.30pm Mon-Sat. **Admission** €4; €2 reductions. No credit cards. **Map** p130 B2 ❷
Established in 1883, Rome's Botanical Garden provides a modestly sized but welcome haven from the rigours of a dusty, hot city. Plants tumble over ancient flights of steps and into fountains and fish ponds, creating luxuriant hidden corners disturbed only by frolicking children.

Palazzo Corsini – Galleria Nazionale d'Arte Antica

Via della Lungara 10 (06 6880 2323, www.galleriaborghese.it). **Open** 8.30am-7.30pm Tue-Sun. **Admission** €4; €2 reductions. No credit cards. **Map** p130 C2 ❸
A 17th-century convert to Catholicism, Sweden's Queen Christina established her glittering court here in 1662. The stout monarch smoked a pipe, wore trousers and entertained female and (ordained) male lovers here. Today, her former home houses part of the national art collection, with scores of Madonnas and Children (the most memorable is a Madonna by Van Dyck). Other works include a pair of Annunciations by Guercino; two St Sebastians (one by Rubens, one by Annibale Carracci), Caravaggio's *St John the Baptist*; and a triptych by Fra Angelico. There's also a melancholy *Salome* by Guido Reni.

San Francesco a Ripa

Piazza San Francesco d'Assisi 88 (06 581 9020). **Open** 7am-noon, 4-7.30pm Mon-Sat; 7am-1pm, 4-7.30pm Sun. **Map** p131 E5 ❹
This church occupies the site of the hospice where St Francis of Assisi stayed when he visited Rome in 1219; a near-contemporary portrait hangs in the cell where the saint slept. The original 13th-century church was rebuilt in the 1680s. It contains Bernini's sculpture of the Beata Ludovica Albertoni (1674), showing the aristocratic Franciscan nun dying in an agonised, sexually ambiguous Baroque ecstasy.

Santa Cecilia in Trastevere

Piazza Santa Cecilia 22 (06 4549 2739). **Open** *Church* 9.30am-1pm, 4-8pm daily. *Crypt & excavations* 9.30am-12.30pm, 4-6.30pm Mon-Sat. *Cavallini frescoes* 10.15am-12.30pm Mon-Sat; 11.30am-12.30pm Sun. **Admission** *Cavallini frescoes* €2.50. *Excavations* €2.50. No credit cards. **Map** p131 E4 ❺
Santa Cecilia stands on the site of a fifth-century building that was itself built over an older Roman house, part of which can be visited. According to legend, it was the home of the martyr Cecilia: after an unsuccessful attempt to suffocate her in her bath, her persecutors tried to behead her with three strokes of an axe (the maximum permitted). She sang for the several days it took her to die, and so became the patron saint of music. Her tomb was opened in 1599, revealing her undecayed body. It disintegrated, but not before a sketch was made, on which Stefano Maderno based the sculpture below the high altar. Her sarcophagus is in the crypt. In the upstairs gallery there remains a small fragment of what must have been one of the world's greatest frescoes. In this 13th-century *Last Judgement*, Pietro Cavallini flooded the apostles with a totally new kind of light – the same that was to reappear in Giotto's work.

Santa Maria in Trastevere

Piazza Santa Maria in Trastevere (06 589 7332, www.santamariaintrastevere.org). **Open** 7.30am-9pm daily. **Map** p130 C3 ❻
Legend has it that a miraculous well of oil sprang from the ground where Santa Maria now stands at the moment that Christ was born, and flowed to the Tiber

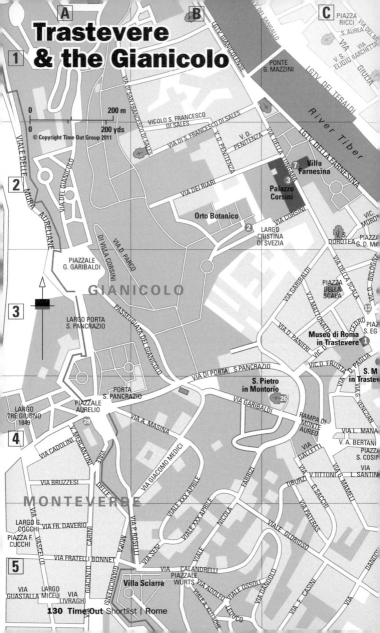

Trastevere
& the Gianicolo

A   B   C

1

PIAZZA RICCI

PONTE G. MAZZINI

VICOLO S. FRANCESCO DI SALES

River Tiber

2

Villa Farnesina

Palazzo Corsini

Orto Botanico

LARGO CRISTINA DI SVEZIA

V. S. DOROTEA

PIAZZA G. D. M.

0   200 m
0   200 yds
© Copyright Time Out Group 2011

GIANICOLO

PIAZZALE G. GARIBALDI

PIAZZA DELLA SCALA

Museo di Roma in Trastevere

3

LARGO PORTA S. PANCRAZIO

PIAZ S. EG

S. M in Traste

S. Pietro in Montorio

PORTA S. PANCRAZIO

PIAZZALE AURELIO

RAMPA DI MONTE AUREO

V. A. BERTANI

PIAZZA S. COSI

4

LARGO TRE GIUGNO 1849

PIAZZA S. COSI

MONTEVERDE

LARGO G. COCCHI

PIAZZA F. CUCCHI

Villa Sciarra

PIAZZALE WURTS

5

LARGO GUASTALLA

LARGO MICELI

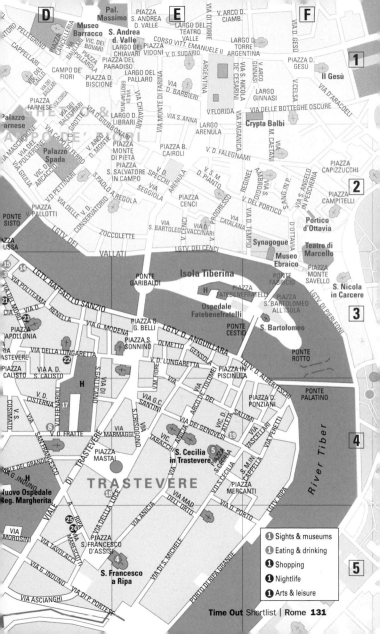

all day. The first church on this site was begun in the early fourth century; the present building was erected in the 12th, and has wonderful mosaics. Those on the façade, from the 12th and 13th centuries, show Mary breastfeeding Christ, and ten women with crowns and lanterns. Inside, the apse has a 12th-century mosaic of Jesus and his mother. Lower down, there are beautiful 13th-century mosaics showing scenes from the life of the Virgin by Pietro Cavallini. The Madonna and Child with rainbow overhead is also by Cavallini. In the chapel to the left of the high altar is a very rare sixth-century painting on wood of the Madonna.

Villa Farnesina

Via della Lungara 230 (06 6802 7267, www.villafarnesina.it). **Open** 9am-1pm Mon-Sat. **Admission** €5; €3 reductions. No credit cards. **Map** p130 C2 ❼
Built in 1508-11 for rich papal banker Agostino Chigi, this palazzo became the property of the powerful Farnese family in 1577. Chigi was one of Raphael's principal patrons; the stunning frescoes in the ground-floor Loggia of Psyche were designed by Raphael, but executed by his followers. The Grace with her back turned (to the right of the door) is attributed to him, and around the corner in the Loggia of Galatea, Raphael created the victorious goddess in her seashell chariot. Also opens the second Sunday of the month.

Eating & drinking

See also **Lettere Caffè** (p138).

Alle Fratte di Trastevere

Via delle Fratte di Trastevere 49-50 (06 583 5775, www.allefratteditrastevere. com). **Meals served** 6-11.30pm Mon, Tue; 12.30-3pm, 6-11.30pm Thur-Sun. Closed 2wks Aug. €€. **Roman/ Neapolitan**. **Map** p131 D4 ❽
The cheerful Alle Fratte does honest Roman trattoria fare with Neapolitan influences. Service is friendly, attentive

and bilingual. First courses come in generous portions, while *secondi* include roast sea bream and veal escalopes in marsala.

Bir & Fud

Via Benedetta 23 (06 589 4016). **Meals served** 6.30pm-midnight daily. Closed 2wks Aug. €€. **Pizzeria/ Roman**. **Map** p130 C3 ❾
Buzzing Bir & Fud serves exactly what the (phonetically spelt) name says: interesting beers from lesser-known breweries, plus food that's super-fresh and additive-free: excellent pizza, bruschetta, mixed salads and some very Roman offal. The venue stays open until 2am at weekends.

Checco er Carrettiere

Via Benedetta 7 (06 581 1413). **Open** 6.30am-1am daily. **Bar/ ice-cream**. **Map** p131 D3 ❿
Historic Checcho has great cakes and some of the best ice-cream this side of the River Tiber. The collection of whiskeys is most impressive, and at *aperitivo* hour, the crisp *crocchette* and fresh quiches are welcome.

Cioccolata e Vino

Vicolo del Cinque 11 (06 5830 1868). **Open** 6.30pm-2am Mon-Fri; 2pm-2am Sat, Sun. **Bar/shop**. **Map** p130 C3 ⓫
Half-shop, half-bar, this tiny emporium is a chocoholic's dream: choose from hot chocolate, an espresso with a piece of bitter chocolate in the bottom of your cup or a tasting of handmade chocs with a glass of wine.

Dar Poeta

Vicolo del Bologna 45 (06 588 0516, www.darpoeta.com). **Meals served** noon-midnight daily. €€. **Pizzeria**. **Map** p130 C3 ⓬
Dar Poeta does high-quality pizza with creative toppings, such as the house pizza with courgettes, sausage and spicy pepper. Healthy salads offer a break from all those carbs. Be prepared to queue, as bookings aren't taken.

Orto botanico p129

Freni e Frizioni

Enoteca Ferrara

*Piazza Trilussa 41 (06 580 3769,
www.enotecaferrara.it).* Open 6pm-
2am daily. **Wine bar**. Map p131 D3 ⓭
Avoid the rather expensive restaurant
and make for the wine bar, with its
good choice of wines by the glass and
an encyclopaedic (though expensive)
bottle menu. From 6pm to 2am, you
can graze through an appetising selection of bar snacks for €7-€10.

Freni e Frizioni

*Via del Politeama 4-6 (06 4549 7499,
www.freniefrizioni.com).* Open 6pm-
2am daily. **Bar**. Map p131 D3 ⓮
In a former mechanic's workshop,
this shabby-chic temple to the *aperitivo* cult is mobbed by crowds of hipsters hitting the generous (free) snack
table (from 7pm) then spilling out of
'Brakes and Clutches' and across the
square, glass and plate in hand.

Friends Art Café

*Piazza Trilussa 34 (06 581 6111,
www.cafefriends.it).* Open 7.30am-
2am Mon-Sat; 6.30pm-2am Sun.
Bar/café. Map p131 D3 ⓯
Habitués meet in this lively bar for
everything from breakfast to after-
dinner cocktails. The chrome detailing
and brightly coloured plastic chairs
lend the place a retro-1980s funhouse
feel. Lunch and dinner menus offer
bruschette, salads and pastas at
reasonable prices. There's an equally
lively branch at via della Scrofa 60.

Glass Hostaria

*Vicolo del Cinque 58 (06 5833 5903,
www.glass-hostaria.it).* **Meals served**
8pm-midnight Tue-Sun. Closed 1wk
Jan, 2wks July-Aug. €€€. **Creative
Italian**. Map p130 C3 ⓰
Ultra-modern Glass kicks against the
traditional Trastevere dining scene,
with unusual, creative pan-Italian
dishes… most of which work. Service
is generally friendly, the wine list is
interesting and it's not bad value, given
its Michelin star.

Top notes

Classical music treats.

Musicians make a pilgrimage to
the magnificent basilica of Santa
Cecilia in Trastevere (see p129)
on 22 November, the feast of
the second-century virgin whose
singing through several attempts
by Roman soldiers to cut off her
head made her the patron saint
of music. Sung mass in this
candle-lit, flower-filled church on
the eve of the *festa* is a treat.

Two other churches with fine
acoustics – Santa Maria in
Trastevere (see p129) and San
Crisogono (piazza Sonino 44) –
make Trastevere a musical hub.
Church concerts are free, and
often packed. Regulars arrive
early, armed with cushions
against the chill of marble steps,
but many devotees are happy to
stand throughout Monteverdi's
Vespers or Verdi's *Requiem*.

On Saturday afternoons, the
great organ of the Pontificio
Istituto di Musica Sacra (piazza
Sant'Agostino 20A, 06 663
8792, www.vatican.va) is
unleashed into the hands of
visiting cathedral organists.
That's free too, as are the
concerts at the auditorium
of the Conservatorio Santa
Cecilia (via dei Greci 18, www.
conservatoriosantacecilia.it).

Another source of (usually)
free, high-class classical music
are Rome's international cultural
institutes. And the Opera di
Roma (see p108) usually gives
one free performance each
summer. Find out what's on
offer at all the city's churches
and other musical venues at
www.info.roma.it.

ROME BY AREA

Libreria del Cinema

Via dei Fienaroli 31D (06 581 77'√,
www.libreriadelcinema√√√√.it). **Open**
3-10pm Mon; 11am-10pm Tue-Fri;
11am-11pm Sat; 11am-10pm Sun. Closed
2wks Aug. **Café**. **Map** p131 D4 **17**
This bookshop is heaven for movie
buffs, with its vast stock of cinema-
related material and its busy events
programme. At the intimate little café,
aficionados swap cinema tales over
light lunches (€€) and *aperitivi*.

Luce 44

Via della Luce 44 (06 580 0846,
www.luce44.it). **Open** 12.30-3pm,
7.45-11.15pm daily. €€€. **Creative
Italian**. **Map** p131 D4 **18**
Luce 44 claims to be Rome's first zero-
impact eaterie, from its sustainably
sourced power to its organic ingredients, produced in the countryside
around Rome. The mod-Med cuisine is
competent, but the standard doesn't
always justify the price tag. More
interesting, perhaps, are the assorted
events, including Sunday brunch with
accompanying bric-a-brac market.

Le Mani in Pasta

Via de' Genovesi 37 (06 581 6017).
Meals served 12.30-3pm, 7.30-11.30pm
Tue-Sun. Closed 3wks Aug, 10 days
Dec. €€€. **Italian**. **Map** p131 E4 **19**
This trat offers decent, creative home
cooking, big portions, friendly service
and great value. Antipasti such as the
chargrilled vegetables or sautéed clams
and mussels, and mountains of pasta,
such as the spaghetti with cuttlefish
and artichokes, may mean you never
get as far as good main courses such as
fillet steak with green peppercorns.

Ombre Rosse

Piazza Sant'Egidio 12 (06 588 4155,
www.ombrerossecaffe.it). **Open** 8am-
2am Mon-Sat; 10am-2am Sun. **Café/
bar**. **Map** p130 C3 **20**
This café is a meeting spot day and
night. Food (€€) is served throughout
the day, but Ombre Rosse is best for

people-watching: snagging a table outside is something of a coup after dark.
Service is slow but amiable.

Shopping

See also **Cioccolata e Vino** (p132)
and **Libreria del Cinema** (left).
Piazza San Cosimato is home to
a produce market (from early on
until about 2pm Mon-Sat) that
manages to retain a local feel in
this tourist-heavy area. On Sunday
mornings, the Porta Portese flea
market engulfs via Portuense and
surrounding streets: watch out for
pickpockets as you root through
bootleg CDs, clothes, bags and
fake designer gear.

Almost Corner Bookshop

Via del Moro 45 (06 583 6942). **Open**
10am-1.30pm, 3.30-8pm Mon-Sat; 11am-
1.30pm, 3.30-8pm Sun. **Map** p131 D3 **21**
This English-language bookshop is
packed with fiction and books on
history, art, archaeology and lots more.
Charming owner Dermot O'Connell is
unfailingly helpful. Check the notice-
board if you're seeking work or lodgings. Closed on Sunday in August.

Roma – Store

Via della Lungaretta 63 (06 581 8789).
Open 10am-8pm daily. **Map** p131 D3 **22**
This blissfully fragrant sanctuary of
lotions and potions stocks an array of
gorgeous scents. Old-school favourites
Floris, Creed and Penhaligon's rub
shoulders with modern classics such
as home-grown Acqua di Parma and
Lorenzo Villoresi.

Valzani

Via del Moro 37A/B (06 580 3792,
www.valzani.it). **Open** 2-8pm Mon,
Tue; 10am-8pm Wed-Sun. Closed
Aug. **Map** p131 D3 **23**
Sachertorte and spicy, nutty *pangiallo*
are the specialities in this Trastevere
institution, but they are the tip of a
sweet-toothed iceberg.

Antico Arco p138

Nightlife

See also **Freni e Frizioni** (p135), **Friends Art Café** (p135) and **Ombre Rosse** (p136).

Big Mama
Vicolo San Francesco a Ripa 18 (06 581 2551, www.bigmama.it). **Open** 9pm-1.30am Tue-Sat. Closed June-mid Sept. **Admission** free with membership (annual €14, monthly €8); extra charge (€8-€22) for big acts. **Map** p131 D5 ㉔

Rome's blues temple, where an array of respected Italian and international artists play regularly, guaranteeing a quality night out. There's jazz too. Food is served: book a table.

Lettere Caffè
Via di San Francesco a Ripa 100-101 (06 9727 0991, www.letterecaffe.org). **Open** 5pm-2am daily. Closed 2wks Aug. No credit cards. **Map** p131 D5 ㉕

Poetry slams and readings compete with live concerts – from rockabilly to jazz, beginning at 10.30pm – and DJ sets in this bookish bar where well-priced wines and spirits and yummy home-made cakes complete the picture.

Gianicolo & Monteverde

The Gianicolo is the highest of central Rome's hills, though not one of the official seven. The view from the summit over the red roofs of the *centro storico* is quite, quite lovely. It's leafy up here and a calm place for a stroll. Only the portrait busts lining the paths, and the cannon fired each day at noon, serve as reminders of the bloody battle fought here between Unification forces and the French in 1849.

To the south, tortuous via Garibaldi passes by the Baroque Fontana Paola, a fountain made in 1612; the columns come from the

original St Peter's. Between the fountain and the church of **San Pietro in Montorio** stands the unlikely Fascist-era Ossario Garibaldino (open 9am-1pm Tue-Sun), containing the remains of heroes of the Risorgimento, Italy's struggle for Unification.

West of here stretches the leafy, well-heeled suburb of Monteverde, home to the vast, green expanses of the Villa Pamphili park. It's a wonderful place for a stroll.

Sights & museums

Tempietto di Bramante & San Pietro in Montorio
Piazza San Pietro in Montorio 2 (06 581 3940). **Open** *Church* 8am-noon, 3-4pm daily. **Map** p130 C4 ㉖

High on the Gianicolo, on one of the spots where St Peter was said to have been crucified (St Peter's is another), San Pietro in Montorio conceals an architectural gem in its courtyard: Donato Bramante's Tempietto, built in 1508. This round construction, with its Doric columns, was the first modern building to follow exactly the proportions of one of the classical orders. In 1628, Bernini added the staircase down to the crypt. To enter the Tempietto, book at the Spanish Academy (06 581 2806). The 15th-century church has a chapel by Bernini (the second on the left).

Eating & drinking

Antico Arco
Piazzale Aurelio 7 (06 581 5274, www.anticoarco.it). **Meals served** 7.30-11.30pm daily. Closed 1wk Aug. €€€€. **Italian**. **Map** p130 A4 ㉗

A 2009 refit gave this place a minimalist but warm interior, accompanied by some interesting innovations in the kitchen. But the old favourites are still there too, from the amazing onion flan with grana cheese sauce, to *primi* such as risotto with castelmagno cheese. Book ahead.

Sistine Chapel p147

The Vatican & Prati

The Vatican & Borgo

The St Peter's that we see today was consecrated in 1626; the previous basilica on this spot was consecrated in the early years of the fourth century. The link between this area and Christianity, however, predates even that earlier church.

In AD 54, Emperor Nero built a circus in the *campus vaticanus*, a marshy area across the river from the city centre. Ten years later, when fire destroyed two-thirds of Rome, Nero blamed the Christians, and the persecution of this new cult began in earnest, with much of the Christian-bashing taking place in Nero's circus: legend says they were covered in tar and burned alive. Top apostle Peter is traditionally believed to have been crucified here and buried close by on the spot where, in 326, Emperor Constantine built the first church of St Peter.

Not all of the following popes resided in the Vatican but, throughout the Christian era, pilgrims have flocked to the tomb of the founder of the Roman Church. Around it, the Borgo district grew up to service the burgeoning Dark Age tourist industry. Pope Leo IV (847-55) enclosed Borgo with the 12-metre-high (40-foot) Leonine Wall, following a series of Saracen and Lombard raids. Pope Nicholas III (1277-80) extended the walls and provided a papal escape route, linking the Vatican to the huge, impregnable Castel Sant'Angelo by way of a long *passetto*, or covered walkway.

After the Sack of Rome in 1527, Pope Paul III got Michelangelo to build bigger, better walls but the popes moved to the Lateran, then the Quirinal, palaces. Only in 1870, with the Unification of Italy, were they forced back across the Tiber once more. Until 1929, the pope

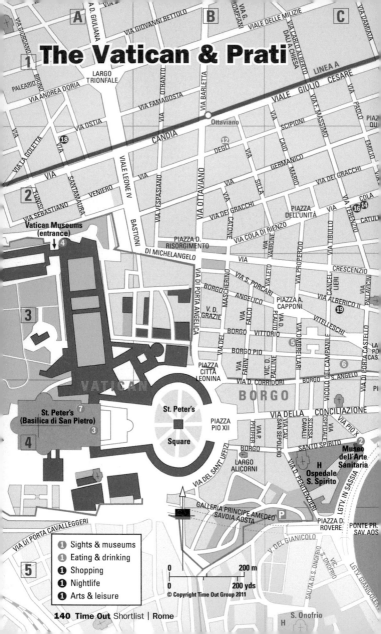

The Vatican & Prati

A A. D. GIULIANA | VIA GIOVANNI BETTOLO | **B** VIA G. GOMPANI | VIALE DELLE MILIZIE | **C**

VIA GIORDANO
PALEARIO
VIA ANDREA DORIA
LARGO TRIONFALE
VIA OSTIA
VIA LA GOLETTA
VIA SANTAMARIA
VIA SEBASTIANO
VIA VENIERO
VIALE LEONE IV
BASTIONI
DI MICHELANGELO

Ottaviano

CANDIA

VIA CARLO ALBERTO DALLA CHIESA

LINEA A

VIALE GIULIO CESARE

VIA PAOLO
PIAZ.
QU
EMILIO

VIA BARLETTA
VIA UTHANTO
VIA FAMAGOSTA

CAIO MARIO
SCIPIONI
VIALE MASSIMO
DEGLI
GERMANICO
VIA COLA DI RIENZO
VIA DEI GRACCHI
PIAZZA DELL'UNITÀ
VIA SILLA
VIA OTTAVIANO
VIA VESPASIANO
VIA CATONE
VIA DEI GRACCHI
COLA
CATUL
VIA TERENZIO
VIA TIBULLO
VIA PROPERZIO
CRESCENZIO
VIA CANCELLIERI
VIA ALBERICO II
VIA PALLAVICINI
LA PO CAS.

PIAZZA D. RISORGIMENTO
DI MICHELANGELO

Vatican Museums (entrance) ↓ 4

PIAZZA D. RISORGIMENTO
VIA DI PORTA ANGELICA
VIA S. PORCARI
VIA DEL MASCHERINO
BORGO ANGELICO
V. D. GRAZIE
VIA FALCO
BORGO VITTORIO
PIAZZA A. CAPPONI
VIA D. PLAUTO
VIA D. UMBELTARI
VITELLESCHI
BORGO S. ANGELO
19

5

6

PIAZZA CITTÀ LEONINA
VIA FARINI
VIC. D. PALLINE
VIA D. CORRIDORI
BORGO PIO
VIA DEL CAMPANILE

VATICAN

BORGO

St. Peter's
(Basilica di San Pietro) 3 · 7

St. Peter's Square

PIAZZA PIO XII

VIA DELLA CONCILIAZIONE

VIA PIO X
VIA SCOSSA CAVALLI
VIA DELL'OSPEDALE
VIA P. PFEIFFER
VIA D. PENITENZIERI
VIA CAV. SAN SEPOLCRO
BORGO SANTO SPIRITO

Museo dell'Arte Sanitaria 2
H **Ospedale S. Spirito**

VIA DEL SANT'UFFIZIO
LARGO ALICORNI

GALLERIA PRINCIPE AMEDEO SAVOIA AOSTA
P
PIAZZA D. ROVERE

VIA DI PORTA CAVALLEGGERI

V. DEL GIANICOLO
SALITA DI S. ONOFRIO
VIC. S. ONOFRIO
PONTE PR. SAV. AOS
LGTV GIANICOLENSE

Key
1 Sights & museums
1 Eating & drinking
1 Shopping
1 Nightlife
1 Arts & leisure

0 — 200 m
0 — 200 yds
© Copyright Time Out Group 2011

S. Onofrio
H

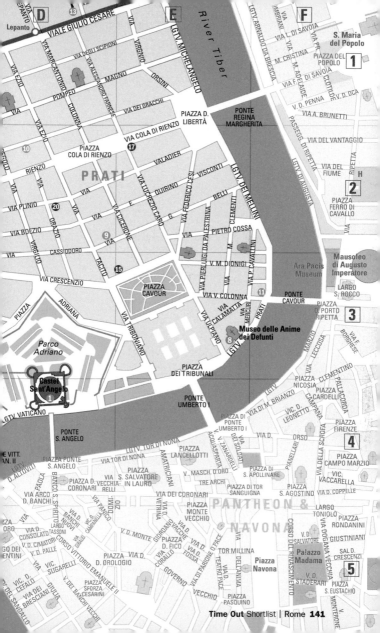

pronounced the Italian state to be sacrilegious. But on 11 February 1929, Pius XII and Mussolini signed the Lateran Pacts, awarding the Church a huge cash payment, tax-free status and a constitutional role that led to an important and continuing influence over legislation on social issues.

The Vatican City occupies an area of less than half a square kilometre, making it the world's smallest state. Despite having fewer than 800 residents, it has its own diplomatic service, postal service, army (the Swiss Guard), heliport, station, supermarket, and radio and TV stations. It has observer status at the UN, and issues its own stamps and currency (Vatican euros have a tiny circulation; the Holy See keeps a few collectors happy with occasional issues of coins that increase exponentially in value). Outside in Borgo, salt-of-the-earth locals mingle with off-duty Swiss Guards and immaculately robed priests from the Vatican *Curia* (administration).

When he's in Rome, the pope addresses crowds in St Peter's Square at noon on Sunday. On Wednesday morning at 10.30, he holds a general audience in St Peter's Square, if the weather is fine, otherwise in the modern Sala Nervi audience hall. Though it's possible to join the crowd at the back of the piazza for outside audiences (there are big screens), you'll need tickets for audiences in the Sala Nervi or for seats close to the pontiff in St Peter's Square. If you want tickets, make your request well in advance by fax to the Prefettura della Casa Pontificia (06 6988 3114, fax 06 6988 5863).

The website www.vatican.va has information on church matters. For more information on the monuments, attractions and institutions of the Vatican state,

visit www.vaticanstate.va. The Vatican walls surround splendid gardens, which can be visited on guided tours (€31, €25 reductions; includes the Vatican Museums). Book online through the Museums section on www.vatican.va, or at the tourist office in St Peter's square.

Sights & museums

Castel Sant'Angelo

Lungotevere Castello 50 (06 689 6003, www.castelsantangelo.com). **Open** 9am-7pm Tue-Sun. **Admission** €5; €3 reductions. Extra charge during exhibitions. No credit cards. **Map** p141 D4 ❶

Begun by Emperor Hadrian in AD 135 as his mausoleum, Castel Sant'Angelo has been a fortress, prison and papal residence. It now hosts temporary art shows, although the real pleasure of a visit lies in wandering from Hadrian's spiralling ramp entrance to the upper terraces, with their superb views. Between, there is much to see: lavish Renaissance salons with spectacular frescoes and trompe l'oeils; the chapel in the *Cortile d'Onore*, designed by Michelangelo; and, halfway up an easily missed staircase, Clement VII's tiny bathroom, painted by Giulio Romano. In the summer the *passetto* – linking the castle to the Vatican – is occasionally open (to the halfway point) and worth a visit.

Museo Storico Nazionale dell'Arte Sanitaria

Lungotevere in Sassia 3 (06 689 3051). **Open** 10am-noon Mon, Wed, Fri. Closed Aug. **Admission** €4. No credit cards. **Map** p140 C4 ❷

A hostel and church were established here in around 726 by King Ine of Wessex to cater for weary and sick pilgrims who descended from the north. Known as the *burgus saxo-num* or 'in Sassia', this became the nucleus of the world's first purpose-built hospital. British funds for the hostel were

Vatican essentials

Top tips for a successful visit.

Huge, forbidding and very security-conscious, the Vatican – including the museums and the basilica – are not the most straightforward places to visit. These tips will help you cope.

■ Entrances to St Peter's basilica and the Vatican Museums are in separate places and involve two lengthy queues, as well as a ten-minute brisk hike around the outside of the Vatican walls to get from one to the other. You can significantly cut your waiting times by booking a ticket and/ or a tour of the museums online (mv.vatican.va) up to 60 days before your visit.

■ Since the post-9/11 introduction of security checks at St Peter's, the queue to enter the basilica is almost always daunting, often wrapping itself most of the way around Bernini's colonnade. Take comfort in the fact that the queue moves reasonably swiftly. But before you join it: (1) make sure you're not going to be turned away when you get to the front because you're unsuitably dressed (you won't get away with shorts, very short skirts or bare midriffs/ shoulders); and (2) bear in mind that the doors close at the advertised times, no matter how many people are waiting outside.

Certain must-have items will make your visit more pleasurable.

■ Sensible shoes: essential if you are to attempt the ascent of the dome. Even if you fork out the extra €2 for the lift, there are still 320 very slippery marble steps to climb after you emerge.

■ Water: only the Galleria degli Arazzi and the Sistine Chapel are air-conditioned, and people have been known to keel over in the summer. There's also a shortage of toilets.

■ Binoculars: a good idea for looking at the details of frescoes in the Sistine Chapel, as well as for appreciating the view if you're planning an ascent of the dome.

■ A museum guidebook or audio guide (€7 from the desk after the ticket barrier): these are possibly the worst labelled museums anywhere.

ROME BY AREA

St Peter's

cut off with the Norman invasion of England in 1066, after which it passed into papal hands and thence to the Templar knight Guy de Montpellier, who founded the Order of the Holy Spirit (Santo Spirito). A few rooms of the modern hospital here house a gruesome array of medical artefacts. See also box p148.

St Peter's (Basilica di San Pietro)

Piazza San Pietro (06 6988 1662, 06 6988 5518). **Map** p140 A4 ❸
Basilica Open *Oct-Mar* 7am-6.30pm daily. *Apr-Sept* 7am-7pm daily. **Admission** free.
Dome Open *Oct-Mar* 8am-5pm daily. *Apr-Sept* 8am-6pm daily. **Admission** €5; €7 with lift.
Grottoes Open *Oct-Mar* 7am-5pm daily. *Apr-Sept* 7am-6pm daily. **Admission** free.
Necropolis Booking obligatory (06 6988 5318, 06 6987 3017 fax, scavi@fsp.va). **Open** *Guided tours* 9am-5pm Mon-Sat. **Admission** €1.
Treasury Museum Open *Oct-Mar* 8am-5.50pm daily. *Apr-Sept* 8am-6.50pm daily. **Admission** €6; €4 reductions.

The current St Peter's was consecrated on 18 November 1626 by Urban VIII, exactly 1,300 years after the consecration of the first basilica on the site. By the mid 15th century, the south wall of the original basilica was collapsing. Pope Nicholas V had 2,500 wagonloads of masonry from the Colosseum carted here, just for running repairs. It took the arrogance of Pope Julius II and his pet architect Donato Bramante to knock the millennia-old basilica down, in 1506.

Following Bramante's death in 1514, Raphael took over the work. In 1547, he was replaced by Michelangelo; he died in 1564, aged 87, after coming up with a plan for a massive dome. Completed in 1590, this was the largest brick dome ever constructed, and is still the tallest building in Rome. In 1607, Carlo Maderno designed a new

façade, crowned by enormous statues of Christ and the apostles.

After Maderno's death, Bernini took over and became the hero of the hour with his sumptuous baldachin and elliptical piazza. This latter was built between 1656 and 1667; the oval measures 340m by 240m (1,115ft by 787ft), and is punctuated by the central Egyptian obelisk and two symmetrical fountains, by Maderno and Bernini. The 284-column, 88-pillar colonnade is topped by 140 statues of saints.

In the portico (1612), opposite the main portal, is a mosaic by Giotto (c1298), from the original basilica. Five doors lead into the basilica: the central ones come from the earlier church, while the others are both 20th century. The last door on the right is opened only in Holy Years by the pope himself.

Inside, a series of brass lines in the floor shows the lengths of other churches around the world that are not as big. Bernini's vast *baldacchino* (1633), cast from bronze purloined from the Pantheon and hovering over the high altar, is the real focal point. Below the altar, two flights of stairs lead to the *confessio*, where a niche contains a ninth-century mosaic of Christ, the only thing from old St Peter's that stayed in its original place. Far below lies the site of what is believed to be St Peter's tomb, discovered during excavations in 1951.

Pilgrims head straight for the last pilaster on the right before the main altar, to kiss the big toe of Arnolfo da Cambio's statue of St Peter (c1296), or to say a prayer by the crystal casket containing the mummified remains of Pope John XXIII, who was beatified in 2002.

To be sure to see everything, follow an anti-clockwise direction. Start by joining the tourist throngs making a beeline for the first chapel on the right, where Michelangelo's *Pietà* (1499) is found. Further along, the third chapel has a tabernacle and two angels by Bernini, plus St Peter's only remaining painting: a *Trinity* by Pietro da Cortona (the others have all been replaced by mosaic copies).

Bernini's Throne of St Peter (1665) stands at the far end of the nave. Encased in it is a wood and ivory chair, probably dating from the ninth century but for many years believed to have belonged to Peter himself. To the right of the throne is Bernini's 1644 monument to his patron Urban VIII.

On the pillars supporting the main dome are venerated relics, including a chip off the True Cross. In the left aisle, beyond the pilaster with St Veronica holding the cloth with which she wiped Christ's face, Bernini's tomb for Pope Alexander VII shows the pope shrouded with a cloth of reddish marble, from beneath which struggles a skeleton clutching an hourglass. Near the portico end of the left aisle is a group of monuments to the Old Pretender James Edward Stuart and family.

Beneath the basilica are the Vatican grottoes – Renaissance crypts containing papal tombs. The Necropolis, where St Peter is said to be buried, lies under these. The small treasury museum off the left nave of the basilica contains stunning liturgical relics. The dome, reached via hundreds of stairs (there's a cramped lift as far as the basilica roof, then 320 steps to climb to get to the very top), offers fabulous views.

Vatican Museums

Viale del Vaticano (06 6988 3860, www.vatican.va). **Open** (ticket office closes 2hrs before) 9am-6pm Mon-Sat; 9am-12.30pm last Sun of mth. Closed Catholic holidays. **Admission** €15; €8 reductions; free last Sun of mth. **Map** p140 A2 **❹**

Begun by Pope Julius II in 1503, this immense collection represents the accumulated fancies and obsessions of a long line of strong, often contradictory personalities. The signposted routes cater for anything from a dash to the Sistine Chapel to a five-hour plod. There are also itineraries for wheelchair users. Wheelchairs can be borrowed at the museum; call in advance on 06 6988 3860 or email accoglienza.musei@scv.va.

Borgia Rooms

This six-room suite was adapted for the Borgia Pope Alexander VI (1492-1503) and decorated by Pinturicchio with a series of frescoes on biblical and classical themes.

Egyptian Museum

Founded in 1839, this selection of ancient Egyptian art from 3,000 BC to 600 BC includes statues of a baboon god, painted mummy cases, real mummies and a marble statue of Antinous, Emperor Hadrian's lover.

Etruscan Museum

This collection contains Greek and Roman art as well as Etruscan masterpieces, including the contents of the Regolini-Galassi Tomb (c650 BC).

Galleria Chiaramonte

Founded by Pius VII in the early 19th century, this is an eclectic collection of Roman statues, reliefs and busts.

Gallerie dei Candelabri & degli Arazzi

The long gallery, studded with candelabra, contains Roman statues, while the next gallery has ten huge tapestries (*arazzi*), woven by Flemish master Pieter van Aelst from cartoons by Raphael.

Galleria delle Carte Geografiche

A 120m-long (394ft) gallery, with the Tower of the Winds observation point at the north end. Ignazio Danti drew the extraordinarily precise maps of Italian regions and cities.

Museo Paolino

Highlights of this collection of Roman and neo-Attic sculpture include a beautifully draped statue of Greek tragedian Sophocles and a trompe l'oeil mosaic of an unswept floor.

Museo Pio-Clementino

The world's largest collection of classical statues fills 16 rooms. Don't miss the first-century BC *Belvedere Torso* by Apollonius of Athens, the Roman copy of the bronze *Lizard Killer* by Praxiteles and, in the octagonal Belvedere Courtyard, the exquisite *Belvedere Apollo* and *Laocoön*.

Pinacoteca

The Pinacoteca (picture gallery) holds many of the pictures that the Vatican managed to recover from France after Napoleon took them in the early 19th century. The collection ranges from Byzantine school works and Italian primitives to 18th-century Dutch and French old masters, and includes Giotto's *Stefaneschi Triptych*; a *Pietà* by Lucas Cranach the Elder; several delicate Madonnas by Fra Filippo Lippi, Fra Angelico, Raphael and Titian; Raphael's last work, *The Transfiguration*; Caravaggio's *Entombment*; and a chiaroscuro *St Jerome* by Leonardo da Vinci.

Sistine Chapel

The world's most famous frescoes cover the ceiling and one immense wall of the *Cappella Sistina*, built by Sixtus IV in 1473-84. For centuries, it has been used for popes' private prayers and papal elections. In the 1980s and '90s, the 930sq m (10,000sq ft) *Creation* (on the ceiling) and the *Last Judgement* (on the wall behind the altar) were subjected to a controversial restoration.

In 1508, Michelangelo was commissioned to paint some undemanding decoration on the ceiling of the chapel. He offered to do far more than that, and embarked upon his massive venture alone, spending the next four-and-a-half years standing (only Charlton Heston lay down) on 18m-high (60ft) scaffolding. A sequence of biblical scenes, from the Creation to the Flood, begins at the *Last Judgement* end; they are framed by monumental figures of Old Testament prophets and classical sibyls.

In 1535, aged 60, Michelangelo returned. Between the completion of the ceiling and the beginning of the wall, Rome had suffered. From 1517, the Protestant Reformation threatened the power of the popes, and the sack of the city in 1527 by Imperial troops was seen by Michelangelo as the wrath of God. The *Last Judgement* dramatically reflects this gloomy atmosphere. In among the larger-than-life figures, Michelangelo painted his own miserable face on the human skin held by St Bartholomew, below and to the right of the powerful figure of Christ.

Before Michelangelo set foot in the chapel, the stars of the 1480s – Perugino, Cosimo Roselli, Botticelli, Ghirlandaio – had created the paintings on the walls.

Raphael Rooms

Pope Julius II gave 26-year-old Raphael carte blanche to redesign four rooms of the Papal Suite. The Study (Stanza della Segnatura, 1508-11) covers philosophical and spiritual themes. The star-packed *School of Athens* fresco has contemporary artists as classical figures: Plato is Leonardo; the glum thinker on the steps at the front – Heraclitus – is Michelangelo; Euclid is Bramante; and Raphael himself is on the far right-hand side behind a man in white.

Raphael next turned to the Stanza di Eliodoro (1512-14), where the portrayal of God saving the temple in Jerusalem from the thieving Heliodorus was intended to highlight the divine protection enjoyed by Pope Julius. The Dining Room (Stanza dell'Incendio; 1514-17) is dedicated to Pope Leo X (the most obese of the popes, he died from gout aged 38). The room is named for the *Fire in the Borgo*, which Leo IV apparently stopped with the sign of the cross. The Reception Room (Sala di Constantino, 1517-24) was completed by Giulio Romano after Raphael's death in 1520, and tells the legend of Emperor Constantine's miraculous conversion.

Pilgrims' progress

In search of miracles.

The Vatican district got an efficient health service 1,200 years ago, when the Saxons set up the riverside complex of Santo Spirito in Sassia (now the Museo Nazionale dell'Arte Sanitaria, p140) to heal and house the thousands of English pilgrims who made their way on foot to the shrine of St Peter.

Even today, the modern hospital beside the magnificent 500-bed ancient hospital with its vast, heavily frescoed wards is where the ambulance takes you if you keel over in the crush on papal audience days.

Pilgrims still flock to St Peter's hoping for a medical miracle: streams of them make their way to the crypt to pray at the marble tomb of Pope John Paul II, the much-loved Polish pope who is moving speedily towards sainthood.

On Wednesdays, the halt and the lame take their place for the general audience. Prayers are offered to saints who specialise in various parts of the body: Lucy for eyes; Blaise for throats; and Agatha for breast cancer. Plastic phials of holy water are carried home to those who are too sick to visit themselves.

Pragmatic locals, meanwhile, make a quick 'pilgrimage' to the well-stocked Vatican pharmacy just inside Porta Sant'Anna to buy many of the new international medicines that the Italian state cannot afford to prescribe.

The Loggia di Raffaello (usually closed) has a beautiful view over Rome; begun by Bramante in 1513 and finished by Raphael, it has 52 small paintings on biblical themes, and leads into the Sala dei Chiaroscuri. The adjacent Chapel of Nicholas V has scenes from the lives of saints Lawrence and Stephen by Fra Angelico (1448-50).

Eating & drinking

Enoteca Nuvolari
Via degli Ombrellari 10 (06 6880 3018). **Open** noon-4pm, 6.30pm-2am Mon-Sat. Closed Aug. No credit cards. **Enoteca**. **Map** p140 C3 ❺
The younger denizens of Borgo hang out in this welcoming *enoteca* with its candle-lit tables and jazz soundtrack. The *aperitivo* hour (6.30-8.30pm) is accompanied by a free buffet; more filling soups and pâtés are on offer next door in the dining room (8pm-midnight, €€). Local workers crowd in here for snacks at lunch time.

Paninoteca da Guido
Borgo Pio 13 (06 687 5491). **Open** 8am-5pm Mon-Sat. Closed 3wks Aug. €. No credit cards. **Snack bar**. **Map** p140 C3 ❻
This hole-in-the-wall joint is one of the best places to grab a snack in the area. Guido does filled rolls, made up while you wait, and there are a couple of pasta dishes each day. You'll have to fight off-duty Swiss guards for one of the few outside tables, though.

Il Ristoro
Basilica di San Pietro (06 6988 3376). **Open** *Oct-Mar* 8.30am-5pm Mon-Sat. *Apr-Sept* 8.30am-6pm Mon-Sat. No credit cards. **Café**. **Map** p140 A4 ❼
Take the St Peter's dome lift for Rome's most unlikely 'cappuccino with a view' – on the roof of the basilica. There's nothing but water, coffee, soft drinks and a dull selection of ice-creams on the menu, but being up here between the giant marble saints is a heady thrill.

Prati

The Prati district was a provocation. Built over meadows (*prati*) soon after Rome became capital of the newly unified Italian state in 1871, its grand *palazzi* housed the staff of the ministries and parliament. But its broad avenues were named after historic figures who had fought against the power of the Papal States, and the largest of its *piazze* – nestling beneath the Vatican walls – was named after the Risorgimento, the movement that had destroyed the papacy's hold on Italy.

A solidly bourgeois district, Prati has a main drag – via Cola di Rienzo – that provides ample opportunities for retail therapy. Imposing military barracks line viale delle Milizie, and the bombastic Palazzo di Giustizia (popularly known as *il palazzaccio*, 'the big ugly building') sits between piazza Cavour and the Tiber. On the riverbank is one of Catholic Rome's truly weird experiences: the **Museo delle Anime in Purgatorio**.

Sights & museums

Museo delle Anime in Purgatorio
Lungotevere Prati 12 (06 6880 6517). **Open** 7.30-11am, 4.30-7.30pm. **Map** p141 E3 ❽
This macabre collection, attached to the church of Sacro Cuore di Gesù in Prati, contains hand- and fingerprints left on the prayer books and clothes of the living by dead loved ones, to request Masses to release their souls from purgatory. Shuts early in summer.

Eating & drinking

L'Arcangelo
Via GG Belli 59-61 (06 321 0992). **Meals served** 1-2.30pm, 8-11.30pm Mon-Fri; 8-11pm Sat. Closed Aug. **€€€. Creative Italian**. **Map** p141 D2 ❾

The sombre L'Arcangelo has dark wood panelling below tobacco-sponged walls, linen tablecloths and a jazz soundtrack. The seasonal dishes are impressive: a tartlet of octopus and potato with olive oil is simple but delicious, and potato gnocchi with lamb and artichokes makes a worthy follow-up. *Secondi*, such as tripe with mint and pecorino, are clever variations on the Roman tradition.

Art Studio Café
Via dei Gracchi 187A (06 3260 9104, www.artstudiocafe.it). **Open** 7.30am-9.30pm Mon-Sat. Closed 2wks Aug. **€-€€. Café/snack bar**. **Map** p141 D2 ❿
There's an arty theme to this bright café, where you can munch your creative lunchtime salad or pasta dish while leafing through chic magazines or art-related tomes. A boutique has attractive handmade jewellery, silk scarves and household objects. There's an *aperitivo* buffet (5.30-9pm), plus lectures and all kinds of crafts courses.

Gran Caffè Esperia
Lungotevere dei Mellini 1 (06 3211 0016). **Open** 7am-9.30pm daily. **Café/bar**. **Map** p141 F3 ⓫
The pavement tables here are hotly contested when the sun shines on them in the morning. Work on your tan while eating toasted *cornetti* with ham and cheese, or smoked salmon sandwiches. The coffee's great.

Isola della Pizza
Via degli Scipioni 43, 45, 47 (06 3973 3483, www.isoladellapizza.com). **Meals served** 12.30-3pm, 7.30pm-midnight Mon, Tue, Thur-Sun. Closed 3wks Aug. **€-€€€. Pizzeria/Italian**. **Map** p140 B2 ⓬
The huge Island of Pizza is a throbbing eating factory, with noisy, hungry hordes digging into immense pizzas (served at lunch too, a rarity in Rome), a range of good pasta dishes or great hunks of meat slung on an open fire.

ROME BY AREA

Ask for their selection of delicious antipasti and you many never even reach the pizza stage.

Settembrini

Via L Settembrini 25 (06 323 2617, www.ristorantesettembrini.it). **Meals served** 12.30-4pm, 8-11.30pm Mon-Fri; 8-11.30pm Sat. Closed 2wks Aug. €€€. **Creative Italian. Map** off p141 D1 **⑬**
Settembrini mixes design and tradition both in its warmly minimalist decor and its menu. In chef Luigi Nastri's Italo fusion approach, flavours of southern Italy are prominent and ingredients are sourced with a strong regard for quality. *Aperitivi* with snacks are served at 7pm. Next door, at nos.19-23, the very urbane Café Settembrini is under the same management.

Shopping

Castroni

Via Cola di Rienzo 196 (06 687 4383). **Open** 8am-8pm Mon-Sat. **Map** p140 C2 **⑭**
Not only does this deli have specialities from all over Italy and foreign staples (Vegemite, real Indian pickles) that are notoriously difficult to find in Rome, it also serves (and sells) excellent coffee, and the ice-cream isn't bad either.

Costantini

Piazza Cavour 16, Prati (06 321 3210, www.pierocostantini.it). **Open** *Shop* 4.30-8pm Mon; 9am-1pm, 4.30-8pm Tue-Sat. *Wine bar* 12.30-3pm, 7.30-11pm Mon-Sat. Closed Aug. **Map** p141 E3 **⑮**
This cavernous cellar has a seriously comprehensive collection of wines, as well as some gourmet extras such as chocolate, olive oil and pasta. The comfortably shadowy wine bar is a good place to enjoy some wine and snacks in situ.

Franchi

Via Cola di Rienzo 200 (06 687 4651, www.franchi.it). **Open** 8am-9pm Mon-Sat. Closed 1wk Aug. **Map** p140 C2 **⑯**

This dream of a deli has just about anything you could ever want to eat: cheeses from everywhere, cured meat and fresh, ready-to-eat seafood dishes.

Iron G

Via Cola di Rienzo 50 (06 321 6798, www.iron-g.com). **Open** 10.30am-7.30pm Mon-Sat. **Map** p141 E2 **⑰**
This boutique supplies clubwear to the fashion victims of this well-heeled neighbourhood. Hip labels mix with ethnic and local accessories.

Nightlife

Alexanderplatz

Via Ostia 9 (06 3974 2171, www.alexanderplatz.it). **Open** 8.30pm-1.30am daily. Closed June-Sept. **Admission** free with monthly (€15) or annual (€45) membership. **Map** p140 A2 **⑱**
One of Rome's longest-running jazz clubs offers nightly concerts with famous names from Italy and beyond. In summer, Alexanderplatz shifts to Villa Celimontana for the park's eponymous Jazz Festival.

The Place

Via Alberico II 27-29 (06 6830 7137, www.theplace.it). **Open** 8.30pm-2.30am Tue-Sun. Closed mid June-mid Sept. **Admission** €10-€20. **Map** p140 C3 **⑲**
A vibrant jazz club with a stage for live acts, the Place draws a thirty- to fortysomething crowd for mostly Italian jazz bands, plus DJs at the weekend. The restaurant serves from 7.30pm during the 'Sound Check' rehearsal session.

Arts & leisure

El Spa

Via Plinio 15C/D (06 6819 2869, www.elspa.it). **Open** 10am-9pm Mon-Thur; 10am-10pm Fri, Sat; noon-9pm Sun. Closed 1wk Aug. **Map** p141 D2 **⑳**
Decorated in Middle Eastern style, this spa focuses on holistic treatments. Try the *mandi lulur*, an ancient Indonesian treatment that leaves skin silky-soft.

Ostia Antica p156

Out of Town

The Appian Way

Striking out from ancient Rome like so many spokes in a massive wheel were the great consular roads. These carried men and weapons and goods and travellers to all corners of the Empire. The first and greatest of these was the via Appia Antica, known as the *Regina viarum* – the 'queen of roads'.

Built in the fourth century BC by statesman and censor Appius Claudius Caecus, the Appia went first to the strategic city of Capua, near Naples, and was then extended to link *Caput mundi* with the Adriatic at Brindisi in 121 BC.

By the time it reached Brindisi, the Appia was the Romans' main route to their eastern Empire, a perfect thoroughfare for speeding troops and supplies to where they were most needed. In 71 BC, 6,600 followers of rebellious gladiator-slave Spartacus were crucified along the Appia as a warning to other underlings with ideas above their station. But well-to-do Romans chose to end their days here too, building their family mausoleums alongside the road, which was soon lined with tombs, vaults and sarcophagi.

Today, only a fraction of this magnificent funerary decoration remains, but it suffices to make this the most fascinating, and the most picturesque, of the ancient roads.

Christians also began burying their dead here (burial was always performed outside a sacred city boundary known as the *pomerium*), initially in necropoli and later underground, creating the 300-kilometre (200-mile) network of tunnels known as the **catacombs**. This system wasn't used for secret worship, as was once thought: authorities were perfectly aware of their existence. A Jewish catacomb still exists at via Appia Antica 119.

ROME BY AREA

Fancy a dip?

Head for the Med.

Most visitors to Rome are so enraptured with culture that they forget the Mediterranean beckons a short train ride away. Granted, it's not always the cleanest or most beautiful bit of the Med. But on a hot day, fleeing the city for a sea breeze and a dip is a great way of passing the time.

Closest is **Ostia**, a sprawling seaside town with some elegant 1930s architecture at its heart. The train from Piramide station to Ostia Lido leaves with its towel-toting passengers every few minutes during the day.

Just south of Ostia lies a long stretch of sand called **Capocotta**. It's a nature reserve, with the presidential country residence on the other side of the road. What you'll find here depends on which kilometre marker you access it from: naturists around km9; a gay stretch a little further north; and a family fun bit down towards the town of Torvaianica. To get here, take the train to the last stop in Ostia, then bus 07 along the coast road.

North of Rome, summer season dormitory town **Fregene** (take the FR5 train from Termini or Ostiense) has a long, if crowded, beach and water which is... well, it's wet. Go just a little further, to **Santa Severa** (mainline trains from Termini or Ostiense), and during the week at least, you may find a quiet corner of the pretty beach. It's a 15-minute walk from the station to the coast.

Via Appia Antica suffered considerably at the hands of marauding Goths and Normans; successive popes did as much damage, grabbing any decent pieces of statuary or marble that remained and reducing the ancient monuments to stumps. But this is still a great place to spend a day, preferably a Sunday or holiday when all but local traffic is banned.

The www.parcoappiaantica.it website provides exhaustive information for visitors.

You can explore the area more extensively by renting a bike at the **Punto Informativo** (via Appia Antica 58-60, 06 513 5316, open daily, €10 per day); or the **Appia Antica Caffè** at via Appia 175 (338 346 5440, www.appiaantica caffe.it, €12 for four hours).

Another ancient route lies nearby: the great Roman aqueduct that brought fresh water to the city from the hills near Tivoli still dominates the **Parco degli Acquedotti**, accessible from viale Appio Claudio.

Getting there

You can take the hop-on, hop-off **Archeobus** (800 281 281, www.trambusopen.com, tickets €10), which leaves from Termini railway station every 30 minutes or so between 9am and 4.30pm, and stops by most major sights. Alternatively, the following regular bus services ply part of the Appian Way:

118 from viale Aventino (Circo Massimo metro) to the catacombs of San Callisto and San Sebastiano.
218 from piazza San Giovanni to Porta San Sebastiano, down the Appia to the Domine Quo Vadis church, then along via Ardeatina.
660 from Colli Albani metro station to the Circus of Maxentius and Tomb of Cecilia Metella.

Sights & museums

Catacombs of San Callisto

Via Appia Antica 110 (06 5130 1580, www.catacombe.roma.it). **Open** 9am-noon, 2-5pm Mon, Tue, Thur-Sun. Closed late Jan-late Feb. **Admission** €8; €5 reductions.

This is Rome's largest underground burial site. Buried in the 20km (12 miles) of tunnels are some 16 popes, dozens of martyrs and thousands of Christians. They are stacked down, with the oldest on the top. Named after third-century Pope Callixtus, the area became the first official cemetery of the Church of Rome. The crypt of St Cecilia is the spot where this patron saint of music is believed to have been buried, before she was transferred to Trastevere (see p129).

Catacombs of San Sebastiano

Via Appia Antica 136 (06 785 0350, www.catacombe.org). **Open** 9am-noon, 2-5pm Mon-Sat. Closed mid Nov-mid Dec. **Admission** €8; €5 reductions.

The name 'catacomb' originated here, where a complex of underground burial sites situated near a quarry was described as being *kata kymbas* – 'near the quarry'. The tour will take you into the crypt of St Sebastian, the martyr always depicted pierced by a hail of arrows (though this was just one of several forms of torture he endured), who was buried here in the third century. Above, the fourth-century basilica of San Sebastiano originally housed the remains of Saints Peter and Paul. On display is the marble slab in which Christ left his footprints during his miraculous apparition at the spot on the via Appia where the Domine Quo Vadis church (06 512 0441, open 8am-7.30pm daily) now stands.

Circus of Maxentius

Via Appia Antica 153 (06 780 1324, www.villadimassenzio.it). **Open** 9am-1.30pm Tue-Sun. **Admission** €3; €1.50 reductions. No credit cards.

This is one of the best-preserved Roman circuses, built by Emperor Maxentius for his private use before his defeat and death at the hands of co-ruler Constantine in AD 312. Remains of the Imperial palace are perched above the track, at its northern end. Also found on this part of the site is the mausoleum Maxentius built for his beloved son Romulus.

Museo delle Mura

Via di Porta San Sebastiano 18 (06 0608, www.museodellemuraroma.it). **Open** 9am-2pm Tue-Sun. **Admission** €3; €2 reductions. No credit cards.

Housed inside the San Sebastiano gate, at the start of the Appian Way, this delightful museum not only charts the history of Rome's walls, but also, in theory, allows visitors to hike along the top of them for 350m (1,150ft). As this guide went to press, the walkway was closed to the public, with no date set for reopening.

Tomb of Cecilia Metella

Via Appia Antica 161 (06 780 0093). **Open** 9am-4.30pm Tue-Sun. **Admission** (includes Baths of Caracalla & Villa dei Quintili) €6; €3 reductions. No credit cards. **Note**: opening hours are erratic.

This colossal cylinder of travertine is the final resting place of a woman from the wealthy Metella family in the first century BC. During the 14th century, the powerful Caetani clan incorporated the tomb into a fortress, adding the crenellations to the top of the structure. The spot where Cecilia was buried is a fine example of brick dome-making. Downstairs, pieces of the volcanic rock used in the construction of via Appia Antica can be seen. Outside and across the way are what's left of the church of San Nicola, a rare example of Gothic architecture in Rome, surrounded by further walls of the fortress.

Villa dei Quintili

Via Appia Nuova 1092 (06 712 9121). **Open** 9am-4.30pm Tue-Sun. **Admission** (includes Baths of Caracalla & Tomb of Cecilia Metella) €6; €3 reductions. No credit cards.

Magnificently situated between the ancient and the modern *vie* Appia (but accessible from the latter), this second-century AD villa was owned by the wealthy, cultured and militarily brilliant Quintili brothers – consuls under Emperor Marcus Aurelius – who were murdered by the Emperor Commodus. The emperor then took over the villa for himself, and essentially ruled from here. The vast structure is set in splendid isolation amid fields strewn with fragments of the many-coloured marble that once faced its mighty halls. A small antiquarium displays statuary and objects which have been found in the vicinity. The villa closes one hour before sunset throughout the summer months.

EUR

Italian Fascism was at once monstrous and absurd, but out of it came some of 20th-century Europe's most fascinating architecture and urban planning.

In the early 1930s, Rome's Fascist governor Giuseppe Bottai had the idea of expanding Rome along via Ostiense towards the sea, some 20 kilometres (12.5 miles) away. Using as an excuse the universal exhibition pencilled in for 1942, he intended to combine cultural and exhibition spaces with a monument to the regime: buildings such as the Palazzo della Civiltà del Lavoro and Palazzo dei Congressi are fine examples.

Architect Marcello Piacentini was charged with co-ordinating the ambitious project, but the planning committee squabbled so much that very little had been achieved by the outbreak of World War II. After the war, work resumed in an entirely different spirit. Still known as EUR (*Esposizione universale romana*), it's now a business district, where unrelieved planes of icy travertine and reinterpretations of classical monuments let you know you're not in Kansas any more.

Several didactic museums – including the **Museo dell'Alto Medioevo**, **Museo della Civiltà Romana** (now containing an astronomy museum), and the **Museo Preistorico ed Etnografico L Pigorini** – allow visitors a glimpse inside these monuments to the hubris of Italian Fascism.

ROME BY AREA

Getting there

Take metro B to EUR Fermi or EUR Palasport, or buses 30Exp, 170, 714.

Sights & museums

Abbazia delle Tre Fontane

Via Acque Salvie 1 (06 540 1655, www.abbaziatrefontane.com). **Open** *Santi Vincenzo e Anastasio* 6.30am-12.30pm, 3-8.45pm daily. *Other churches* 8am-1pm, 3-6pm daily. *Shop* 9am-1.30pm, 3.30-7pm daily. **Admission** free.

North-east of EUR centre (and reachable by bus 767) lies a haven of ancient, eucalyptus-scented green, with three churches commemorating the points where St Paul's head supposedly bounced after it was severed in AD 67. (A Roman citizen, Paul was eligible for the quick head-chop, as opposed to a lengthy crucifixion.) Active from the fifth century, this Trappist monastery's church of San Paolo delle Tre Fontane is said to be built on the spot where the apostle was executed; apart from a column to which Paul was supposedly tied, all traces of the earlier church were destroyed in 1599 by architect Giacomo della Porta, who also designed the two other churches. Monks planted the eucalyptus trees in the 1860s, believing they would drive away malarial mosquitoes; a liqueur is now brewed from the trees and sold in a little shop.

Museo dell'Alto Medioevo

Viale Lincoln 3 (06 5422 8199). **Open** 9am-2pm Tue-Sun. **Admission** €2; €1 reductions. No credit cards.

Focusing on the decorative arts from the period between the fall of the Roman Empire and the Renaissance, this museum has gold- and silver-decorated swords, buckles and horse tackle, plus more mundane objects: ceramic bead jewellery and the metal frames of what may be Europe's earliest folding chairs.

Museo della Civiltà Romana

Piazza G Agnelli 10 (06 5422 0919, www.museociviltaromana.it). **Open** *Museum* 9am-2pm Tue-Sun. *Planetarium* 9am-2pm Tue-Fri; 9am-7pm Sat, Sun. **Admission** *Museum* €6.50; €4.50 reductions. *Planetarium* (booking obligatory 06 0608) €6.50; €4.50 reductions. *Joint ticket* €8.50; €6.50 reductions. No credit cards.

With its blank white walls and lofty, echoing corridors, this building, from 1937, is Fascist-classical at its most grandiloquent. There's a fascinating cutaway model of the Colosseum's maze of tunnels and lifts, as well as casts of the intricate reliefs on Trajan's column. The centrepiece is a giant model of Rome in the fourth century AD, which puts the city's scattered fragments and artefacts into context. The palazzo also contains the Museo dell'Astrologia and a planetarium (www.planetarioroma.it).

Museo Preistorico ed Etnografico L Pigorini

Piazzale G Marconi 14 (06 549 521, www.pigorini.beniculturali.it). **Open** 10am-6pm daily. **Admission** €6; €3 reductions. No credit cards.

Prehistoric Italian artefacts, together with material from various world cultures, are on display here. In the lobby is a reconstruction of the prehistoric Guattari cave near Monte Circeo, south of Rome, with a genuine Neanderthal skull.

Ostia Antica

Substitute a trip to Pompeii with a jaunt to ancient Rome's port instead: there's no looming volcano but the excavated ruins (*scavi*) of Ostia Antica convey the everyday life of a working Roman town every bit as well.

Five minutes' walk from the entrance to the excavations, the medieval village of Ostia Antica has a castle (built in 1483-86 for

Medieval miracle

Sleepy Viterbo was once a papal powerhouse.

It was only briefly, in the 13th century, that Viterbo became the centre of the Christian world. But this short burst of glory explains the medieval magnificence of this sleepy city north of Rome.

Transport links back then were good: Viterbo straddled the via Francigena pilgrim route from Canterbury to Rome. Nowadays, a single-track railway line from San Pietro or Ostiense stations (€9 return) takes you there.

While *Caput mundi* shuddered from one wave of anarchy after another, the 100km (62 miles) that separated it from Viterbo made popes feel safe there... until 1305, when they gave up on Italy completely, and removed the papacy to Avignon.

The walled city was built to last, in massive dark grey blocks of volcanic tufa. Some of the earliest masonry is still visible in piazza del Palazzo dei Papi, where it formed the foundations of the Roman temple of Hercules. This main square looks like a film set, with its crenellated loggia and the

vast conclave hall (five popes were elected in Viterbo between 1266 and 1281), plus its stripy two-tone belltower and its Romanesque cathedral, given a fashionable new façade in the 16th century.

A second wave of money poured into the city under Renaissance Pope Sixtus IV: you can see the oak-tree coat of arms of his Della Rovere family on the magnificent Palazzo dei Priori in piazza del Plebiscito. The city has 100 impressive fountains, and many fine early churches, such as the tiny jewel-like San Sisto, Santa Maria Nuova, San Francesco alla Rocca, and the cloistered monastery buildings of Santa Maria in Gradi, where St Thomas Aquinas preached and wrote.

Since then, Viterbo has been very much a backwater, which makes its wonderful state of preservation a surprise. In fact, it wasn't until the Allies' carpet bombing of railway yards on two sides of the city in World War II that Viterbo suffered much damage or underwent any change.

ROME BY AREA

the bishop of Ostia, the future Pope Julius II) and picturesque cottages, which were inhabited by the people who worked in the nearby salt pans.

Getting there

Ostia Antica is a 20-minute train ride from Roma-Lido station, next to Piramide metro.

Sights & museums

Scavi di Ostia Antica

Viale dei Romagnoli 717, Ostia Antica (06 5635 2830, www.itnw.roma.it/ostia/scavi). **Open** Nov-Mar 8.30am-5pm Tue-Sun. Apr-Oct 8.30am-7.30pm Tue-Sun. **Admission** €6.50; €3.25 reductions. No credit cards.

Legend has it that Ostia was founded by Ancus Martius, the fourth king of Rome, in the seventh century BC, although the oldest remains date from 'only' c330 BC. Ostia was Rome's main port for more than 600 years.

Abandoned after sackings by barbarians in the fifth century, the town was gradually buried by river mud. Over the centuries, the coastline has receded, leaving Ostia landlocked and obsolete. Visit on a sunny weekday and bring a picnic (not allowed, but keep a low profile and you probably won't be ejected). It's open until 7.30pm in summer.

The *decumanus maximus* (high street) runs from the Porta Romana for almost a kilometre (half a mile), past the theatre and forum, before forking left to what used to be the seashore. The right fork, via della Foce, leads to the Tiber. Either side of these main arteries lies a network of intersecting lanes where the best discoveries can be made.

Behind the theatre is one of Ostia's most interesting features: the Forum of the Corporations. Here the trade guilds had their offices, and mosaics on the floors of shops that ring the open square refer to the products each guild dealt in – shipowners had ships on the floor, ivory dealers had elephants. Further along on the right is the old mill, where the furrows ploughed by the blindfolded donkeys that turned it are still visible. In the tangle of streets between the decumanus and the museum, don't miss the *thermopolium* – an ancient Roman bar. Located off the forum to the south-east are the forum baths and nearby is the *forica*, or ancient public latrine. Off via della Foce, the House of Cupid and Psyche is an elegant fourth-century construction; the House of the Dioscuri has beautiful mosaics; the Insula of the Charioteers still has many of its frescoes.

A dusty old museum (same hours) contains bits of statuary from the digs, plus there's a shiny new café and bookshop… though mangy dogs may bar your path as you approach.

Tivoli

Just 20 kilometres (12.5 miles) from Rome, Tivoli (ancient Tibur) is home to two UNESCO World Heritage Sites – **Villa d'Este**, in Tivoli itself, and **Hadrian's Villa**, five kilometres (three miles) down the hill – which make it an ideal destination for a day trip.

Getting there

Take the COTRAL bus from Ponte Mammolo metro station; note that the bus marked *autostrada* is a quicker service. If you're travelling by bus, visit Tivoli town first (the regular service is marked 'via Tiburtina' and takes about 45mins to Tivoli) and get off at the main square (piazza Garibaldi) for Villa d'Este. From the bus stop in front of the tourist office in piazza Garibaldi, frequent orange (local) buses serve Villa Adriana (10 mins) down the hill. From Villa Adriana, both local and COTRAL buses travel to Rome.

The Appian Way p151

RAbIRIA VSIA
DEMARIS

Local trains go to Tivoli from Tiburtina station; bus 4 goes from Tivoli station to the centre of town for the Villa d'Este.

Sights & museums

Hadrian's Villa (Villa Adriana)
Via di Villa Adriana, Villa Adriana (0774 382 733). **Open** 9am-6pm daily. **Admission** €6.50; €3.25 reductions; extra charge during exhibitions. No credit cards.

Villa Adriana, the retreat of Emperor Hadrian, is strewn across a gentle slope. Built from AD 118 to 134, it has some fascinating architectural spaces and water features.

Hadrian was an amateur architect, and it is believed that he designed many of the elements in his magnificent villa himself. In the centuries following the fall of the Roman Empire, the villa became a luxury quarry for treasure-hunters. At least 500 pieces of statuary in collections around the world have been identified as coming from this site. The restored remains lie amid olive groves and cypresses and are exceedingly impressive. The model in the pavilion up the hill from the entrance gives an idea of the villa's original size.

Where the villa's original entrance lay is still uncertain; today, the first space you'll encounter after climbing the road from the ticket office is the *pecile* (or *poikile*), a large pool that was once surrounded by a portico with high walls, of which only one remains. East of the *pecile*, the *Teatro marittimo* (Maritime Theatre) is one of the most delightful inventions in the villa. A circular brick wall encloses a moat, at the centre of which is an island of columns and brick-work; a cement bridge crosses the moat, but originally there would have been wooden bridges that could be removed.

Beneath the building called the winter palace, visitors can walk along the perfectly preserved *cryptoporticus* (covered corridor).

In the valley below is the lovely *canopus*: a narrow pool, framed on three sides by columns and statues, including a marble crocodile. At its southern end is a structure called the *serapeum*, used for lavish entertaining. Summer guests enjoyed an innovative form of air-conditioning – a sheet of water poured from the roof over the open face of the building, enclosing the diners.

Villa d'Este
Piazza Trento 1, Tivoli (0774 332 920, 0774 335 850, www.villadestetivoli. info). **Open** 8.30am-1hr before sunset Tue-Sun. **Admission** €6.50; €3.25 reductions; extra charge during exhibitions. No credit cards.

Dominating the town of Tivoli is the Villa d'Este, a lavish pleasure palace built in 1550 for Cardinal Ippolito d'Este, son of Lucrezia Borgia, to a design by architect Pirro Ligorio. Inside the villa there are frescoes and paintings by Correggio, Da Volterra and Perin Del Vaga (including views of the villa just after its construction). But the gardens are the main attraction. Ligorio developed a complex 'hydraulic machine' that channelled water from the River Aniene (still the source today) through a series of canals under the garden. Using know-how borrowed from the Romans, he created 51 fountains spread around the terraced gardens. The sibyls (pagan high-priestesses) are a recurring theme – it was at Tivoli that the Tiburtine sibyl foretold the birth of Christ – and the grottoes of the sibyls behind the vast fountain of Neptune echo with thundering artificial waterfalls.

Technological gimmickry was also a big feature; the Owl Fountain (operates every two hours from 10am) imitated an owl's song using a hydraulic mechanism, while the *Fontana dell'organo idraulico* (restored and in operation every two hours from 10.30am) used water pressure to compress air and play tunes.

Electric carts are provided free for disabled visitors to tour the gardens; booking is essential (0774 335 850).

Essentials

Dear Travellers,

Since 1998 we assist you in finding the best holiday home solution.

We offer a wide range of elegant and well furnished apartments throughout Italy.

Specialized in Rome, Venice and Florence.

See you soon in Italy.

Kinds regards

2010 in numbers:

3667 bookings

231 apartments in Rome

134 apartments in Florence

125 apartments in Venice

698 reviews on Flipkey.com

Rated Excellent 2011 by Tripadvisor.com

7780 people slept in our accommodation.

CONTACTS:
web site : www.sleepinitaly.com
email : info@sleepinitaly.com
phone - fax : +39 06 32650922

New opening : www.sleepinparis.co bb in Paris

Crossing Condotti p167

Hotels

Not even the recession has made much of a dent in Rome's high hotel prices, although many hostelries will now slash prices in the lowest of low season (see box p171). Nor has it driven standards up greatly: with a few exceptions – on both the positive side and the negative – you will get what you pay for.

There are four- and five-star options aplenty, awash with high concept design, while cheap (though not always salubrious) backpacking options abound around the Termini station area. The gap in the centre where charming two- and three-stars should cater to more demanding travellers with lower credit limits is filling out only slowly.

Even before the recession hit, competition from some boutique hotels popping up around the *centro storico* meant that older-style hotels

and *pensioni* did upgrade both amenities and decor in order to stay in business. The appearance on the scene of such small gems as **Casa Montani** (see p171) doubtlessly helped this process along.

It's only at the lower end that Rome is still lagging behind: in all but a few notable cases – for example, the **Beehive** (see p175) and **Casa Romana** (see p175) – the gulf in standards between rock bottom and the lower edge of moderate is immense: in Rome, it's worth paying just that little bit more. Either that, or go out on a limb, for example with a very un-Roman camping experience.

Location

There are three five-star hotels close to Termini station, but the vast majority of hotels in this area – the **Esquilino** – are cheap *pensioni*

ESSENTIALS

swarming with backpackers. It's not Rome's most picturesque corner, and almost certainly not what you dreamed of for your Roman holiday. It could well be worth considering looking further afield.

A room in the *centro storico* offers many advantages, not least of which are a shower between sightseeing and dinner, and a pleasant stroll (rather than a bus or taxi) back to the hotel afterwards. The area around **campo de' Fiori** offers mid-priced hotels with lots of character, and a central piazza that is a lively market by day and a hip Roman hangout by night (though don't stay too late, as it tends to get rowdy as the evening wears on); the area around the **Pantheon** and **piazza Navona** is generally a bit pricier.

Moving distinctly up the price range, Rome's top-end hotels have traditionally clustered around **via Veneto**; it's nothing like as lively as it was in its *dolce vita* heyday, and there's a strong whiff of expense account in the air. But the street definitely has a certain grandeur. The **Tridente** area near the Spanish Steps, hub of designer

shopping, is full of elegant hotels at the upper end of the price scale.

If you're looking for some peace and quiet, the **Celio**, just beyond the Colosseum, offers a break from the frantic activity of the *centro storico*, as does another of Rome's seven hills: the **Aventine**, an exclusive residential outpost no distance at all from the *centro*.

Heading across the river, the characterful **Trastevere** district is a pleasant place to stay, with good bus and tram connections to the major sights; in recent years it has blossomed from hotel-desert to hotel-bonanza, offering an array of price options. Just north of here, the medieval alleys around the **Vatican** give on to the busy retail thoroughfares of **Prati**: it's lively during the day but hushed at night.

Booking a room

Always reserve a room well in advance, especially at peak times – which now means most of the year, with lulls during winter (January to March) and in the dog days of August. If you're coming at the same time as a major Christian holiday (Christmas or Easter), it's advisable to book weeks, or even months, ahead.

Booking is almost always via hotel websites, but smaller places may ask for a fax confirming a booking, with a credit card number as deposit. The www.venere.com booking service offers hotels in all price ranges. **Hotel Reservation** (06 699 1000, www.hotelreservation. it), which has desks at Fiumicino airport and at Termini station, offers a €3 booking service.

Avoid the touts that hang around Termini: you're likely to end up paying more than you should for a very grotty hotel.

Standards & prices

Italian hotels are classified on a star system, from one to five. One star usually indicates *pensioni*, which are cheap but have very few facilities; you may have to share a bathroom. The more stars, the more facilities a hotel will have, but bear in mind that it's a box-ticking exercise: a higher rating doesn't guarantee friendliness, cleanliness or decent service.

Price rises have slowed right down in Rome recently. It's worth keeping an eye out for good deals on hotel websites: many now operate a booking system similar to low-cost airlines, with room prices determined by demand in any given period. If you're in a group or staying for a longish period, ask about discounts.

If you're visiting with children, most hotels will be happy to squeeze a cot or camp bed into a room, but they will probably charge 30 to 50 per cent extra for the privilege.

Alternative accommodation

If you're travelling with children and/or staying for a while, you

S H O R T L I S T

Recent arrivals
- Casa Romana (see p175)
- Crossing Condotti (see p167)
- Grand Hotel Via Veneto (see p173)

Utter luxury
- De Russie (see p171)
- Hassler Villa Medici (see p173)
- St Regis Grand (see p176)
- Villa Spalletti Trivelli (see p176)

Stellar chefs
- Filippo la Mantia at Hotel Majestic (see p177)
- La Pergola at Rome Cavalieri (see p177)

Cool pools
- Exedra (see p176)
- Radisson SAS es. Hotel (see p176)

Chic & cheap
- Beehive (see p175)
- Casa Montani (see p171)
- Casa Romana (see p175)
- Daphne Inn (see p171)
- Relais Palazzo Taverna (see p169)

Bargain beds
- Artemide (no frills rooms – see 175)
- Foresteria Orsa Maggiore (women only – see p178)
- Pensione Paradise (see p178)

Stunning suites
- Garden Suite at the Inn at the Roman Forum (see p176)
- Royal Suite at the St Regis Grand (see p176)
- Villa La Cupola at the Westin Excelsior (see p175)

ESSENTIALS

World Class

Perfect places to stay, eat and explore.

might prefer to rent an apartment. Sites such as www.flatinrome.com and www.romanreference.com have many on their books; London-based www.aplaceinrome.com has a delightful few. For B&Bs, check out www.bbitalia.it or www.b-b.rm.it. Both apartments and B&Bs are listed on www.romedowntown.it. For information on camping and other less expensive forms of accommodation, see box p171.

Our choice

The hotels listed in this guide have been chosen for their location, because they offer value for money, or simply because they have true Roman character. Unless stated, rates are for rooms with bathrooms, and include breakfast. Our price categories refer to standard double rooms in high season; at quieter times, many hotels cut prices by as much as 50 per cent.

In the deluxe category (€€€€) the emphasis is firmly on luxury; a standard double will cost over €400. Those in mid- to upper-price ranges are smaller, many in old *palazzi*, with pretty, though often small, bedrooms. Expect to pay €120 to €250 for a moderately priced hotel (€€), and anywhere from €250 to €400 for an expensive room (€€€). *Pensioni* are fairly basic, but those listed here are friendly and usually family-run; you'll be very hard pressed to find a half-decent double room in mid-to-high season for less than €120 per night.

Few Roman hotels – bar the grander ones – have access for disabled guests. Though staff are generally very willing to help guests with mobility difficulties, the real problem is that most places have so many stairs that there's not much they can do. As hotels renovate, they do tend to add an accessible room if they can.

A no-smoking law introduced in 2005 applies to hotels' public areas. Some hotels are still fairly laissez-faire when it comes to guests lighting up in the rooms so long as they open a window, but if you can't do without your nicotine, check this before booking.

Il Centro

Abruzzi
Piazza della Rotonda 69 (06 9784 1351, www.hotelabruzzi.it). **€€**.
Its location is this hotel's main draw, though recent renovations have upgraded what used to be a dingy establishment. Many rooms have views of the Pantheon; some are very small.

Campo de' Fiori
Piazza del Biscione 6 (06 6880 6865, www.hotelcampodefiori.com). **€€**.
Just off busy campo de' Fiori, this hotel underwent a complete renovation in 2006: though not large, its rooms are finely fitted out in rich colours. The small but elegant bathrooms have bronze-effect tiles with antique mirrors. The pretty roof terrace has great views.

Crossing Condotti
Via Mario de' Fiori 28 (06 6992 0633, www.crossingcondotti.com). **€€€**.
This five-room hotel is remarkably central: a short stroll from Prada, Bulgari and other fashion heavyweights. It has free Wi-Fi and antique furniture, but the decor may be a little too conventional for some tastes. It's at the lower end of this price range.

Due Torri
Vicolo del Leonetto 23 (06 6880 6956, www.hotelduetorriroma.com). **€€**.
In a labyrinth of cobbled streets, the Due Torri has a welcoming feel. The 26 rooms are cosy rather than spacious, and kitted out with dark wooden furniture. If you're persistent, you might get one of the rooms with a private terrace overlooking the rooftops.

Aleph

Pensione Barrett

Largo Argentina 47 (06 686 8481, www.pensionebarrett.com). €€.

A bewildering number of antiques and curios decorate this hotel, giving it an eccentric feel. Rooms are a mishmash of faux-classical columns and mouldings, dark wood furniture, beamed ceilings and pastel walls; some have great views over largo Argentina. Breakfast is not included.

Relais Palazzo Taverna & Locanda degli Antiquari

Via dei Gabrielli 92 (06 2039 8064, www.relaispalazzotaverna.com). €€.

In a 15th-century building, these twin *residenze* have sleek, modern decor. Spacious bedrooms feature white-painted wood ceilings, wallpaper with bold graphics and bed linen in spicy tones. Breakfast is served in the rooms.

Residenza in Farnese

Via del Mascherone 59 (06 6821 0980, www.residenzafarneseroma.it). €€.

This converted convent in a narrow ivy-lined alley has been refurbished without losing its charm. A chandelier in the lobby lends a sense of opulence; own-made jams for breakfast reflect the homely appeal of the place. Rooms run the gamut from basic updated cells with small marble bathrooms to more comfortable pastel-hued rooms with hand-painted furnishings. It's at the higher end of this price range.

St George Roma

Via Giulia 62 (06 686 611, www.stgeorgehotel.it). €€€€.

This five-star on gorgeous via Giulia is a study in coolly elegant designer neutrals and dark wood, with swathes of travertine in the public spaces and bathrooms, and the odd deco-inspired detail (and, in places, a whiff of style over substance). The basement spa has a small indoor pool; there's a cigar lounge and a rooftop terrace. Air-con can be erratic.

Sole al Pantheon

Piazza della Rotonda 63 (06 678 0441, www.hotelsolealpantheon.com). €€€.

Dating back to the 15th century, the Sole al Pantheon is one of Europe's oldest hotels. Rooms have a fresh feel, though, with tiles and pretty frescoes. Bathrooms are not luxurious but they do have whirlpool baths. Rooms at the front have great views of the Pantheon.

Teatro di Pompeo

Largo del Pallaro 8 (06 6830 0170, www.hotelteatrodipompeo.it). €€.

This small, friendly hotel occupies a palazzo that was built on the site of the ancient Teatro di Pompeo; its *pièce de résistance* is its cave-like breakfast room, tucked away inside the ancient ruins. The guest rooms are simply appointed in neutral tones, with terracotta floors and high, beamed ceilings. Opt for one of the rooms in the main hotel building rather than those in the more basic annexe a few streets away.

Teatro Pace

Via del Teatro Pace 33 (06 687 9075, www.hotelteatropace.com). €€.

On a cobbled alley near piazza Navona, this 17th-century former cardinal's residence has a Baroque spiral staircase that winds up four floors (there's no lift, but chairs are provided every couple of floors so you can catch your breath). Rooms are spacious and elegantly decorated with wood floors, heavy drapes and marble bathrooms; all have their original beamed ceilings. Breakfast is served in the rooms. Good low-season deals can be had on the hotel website.

Tridente & Borghese

Aleph

Via di San Basilio 15 (06 422 901, www.boscolohotels.com). €€€€.

This Adam Tihany-designed hotel with a theme – heaven and hell – has common areas in various intensities of devil-red, and bright, 'heavenly' bedrooms. It's a favourite with the fashion

set. A top-floor terrace bar and restaurant operate during the warmer months; there's also a subterranean spa in white and icy blue. Rooms are modern and luxurious.

Casa Howard

Via Capo le Case 18 (06 6992 4555, www.casahoward.com). €€.

All rooms in this beautiful *residenza* near piazza di Spagna have been designed with an emphasis on quality; note that some rooms have (private) bathrooms along the hall. There's a Turkish bath too. The five (slightly more expensive) rooms around the corner at via Sistina 149 have ensuite bathrooms. Massages can be arranged at both properties. Prices can leap to €€€ in high season.

Casa Montani

Piazzale Flaminio 9 (06 3260 0421, www.casamontani.it). €€.

This delightful five-room townhouse overlooking the Porta del Popolo gate is a rarity in Rome: charming, exquisitely decorated, impeccably run... and good value. A delicious breakfast is served in the rooms, and Wi-Fi is free.

Daphne Inn

Via degli Avignonesi 20; via di San Basilio 55 (06 4782 3529, www.daphne-rome.com). €€.

The Daphne Inn has two locations: one near the Trevi Fountain, the other off via Veneto. Each has seven rooms (some with ensuite baths and some that share), fitted out in organic-modern style with terracotta floors, neutral tones and framed leaf prints on the walls. Both offer great value and a warm welcome.

De Russie

Via del Babuino 9 (06 328 881, www.hotelderussie.it). €€€€.

The De Russie's modern elegance is a million miles away from the luxury-schmaltz of many hotels on via Veneto. Fabulous gardens and a state-of-the-art

Sleep on the cheap

How to bag yourself a bargain bed in Rome.

To see the Eternal City without crashing through your credit limit, there are a few rules to follow. First of all, plan your visit to avoid high season – that includes big religious feast days and major Vatican shindigs. Click on 'Prefecture' on the Vatican website (www.vatican.va) for a calendar of papal events and steer clear, in particular, of beatifications and canonisations. August can be a great month to come: hot, certainly, but the Roman crowds are off on holiday.

Secondly, remember there are alternatives to hotels. In the summer months, you could try camping: **Flaminio Village** (via Flaminia Nuova 821, 06 333 2604, www.villageflaminio.it) offers tent pitches, as well as bungalows to rent, in landscaped gardens with a large pool and good facilities. And year-round there are religious institutes offering accommodation. Find them through www.monastery stays.com, www.santasusanna. org or www.hospites.it.

But if you really want a hotel, even there you'll find bargains. The swish **Artemide** (see p175) has 'no frills' rooms; the **Relais Palazzo Taverna** (see p169) is a well-priced designer option; **Pensione Panda** (see p175) and **Okapi Rooms** (see p173) are central, and the **Beehive** (see p175) and **Casa Romana** (see p175) are stylish and handy for the Ciampino airport bus.

health centre make it a star magnet, although some rooms are smaller and less opulent than you might expect.

Eden

Via Ludovisi 49 (06 478 121, www.edenroma.com). €€€€€.
Elegantly understated, the Eden offers the attentiveness and attention to detail of a top-notch hotel without the stuffiness. Handsome reception rooms, tastefully decorated bedrooms, and a roof terrace with restaurant, piano bar and truly spectacular views are plus points.

Fontanella Borghese

Largo Fontanella Borghese 84 (06 6880 9504, www.fontanella borghese.com). €€.
This hotel is elegantly done out in relaxing cream and muted colours. Shopping destinations via del Corso and via Condotti are just around the corner: it's an ideal bolthole when the credit cards start to melt.

Grand Hotel Via Veneto

NEW *Via Veneto 155 (06 487 881, www.ghvv.it). €€€€*
The newest addition to the via Veneto luxe market, the GHVV has an art deco theme in the striking public spaces, and a more contemporary bent in bedrooms, even the smallest of which are spacious by Rome standards. The huge bathrooms are in Carrara marble. Multilingual staff are remarkably charming, and the street level bar-restaurant buzzes at cocktail hour. There's a whirlpool tub in the solarium on the roof.

Hassler Villa Medici

Piazza Trinità dei Monti 6 (06 699 340, www.hotelhasslerroma.com). €€€€.
This is one of Rome's classic hotels, with all the trimmings you'd expect: chandeliers, polished wood and marble, plush fabrics and grand oil paintings, and a garden out back. The attentiveness of the staff distinguishes the Hassler from the impersonal top

chain hotels in Rome. A few steps away, and with a royal-box view over the Spanish Steps, is Il Palazzetto (vicolo del Bottino 8, www.ilpalazzetto roma.com), an annexe under the same ownership.

Hotel Art

Via Margutta 56 (06 328 711, www.hotelart.it). €€€.
On a street famed for its art studios, this hotel's lobby has white pods serving as check-in and concierge desks. Hallways are in retina-burning shades, but the bedrooms have creamy bed linens and dark wood furniture. There's a small gym.

Inn at the Spanish Steps

Via Condotti 85 (06 6992 5657, www.atspanishsteps.com). €€€€.
The Inn at the Spanish Steps offers luxury boutique-hotel accommodation on one of the world's most famous shopping streets. Rooms are an extravagant mix of rich fabrics and antiques; some of the deluxe rooms have 17th-century frescoes. Just down the road, its sister establishment – View at the Spanish Steps – is more restrained, with sober grey and blue fabrics, dark wood floors and black-and-white tiled bathrooms. Prices plunge in low season.

Modigliani

Via della Purificazione 42 (06 4281 5226, www.hotelmodigliani.com). €€.
A charming garden, walls covered with artworks by owner Marco di Tillo and grateful guests, and a real family-friendly feel make this 23-room hotel a special find. It's handily located, near the Spanish Steps.

Okapi Rooms

Via della Penna 57 (06 3260 9815, www.okapirooms.it). €.
Sticking with the exotic beast theme, the owners of the Pensione Panda (see p175) have opened this fresh, bright outpost a stone's throw from piazza del Popolo. Though pretty basic and

Inn at the Roman Forum p176

reportedly noisy at times, Okapi Rooms offers air-con and internet access, and one room has a little terrace.

Pensione Panda

Via della Croce 35 (06 678 0179, www.hotelpanda.it). €.
Panda's location, near the piazza di Spagna, is its main selling point. Bedrooms are clean but very basic; newly renovated rooms have lofty beamed ceilings and terracotta floors. *Centro storico* bargains are hard to come by, and it is usually booked solid in high season.

Portrait Suites

Via Bocca di Leone 23 (06 6938 0742, 055 2726 4000 reservations, www.lungarnohotels.com). €€€€.
Stylish Portrait Suites belongs to the Ferragamo fashion group. Memorabilia from the company archives decorate the hallways; in the bedrooms, a black and slate colour scheme is offset with touches of pink and lime. There are spacious marble bathrooms, walk-in wardrobes and a glamorous kitchenette. Breakfast is served in the rooms or on the spectacular terrace.

Residenza A

Via Veneto 183 (06 486 700, www.hotelviaveneto.com). €€.
Set on the first floor of an imposing palazzo, Residenza A is a boutique hotel with splashy modern art enlivening its grey and black colour scheme. The rooms have been luxuriously finished, with perks such as flatscreen computers and free internet, roomy showers and Bulgari bath products.

Residenza Cellini

Via Modena 5 (06 4782 5204, www.residenzacellini.it). €€.
This luminous and spacious *residenza* has huge guest rooms, decorated with faux-antique wooden furniture. The bathrooms have jacuzzis or showers with hydro-massage. On the floor that opened in 2007, three rooms have

balconies and all are decorated in the same classic style; there's a terrace too.

Westin Excelsior

Via V Veneto 125 (06 47081, www.westinrome.com). €€€€.
The Excelsior's public spaces are lavish and its rooms – with marble bathrooms – are a Hollywood-style fantasy. The Villa La Cupola suite is the priciest bed in Rome, rumoured to cost over €20,000 a night.

Esquilino & Celio

Artemide

Via Nazionale 22 (06 489 911, www.hotelartemide.com). €€-€€€.
A classically stylish haven on a busy shopping street, with charming, professional staff (and free mini-bars) to ensure a pleasant stay. Smaller 'no frills' rooms without breakfast cost much less than the regular rooms.

Beehive

Via Marghera 8 (06 4470 4553, www.the-beehive.com). €.
American owners Steve and Linda Brenner mix their penchant for design-icon furnishings with reasonable rates and basic amenities to create a 'youth hostel meets boutique hotel' vibe. There's a sunny garden, plus free internet access. Breakfast not included.

Capo d'Africa

Via Capo d'Africa 54 (06 772 801, www.hotelcapodafrica.com). €€€.
The lobby may be somewhat underwhelming but the location, on a quiet street near the Colosseum, is terrific. Rooms are spacious and comfortable, if bland; the rooftop breakfast room has stellar views of the Colosseum.

Casa Romana

Via dei Mille 41A (329 228 0626, www.myromeapartment.com). €.
Simply stylish, this three-roomer not far from Termini station offers facilities rarely found in this price bracket,

ESSENTIALS

plus a friendly welcome, excellent breakfast and expert tourist advice from host Fulvia Angelini.

Exedra
Piazza della Repubblica 47 (06 489 381, www.boscolohotels.com). €€€€.
From its porticoed exterior to its opulent lobby, the Exedra is very glam; rooms run from plush and utterly comfortable to outrageous. In summer, the rooftop bar/restaurant and pool offer superb views, and there's a spa. The one drawback is the location: the hotel is a little too close to Termini station for comfort.

Inn at the Roman Forum
Via degli Ibernesi 30 (06 6919 0970, www.theinnattheromanforum.com). €€€€.
This boutique hotel's location, on a quiet, picturesque street, gives it an exclusive feel. Rooms are a sumptuous mix of luxe fabrics and antiques; the pricier bedrooms have canopied beds and marble bathrooms. On sunny days, breakfast is served on the roof terrace. The two executive suites can be booked together as the Master Garden Suite, an exclusive apartment with a walled garden. Smaller rooms with no breakfast are in the €€ bracket.

Lancelot
Via Capo d'Africa 47 (06 7045 0615, www.lancelothotel.com). €€.
This beautifully kept family-run hotel has an elegant mix of linen, wood and tiles in the bedrooms, some of which have terraces facing the Palatine and Colosseum. The elegant reception has tiled floors and antique furniture, along with some unusual *objets*.

Nerva
Via Tor de' Conti 3 (06 678 1835, www.hotelnerva.com). €€.
The family-run Nerva is handy for the Forum, and the rather old-fashioned rooms have all been refurbished. The staff are a friendly bunch.

Radisson SAS es. Hotel
Via F Turati 171 (06 444 841, www.rome.radissonsas.com). €€€.
Built on the site of an ancient cemetery, this 'concept' hotel caters for business clients – who don't baulk at the location by the train station – and diehard design fans. The stunning rooftop has a bar and a pool. In the all-white rooms, the bed is on a low platform, divided from the bathroom by a glass screen.

St Regis Grand
Via VE Orlando 3 (06 47091, www.stregis.com/grandrome). €€€€.
The hotel's original chandeliers dazzle in massive marbled reception rooms, decorated in opulent gold, beige and red. Rooms have been individually designed using rich fabrics, and are filled with silk-covered Empire and Regency-style furnishings. There's a gym and a sauna.

Villa Spalletti Trivelli
Via Piacenza 4 (06 4890 7934, www.villaspalletti.it). €€€€.
The aristocratic Spalletti Trivelli clan has turned its family home – with views across a little park to the Quirinale palace – into a sumptuously elegant 12-roomer with such high-class extras as an historic library, a formal garden where breakfast or *aperitivi* can be served and a marvellous spa in the basement. There's a chef on hand to whip up special meals on request.

Aventine & Testaccio

Sant'Anselmo, Villa Pio & Aventino
Piazza di Sant'Anselmo 2/via di Santa Melania 19 (06 570 057, www.aventinohotels.com). €€-€€€.
The three hotels in this group are within a stone's throw of one another in an exclusive residential area. The more ornate Sant'Anselmo recently reopened after refurbishment. Villa San Pio consists of three separate buildings that share the same pretty gardens and an airy breakfast room; it has a light

Star food

Rome's hotel restaurants are going gourmet.

Filippo La Mantia

Rome boasted 14 Michelin stars in 2011, and of those, five went to hotel restaurants. With one notable exception (La Pergola, see below), this indicates a fairly recent shift in the perception of what hotels should offer – from comfort food for globe-trotters with tired tastebuds to cutting-edge gourmet. But whether Michelin is picking the right hotels is quite another matter.

Losing its star in 2011 was **baby**, the restaurant in the Hotel Aldrovandi helmed by chef Alfonso Iaccarini, who has returned full-time to his excellent eaterie on the Amalfi Coast. Rome's hotel dining options are all the poorer for this.

Thank goodness, then, that we still have **La Pergola** in the Rome Cavalieri (via Cadlolo 101, 06 35 091, www.romecavalieri.com), the only restaurant in this city of food to boast three Michelin stars. Given the position – high up on Monte Mario – you might think people go for the view. But with food like this on your plate (dinner for two €400 plus wine), the panorama pales. German chef Heinz Beck creates a menu of daring perfection. There is also an award-winning cellar of (very pricey) wine.

The French food bible has given a star each to **Imàgo** at the Hotel Hassler (see p173) and **Mirabelle** at the Hotel Splendide Royale (via di Porta Pinciana, Veneto, 06 4215 8838, www.mirabelle.it) – two choices which are, in our opinion, questionable. On the plus side, both offer fantastic views over the city. This doesn't, however, compensate for service which can be inattentive, food which can be mediocre and tabs which can leave you reeling.

Not (yet) a starred chef, former news photographer **Filippo La Mantia** (see p95) burst on to the hotel food scene in 2009 with his irrepressible Sicilian ebullience, taking over the restaurant at the Hotel Majestic on via Veneto. The dining room is an extravaganza of burnished mirrors, Empire furniture and potted palms. La Mantia's delicate, citrus-perfumed touch is the keynote here. Try it for lunch, when the €38-a-head price tag is slightly less painful than the evening à la carte.

ESSENTIALS

Radisson SAS es. Hotel p176

feel, making it a pleasant place to stay. The Aventino is less manicured. Some rooms have jacuzzis.

Trastevere & the Gianicolo

Arco del Lauro
Via dell'Arco de' Tolomei 27-29 (06 9784 0350, 346 244 3212, www.arcodellauro.it). €.
Situated on a picturesque backstreet, Arco del Lauro has six tasteful bedrooms decorated in modern, fresh neutrals. Budget-priced *residenze* options are few and far between in chichi Trastevere: this one is airy and spotlessly clean. Breakfast is taken in a bar in a nearby piazza.

Casa di Santa Francesca Romana
Via dei Vascellari 61 (06 581 2125, www.sfromana.it). €.
This ex-convent is now a hotel with a noticeably churchy feel. It's popular with businessmen on a budget and

with families (thanks to the spacious quad rooms). Breakfast is served in a lovely courtyard.

Donna Camilla Savelli
Via Garibaldi 27 (06 588 861, www. hoteldonnacamillasavelli.com). €€€.
This former convent, designed by Borromini, is now a plush 4-star hotel but there's still a slight air of nunnery around the echoing corridors. The position – in a quiet corner but a short stroll from Trastevere's lively alleyways – is great, there's a pretty garden, and the view from the roof terrace is amazing.

Foresteria Orsa Maggiore
Via San Francesco di Sales 1A (06 689 3753, www.foresteriaorsa. altervista.org). €.
Inside a 16th-century convent that for years has been home to a feminist cultural centre, this women-only hostel offers B&B lodgings in bright, clean single, double and dorm rooms at rock-bottom prices. The right-on complex also has eateries, exhibition spaces, a bookshop and a fair-trade store.

ESSENTIALS

Hotel Santa Maria

Vicolo del Piede 2 (06 589 4626, www.hotelsantamaria.com). €€.
On the site of a 16th-century convent, the Santa Maria has rooms with tiled floors, floral print decor and spacious bathrooms. All open on to a courtyard with orange trees. Around the corner, at via dell'Arco di San Calisto 20 (06 5833 5103, www.residenzasanta-maria.com, €€), the Residenza Santa Maria is this hotel's charming offshoot.

Residenza Arco de' Tolomei

Via dell'Arco de' Tolomei 27 (06 5832 0819, www.bbarcodeitolomei.com). €€.
This bijou *residenza* projects a cosy, welcoming feel. There's beautiful wood flooring, plentiful antiques and a sunny breakfast room. All of the bedrooms are individually designed in a whimsical, English country-house style; the three on the upper floor have terraces.

Vatican & Prati

Bramante

Vicolo delle Palline 24 (06 6880 6426, www.hotelbramante.com). €€.

Once home to 16th-century architect Domenico Fontana, this place became an inn in 1873. It has a large, pleasant reception and a little patio for the summer. The 16 rooms of varying sizes are simple yet elegant in style; most have high-beamed ceilings, and some feature wrought-iron beds.

Colors Hotel & Hostel

Via Boezio 31 (06 687 4030, www.colorshotel.com). €.
A short walk from St Peter's, Colors has bright, clean dorm and hotel accommodation, plus self-catering kitchen facilities and a terrace. Superior rooms have breakfast included. All rooms have air-con. Credit cards are accepted for the superior rooms only.

Pensione Paradise

Viale Giulio Cesare 47 (06 3600 4331, www.pensioneparadise.com). €.
Rooms in this budget hotel may be a little on the poky side, but friendly staff and a decent location ensure that back-packers keep on coming. There's no breakfast and no air-con, but if you're willing to rough it a little, you could do far worse.

Residenza Arco de' Tolomei

ESSENTIALS

Getting Around

Arriving & leaving

Airports

Aeroporto Leonardo da Vinci, Fiumicino

Via dell'Aeroporto di Fiumicino (06 65951, www.adr.it). **Open** 24hrs daily.
There is an express **rail** service between Fiumicino airport and Termini railway station, which takes 31mins and runs every 30mins from 6.36am until 11.36pm daily (5.52am-10.52pm to Fiumicino). A one-way ticket costs €14. Note that at Termini the train leaves from platforms 27-28, a good ten-minute hike from the main entrance.

The regular service from Fiumicino takes 25-40mins, and stops at Trastevere, Ostiense, Tuscolana and Tiburtina stations. Trains leave about every 20mins (less often on Sun) between 5.57am and 11.27pm (5.05am-10.33pm to Fiumicino). A single ticket costs €8.

Tickets for either service can be bought with cash or credit card from ticket booths or self-ticketing machines. Stamp your ticket in the machines at the head of the platform before boarding, or you risk a fine.

SIT Bus Shuttle (06 591 6826, www.sitbusshuttle.it) runs frequent services from Fiumicino to Termini railway station (in via Marsala, in front of the Hotel Royal Santina, 8.30am-12.30am) and vice versa (5am-8.30pm). Tickets cost €8 single, €15 return.

During the night, a Cotral **bus** service runs between Fiumicino (outside Terminal C) and Termini and Tiburtina railway stations in Rome; tickets cost €4.50 on newsstands, €7 on board. Buses leave Tiburtina at 12.30am, 1.15am, 2.30am and 3.45am, stopping at Termini railway station 10mins later. Departures from Fiumicino are at 1.15am, 2.15am, 3.30am and 5am. Neither Termini nor Tiburtina are attractive places at night, so it's advisable to get a taxi on from there to your final destination.

Aeroporto GB Pastine, Ciampino

Via Appia Nuova 1651 (06 65951, www.adr.it). **Open** 24hrs daily.
Though bus services claim to run into the early morning, often they don't. Booking tickets online before you leave home may signal to bus drivers not to pack up early. Taxi drivers at this airport have a reputation for preying on tourists.

On paper at least, the most hassle-free way to get into town from Ciampino is to take a coach. **Terravision** (www.terravision.eu) runs services to Termini station (journey time 40mins). Buses leave from outside the arrivals hall after each arrival. Buses from Termini to Ciampino leave from via Marsala. This is a dedicated service for low-cost airlines, so you'll need to show your ticket or boarding pass to buy a ticket (€4 single), which can be booked online with a discount, or bought (cash only) in Arrivals at Ciampino, at the Terravision office in the Termini forecourt or on the bus.

SIT Bus Shuttle (06 591 6826, www.sitbusshuttle.it) is a frequent service from Termini (via Marsala) to Ciampino (45 minutes, €6, 4.30am-9.30pm), and Ciampino to Termini (8.45am-11.45pm). Tickets can be bought on the bus or online.

Schiaffini buses (800 700 805, www.schiaffini.it) runs a service between Ciampino and Anagnina metro station every 30-40mins (6am-10.40pm daily), and to Ciampino station (where frequent trains depart for Rome Termini) 5.45am-11.25pm daily; both cost €1.20. It also runs regular services (€4.50) between the airport and Termini station. Very early morning services cost €1.20 and €5 respectively. Buy tickets on board.

Cotral (www.cotralspa.it) buses run regularly between the airport and Anagnina metro station, and between the airport and Ciampino town's railway station (both €1.20).

By bus

There is no central long-distance bus station in Rome. Most coach services terminate outside the following metro stations: Saxa Rubra (routes north); Cornelia, Ponte Mammolo and Tiburtina (north and east); Anagnina and Laurentina (routes south).

By train

Most long-distance trains arrive at Termini station, also the hub of Rome's transport network. Beware of pickpockets. Night trains may arrive at Tiburtina or Ostiense.

For bookings and information on mainline rail services across Italy, call **Trenitalia** (24hrs daily) on 892 021 (06 6847 5475 from abroad) or go to www.trenitalia.it. Tickets can be bought at stations (credit cards accepted over the counter and by ticket machines) or online. Under-12s pay half fare; under-fours travel free.

Slow trains (*diretti, espressi, regionali* and *interregionali*) are cheap; fast services – InterCity (IC), EuroCity (EC), Eurostar Italia (ES) – are closer to the European norm.

You must stamp your ticket in the yellow machines at the head of the platform before boarding. You risk being fined if you don't.

Rome's main stations are **Ostiense** (piazzale dei Partigiani),

Termini (piazza dei Cinquecento), **Tiburtina** (circonvallazione Nomentana) and **Trastevere** (piazzale Biondo).

Public transport

Rome's transport system is co-ordinated by **ATAC** (06 57003, 800 431 784 toll-free, 800 154 451 disabled information, www.atac.roma.it). You can download maps of the transport network from the website (click on *Linee e mappe*), which also has a useful journey planner.

City-centre and inner-suburb routes are served by the buses and trams of the **Trambus** transport authority. The system is relatively easy to use and as efficient as the traffic-choked streets allow.

Pickpocketing is a problem on buses and metros, particularly on major tourist routes, notoriously the 64 and 40 Express between Termini station and the Vatican.

For hop-on, hop-off city bus tours, see www.trambusopen.com.

Tickets

The same tickets are valid on all city bus, tram and metro lines, whoever the operator is. They are not valid on services to Fiumicino airport. Though the latest generation of buses has ticket dispensers on board, in most cases you'll have to buy before you board, from ATAC automatic ticket machines, information centres, some bars and newsstands, and all *tabacchi*. Before purchasing a three-day ticket, consider whether the three-day **Roma Pass** (see p11) might not be better value.

BIT valid for 75mins, during which you can take an unlimited number of city buses, plus one metro trip; €1.
BIG valid for one day, until midnight; covers the whole urban network; €4.

ESSENTIALS

BTI three-day pass, covering all bus and metro routes, and local mainline trains to Ostia; €11.

CIS valid for seven days; it covers all bus routes and the metro system, including the lines to Ostia; €16.
You must stamp tickets on board. Under-tens travel free; older kids and pensioners must pay the adult fare. If you are caught without a stamped ticket, you'll be fined €51 on the spot, or €104.40 if you opt to pay later at a post office.

Buses

Bus is the best way to get around. The system is easy to use; a sign at each bus stop tells you the routes each line stopping there takes. Most services run 5.30am-midnight daily, every 10-45mins. The doors for boarding (usually front and rear) and alighting (usually centre) are clearly marked. 'Express' buses make few stops along their route: check before boarding so you don't get whisked past your destination.

For hop-on, hop-off city bus tours, see www.trambusopen.com; for tours along the Appian Way, see p152.

Trams

Tram routes mainly serve suburban areas. An express tram service – No.8 – links largo Argentina to Trastevere and the western suburbs.

Metro

Rome's two metro lines cross beneath Termini train station (for information 06 57003, 800 431 784, toll-free, www.atac.roma.it). Line A runs from south-east to north-west; line B from EUR to the north-east. Both are open 5.30am-11.30pm (until 1.30am Fri & Sat). From 11.30pm (1.30am Fri & Sat) until 5am, buses N1 and N2 ply the same routes as lines A and B respectively.

Taxis

Licensed taxis are white and have a meter. Touts are rife at major tourist magnets; ignore them if you don't want to risk an extortionate fare.

Recent changes in taxi tariffs have made them super-complicated. When you pick up a taxi at a rank or hail one in the street, the meter should read zero. The minimum fare is currently €2.80 (€4 on Sundays and public holidays), or €5.80 if you board 10pm-7am. Each kilometre after that is €0.92. The first piece of luggage put in the boot is free, then it's €1 per piece. Tariffs outside the GRA, Rome's major ring road, are much higher. There's a ten per cent discount for trips to hospitals, and for women travelling alone 9pm-1am, and a €2 surcharge for any trip starting at Termini station.

Fixed airport tariffs from anywhere inside the Aurelian walls (ie most of the *centro storico*) are €45 to/from Fiumicino, €35 to/from Ciampino. This is for up to four people and includes luggage: don't let taxi drivers tell you otherwise.

Most of Rome's taxi drivers are honest; if you think you're being fleeced, take down the driver's details from the metal plaque inside the rear door. The more obviously you do this, the more likely you are to find the fare returning to its proper level. Report complaints to the drivers' co-operative (phone number on the outside of each car) or, in serious cases, the police.

When you phone for a taxi, you'll be given the taxi code-name (always a location followed by a number) and a time, as in *Bahama 69, in tre minuti* ('Bahamas 69, in three minutes'). Besides the minimum fare, you'll be charged the following 'call' rates depending on how long your taxi takes to arrive: €2 (up to five mins), €4 (five-ten mins) or €6 (more than ten mins). If the meter shows more than this when the taxi arrives, the difference must be deducted at the end of the trip.

Cooperativa Samarcanda *06 5551*.
Cosmos Radio Taxi *06 88 177, 06 8822*.
Società Cooperativa Autoradio Taxi Roma *06 3570, www.3570.it*.
Società la Capitale Radio Taxi *06 49 94*.

Driving

Much of central Rome is off-limits during the day for anyone without a permit. Police and cameras guard these ZTL (*zone a traffico limitato*) areas; any car without a pass will be fined €70 if it enters at restricted times. A strict no-car policy applies in the centre on some Sundays too; check www.comune.roma.it or www.atac.roma.it for information.

Most motoring associations have breakdown service agreements with **Automobile Club d'Italia** (24hr information and emergency toll-free 800 116, www.aci.it). Remember:
▪ You are required to wear a seatbelt at all times, in front and back seats, and to carry a warning triangle and reflective jacket in your car.
▪ You must keep your driving licence, vehicle registration and ID documents on you at all times.
▪ Traffic lights flashing amber mean stop and give way to the right.

Parking

Residents park for free and visitors pay to park in many areas. It's well policed – look for the blue lines. Buy parking tickets (€1/hr; €1.20/hr in most ZTL areas) at pay-and-display ticket dispensers or from *tabacchi*. In most areas, you can park for free at certain times. Hourly parking cards (*scheda per il parcheggio*), available from *tabacchi*, save you the bother of scrabbling for small change.

In zones with no blue lines, anything resembling a parking place is up for grabs, with some exceptions: watch out for *Passo carrabile* ('access at all times') or *Sosta vietata* ('no parking') signs and disabled parking spaces (marked by yellow stripes). The sign *Zona rimozione* ('tow-away zone') means no parking, and is valid for the length of the street or until the sign is repeated with a red line through it. If a street or square has no cars parked in it, assume it's a strictly enforced no-parking area.

In some areas, self-appointed *parcheggiatori* will 'look after' your car for a small fee; it may be illegal, but it's worth paying up to ensure your tyres remain intact.

Cars are safe in most central areas, but you may prefer to use a car park to keep your car off the street. The following are central:

Parking Ludovisi *via Ludovisi 60 (06 474 0632)*. **Rates** €2.20/hr for first five hours, €1/hr thereafter. No credit cards.
Terminal Park *via Marsala 20 (06 444 1067)*. **Rates** €3 first hour; €2 second hour; €1/hr thereafter; €26 daily rate. No credit cards.

Vehicle removal

If your car isn't where you left it, it may have been towed. Phone the municipal police (*Vigili urbani*) on 06 67691 and quote your number plate to find out which pound it's in, or check on www.comune.roma.it: click on '*Dipartimenti e altri uffici*', then '*Corpo di Polizia Municipale*'.

Vehicle hire

Avis *06 481 4373, 06 4521 08391, 199 100 133, www.avisautonoleggio.it*.
Europcar *199 307 030, 06 488 2854, www.europcar.it*.
Maggiore *06 2245 6060, 06 488 0049, 199 151 120, www.maggiore.it*.

ESSENTIALS

Resources A-Z

For information on travelling to Italy from within the European Union, including details of visa regulations and healthcare provision, see the EU's travel website: http://europa.eu/travel.

Accident & emergency

For an **ambulance**, dial 118; for the **fire brigade**, dial 115; for **police**, see p185.

The hospitals listed below offer 24-hour casualty services. If your child needs emergency treatment, go to the Ospedale Bambino Gesù.

Ospedale Fatebenefratelli
Isola Tiberina (06 68 371).
Ospedale Pediatrico Bambino Gesù *Piazza Sant'Onofrio 4 (06 68 591, www.opbg.net).*
Ospedale San Camillo-Forlanini *Via Portuense 332 (06 55 551, 06 58 701, www.scamillo forlanini.rm.it).*
Ospedale San Giovanni *Via Amba Aradam 8 (06 77 051, www.hsangiovanni.roma.it).*
Policlinico Umberto I *Viale Policlinico 155 (06 49 971, www.policlinicoumberto1.it).*

Pharmacies

Normal opening hours are 8.30am-1pm, 4-8pm Mon-Sat. Out of hours, a duty rota system operates. A list by the door of any pharmacy (and also in the local papers) indicates the nearest.

Farmacia della Stazione *Piazza dei Cinquecento 49-51 (06 488 0019).* **Open** 24hrs daily.
Piram *Via Nazionale 228 (06 488 0754).* **Open** 24hrs daily.

Credit card loss

American Express *06 7290 0347, 800 874 333 US cardholders*
Diners Club *800 393 939*
MasterCard *800 870 866*
Visa *800 877 232*

Customs

Travellers in EU countries are not required to declare goods imported into or exported from Italy if they are for personal use, up to the following limits:
- 800 cigarettes or 400 cigarillos or 200 cigars or 1kg of tobacco.
- ten litres of spirits (over 22% alcohol) and ten litres of fortified wine (under 22% alcohol).

For people arriving from non-EU countries, the following limits apply:
- 200 cigarettes or 100 cigarillos or 50 cigars or 250g of tobacco.
- one litre of spirits or two litres of wine.
- One bottle of perfume (50ml), 25cl of eau de toilette or various merchandise not exceeding €175.

Anything above these limits will be subject to taxation at the port of entry. There are no restrictions on the importation of cameras, watches or electrical goods. Check the Italian customs website (www.agenzia dogane.it) for further information.

Dental emergency

For serious dental emergencies, use hospital casualty departments (see left). Children should be taken to the Ospedale Bambino Gesù.

Disabled

With cobbled streets, narrow pavements and old buildings,

ESSENTIALS

Rome is difficult for disabled people. That said, many city-centre buses are now wheelchair accessible, and most museums and larger hotels have facilities.

Rome city council's Osservatorio Permanente sull'Accessibilità has an excellent website, in English, showing accessibility and facilities in all the city's major tourist sites. Check out www.handyturismo.it.

The non-profit **CO.IN** (www.coinsociale.it) can provide details of disabled facilities at museums, restaurants, shops, theatres, stations and hotels. It also organises transport for disabled people (up to eight places), which must be booked several days in advance. It runs a phone service in Italian and English (toll-free 800 271 027, from within Italy only).

Roma per Tutti (06 5717 7094, www.romapertutti.it) is run by CO.IN and the city council. English-speaking staff answer questions on accessibility in hotels, buildings and monuments. Guided tours with transport can be booked. Its site (Italian only) also contains useful information on events.

Electricity

Italy uses 220V – compatible with British-bought appliances (with a plug adaptor); US 110V equipment requires a current transformer.

Embassies & consulates

For a full list of embassies, see *Ambasciate* in the phone book.

Australia *Via Antonio Bosio 5 (06 852 721, www.italy.embassy.gov.au).*
Britain *Via XX Settembre 80 (06 4220 0001, www.ukinitaly.fco.gov.uk).*
Canada *Via Zara 30 (06 854 441, www.canada.it).*
Ireland *Piazza Campitelli 3 (06 697 9121, www.ambasciata-irlanda.it).*
New Zealand *Via Clitunno 44 (06 853 7501, www.nzembassy.com).*
South Africa *Via Tanaro 14 (06 852 541, www.sudafrica.it).*
US *Via Vittorio Veneto 119 (06 46 741, www.usembassy.it).*

Internet

Much of central Rome, plus major parks (*ville* Borghese, Pamphili, Ada, Torlonia), EUR and the Auditorium – Parco della Musica zone, is covered by the ever-growing city-sponsored free wireless network. When you open your browser in one of the hotspots, you'll be asked to log on. Initially, you'll need to register, giving a mobile phone number. For information, including a map of available hotspots, see www.romawireless.com.

Opening hours

For shopping hours, see p23; for pharmacies, see p184.

Most banks open 8.30am-1.30pm, 2.45-4.30pm Mon-Fri. Some central branches also open until 6pm Thur and 8.30am-12.30pm Sat. All banks work reduced hours the day before a holiday (many close by 11am).

Police

For emergencies, call one of the following helplines:

Carabinieri *(English-speaking helpline) 112*
Polizia di stato *113*
The principal *Polizia di Stato* station, the Questura Centrale, is at via San Vitale 15 (06 46 861, www.poliziadistato.it). Others, and the Carabinieri's *Commissariati*, are listed in the phone directory under *Polizia* and *Carabinieri*. Incidents can be reported to either.

ESSENTIALS

Post

The postal service is fairly efficient (try the Vatican Post Office, run in association with the Swiss postal service, if in doubt). For postal information, call 803 160 (8am-8pm Mon-Sat) or visit www.poste.it.

There are large post offices (*ufficio postale*) in each district; opening hours are generally 8.30am-6pm Mon-Fri (8.30am-2pm Aug), 8.30am-1.30pm Sat and any day preceding a public holiday. All offices close up to two hours earlier than normal on the last day of each month. Some services are available via the website (www.poste.it); check it first to avoid the queues.

Posta Centrale *Piazza San Silvestro 19 (information 803 160).*
Vatican Post Office *Piazza San Pietro (06 6988 3406).* **Open** 8.30am-6.30pm Mon-Fri; 8.30am-6pm Sat.

Smoking

Smoking is prohibited in all public places in Italy except for those that provide a distinct, ventilated smokers' room. Fines of €27.50-€275 (or up to €550 if you smoke in the presence of children or pregnant women) are possible.

Tabacchi

Tabacchi, identified by signs with a white T on a black background, are the only places where you can legally buy tobacco products. They also sell stamps, phone cards, tickets for public transport and lottery tickets.

Telephones
Dialling & codes

• Rome landlines have the area code 06, which must be used whether calling from within or outside the city. When phoning Rome from abroad, do *not* omit the initial 0.
• Numbers beginning with 800 are toll-free. Numbers starting with 840 and 848 are charged at low set rates but can only be called within Italy.
• Mobile numbers begin with a 3. GSM phones can be used on both 900 and 1800 bands; British, Australian and New Zealand mobiles work fine, but US phones (unless they're tri-band) don't work.
• For international calls, dial 00, followed by the country code, area code (omitting the initial zero, if applicable) and number. Codes include: Australia 61; Canada 1; Irish Republic 353; New Zealand 64; United Kingdom 44; United States 1.

Directory enquiries

Charges for information given over the phone are steep. Major services are 1254 (Italian and international numbers, in Italian) and 892 412 (international numbers, in Italian and English, from mobile phones). Italian directory information can be accessed for free at www.1254.it and www.paginebianche.it.

Public phones

Rome has no shortage of public phone boxes, and many bars have payphones, which are rarely busy as locals are addicted to mobiles. Most only accept phone cards (*schede telefoniche*); a few also accept major credit cards. Phone cards cost €5, €15 and €30 and are available from *tabacchi*, some newsstands and some bars.

Tickets

For pre-booking tickets for sights, galleries and exhibitions, see p11, and Tourist Information (see p187).

Expect to pay *diritti di prevendita* (booking fees) on tickets bought anywhere except at the venue on the night. **Feltrinelli Libri e Musica** (Galleria Alberto Sordi, piazza Colonna, 06 679 4957) sells tickets for classical concerts and for rock, jazz and other events.

Hello Ticket (800 907 080, www.helloticket.it) takes bookings over the phone and online for most concerts, theatre and sporting events.

Time

Italy is on Central European Time, making it an hour ahead of GMT and six hours ahead of Eastern Standard Time. In all EU countries, clocks move forward an hour in early spring, and then back again in late autumn.

Tipping

Foreigners are generally expected to tip more than Italians, but the ten or more per cent usual in many countries is seen as generous even for the richest-looking tourist. Anything between €1 and €5 is normal; some smarter places now include a 10-15% service charge. For drinks, leave 10¢-20¢ when ordering at the counter. Taxi drivers will be happy if you round the fare up to the nearest euro.

Tourist information

The city council operates well-stocked, green tourist information kiosks (**PIT**), 9.30am-7/7.30pm daily; the most central are in piazza Pia (by Castel Sant'Angelo), piazza delle Cinque Lune (by piazza Navona), via del Corso and piazza Sonnino (in Trastevere).

The fastest one-stop shop for tourist information, however, is a phone service, 060608, sponsored by the city council. Information on sights, opening times, shows and

much else is dispensed in English and Italian; phone operators will put callers through to the appropriate booking agency if they want to reserve tickets or seats. The www.060608.it website is an excellent source of information.

The APT tourist board's website (www.turismoroma.it) is also worth checking out.

Ufficio Pellegrini e Turisti (Vatican Tourist Office) *Piazza San Pietro (06 6988 1662, www.vatican.va).* **Open** 8.30am-6pm Mon-Sat.

Visas

EU nationals and citizens of the US, Canada, Australia and New Zealand do not need visas for stays of up to three months. For EU citizens, a passport or national ID card valid for travel abroad is sufficient; non-EU citizens must have full passports. In theory, all visitors must declare their presence to the local police within eight days of arrival. If you're staying in a hotel, this will be done for you.

What's on

The listings magazines *Roma C'è* (www.romace.it, out Wed) and *Trovaroma* (free with *La Repubblica* on Thur) are the best sources of information about shows, concerts and nightlife. The latter has an English section.

Major events are listed on the official tourist board website – www.romaturismo.it – and on www.060608.it. For an alternative look at Rome's nightlife, check out www.romastyle.info and www.musicaroma.it. For more information on Rome's gay scene, contact **Arcigay Roma** (www.arcigayroma.it) or **Arci-Lesbica Roma** (www.arcilesbica.it/roma). See also p28.

ESSENTIALS

Vocabulary

Pronunciation

a – like a in ask
e – like a in age or e in sell
i – like ea in east
o – like o in hotel or hot
u – like oo in boot
c – as in cat before a, o and u;
otherwise like ch in cheat
g – as in good before a, o and u;
otherwise like g in giraffe; **gl** – like lli
in million; **gn** – like ny in canyon
h – not pronounced; after any consonant
makes it hard (ch – cat; gh – good); **sc** –
like sh in shame; **sch** – like sc in scout

Useful phrases

hello/goodbye (informal) *ciao, salve;*
good morning *buon giorno;* **good
evening** *buona sera;* **good night**
buona notte; **please** *per favore, per
piacere;* **thank you** *grazie;* **you're
welcome** *prego;* **excuse me, sorry**
pardon, (formal) *mi scusi,* (informal)
scusa; **I don't speak Italian** *non parlo
l'italiano* **do you speak English?**
parla inglese?; **can I use/where is
the toilet?** *posso usare/dov'è il bagno?;*
open *aperto;* **closed** *chiuso;* **entrance**
entrata; **exit** *uscita*

Transport

bus *autobus, auto;* **car** *macchina;* **coach**
pullman; **plane** *aereo;* **taxi** *tassì, taxi;*
train *treno;* **tram** *tram;* **bus stop**
fermata (dell'autobus); **platform**
binario; **station** *stazione;* **ticket**
biglietto; **one-way** *solo andata;*
return *andata e ritorno*

Directions

where is? *dov'è?;* **(turn) left** *(giri a)
sinistra;* **(it's on the) right** *(è a/sulla)
destra;* **straight on** *sempre dritto;* **is it
near/far?** *è vicino/lontano?*

Communications

attacco per il computer *dataport;*
broadband *ADSL (adiesselle);*
cellphone *telefonino;* **courier**
corriere, pony; **fax** *fax;* **letter** *lettera;*
phone *telefono;* **postcard** *cartolina;*
stamp *francobollo;* **a stamp for
England/the US** *un francobollo
per l'Inghilterra/gli Stati Uniti*

Days

Monday *lunedì;* **Tuesday** *martedì;*
Wednesday *mercoledì;* **Thursday**
giovedì; **Friday** *venerdì;* **Saturday**
sabato; **Sunday** *domenica;* **yesterday**
ieri; **today** *oggi;* **tomorrow** *domani;*
weekend *fine settimana, weekend*

Numbers, weights & sizes

0 *zero;* 1 *uno;* 2 *due;* 3 *tre;* 4 *quattro;* 5
cinque; 6 *sei;* 7 *sette;* 8 *otto;* 9 *nove;* 10
dieci; 11 *undici;* 12 *dodici;* 13 *tredici;*
14 *quattordici;* 15 *quindici;* 16 *seidici;*
17 *diciasette;* 18 *diciotto;* 19 *dicianove;*
20 *venti;* 30 *trenta;* 40 *quaranta;* 50
cinquanta; 60 *sessanta;* 70 *settanta;* 80
ottanta; 90 *novanta;* 100 *cento;* 200
duecento; 1,000 *mille;* 2,000 *duemila*
I take (shoe/dress) size *porto il
numero/la taglia…;* **100 grams of…**
un'etto di…; **300 grams of…** *tre etti
di…;* **a kilo of…** *un kilo di…;* **five
kilos of…** *cinque chili di…*

Booking & paying

booking, reservation *prenotazione;*
I'd like to book… *vorrei prenotare…;*
…a table for four at eight *un tavolo
per quattro alle otto* **…a single/twin/
double room** *una camera singola/
doppia/matrimoniale* **how much is it?**
quanto costa?

Menu Glossary

Sauces & toppings

aglio, olio e peperoncino *garlic, oil and chilli*; **alle vongole** *clams*; **al pomodoro fresco** *fresh/raw tomatoes*; **al ragù** *'bolognese' (a term that doesn't exist in Italian)*; **al sugo** *puréed cooked tomatoes*; **all'amatriciana** *tomato, chilli, sausage and onion*; **alla gricia** *as above without tomato*; **all'arrabbiata** *tomato and chilli*; **alla carbonara** *egg, bacon and parmesan*; **alla puttanesca** *olives, capers and garlic*; **cacio e pepe** *cheese and black pepper*; **in bianco** *with oil or butter and parmesan*; **(ravioli) ricotta e spinaci** *filled with curd cheese and spinach*

Meat & meat dishes

abbacchio, agnello *lamb*; **animelle** *fried pancreas and thymus glands*; **bresaola** *thinly sliced cured beef*; **coda alla vaccinara** *oxtail in celery broth*; **coniglio** *rabbit*; **lardo** *fatty bacon*; **lingua** *tongue*; **maiale** *pork*; **manzo** *beef*; **ossobuco** *beef shins with marrow jelly inside*; **pajata** *veal/lamb intestines*; **pollo** *chicken*; **porchetta** *roast suckling pig*; **prosciutto cotto** *ham*; **prosciutto crudo** *Parma ham*; **straccetti** *thin strips of pan-tossed beef*; **trippa** *tripe*; **vitello** *veal*

Fish & seafood

alici, acciughe *anchovies*; **aragosta, astice** *lobster*; **arzilla, razza** *skate*; **baccalà** *salt cod*; **branzino, spigola** *sea bass*; **calamari** *squid*; **cernia** *grouper*; **dentice, fragolino, marmora, orata, sarago** *forms of bream*; **cozze** *mussels*; **gamberi** *prawns*; **granchio** *crab*; **mazzancolle** *king prawns*; **merluzzo** *cod*; **moscardini** *baby octopus*; **ostriche** *oysters*; **pesce sanpietro** *john dory*; **pesce spada** *swordfish*; **polpo, polipo** *octopus*; **rombo** *turbot*; **salmone** *salmon*; **seppie** *cuttlefish*; **sogliola** *sole*; **tonno** *tuna*; **trota** *trout*; **vongole** *clams*

Vegetables

asparagi *asparagus*; **broccoli siciliani** *broccoli*; **broccolo** *green cauliflower*; **broccoletti** *turnip tops*; **carciofo** *artichoke*; **cavolfiore** *cauliflower*; **cicoria** *green leaf vegetable, like dandelion*; **cipolla** *onion*; **fagioli** *beans*; **fagiolini** *green beans*; **fave** *broad beans*; **funghi** *mushrooms*; **insalata verde/mista** *green/mixed salad*; **melanzana** *aubergine, eggplant*; **patate** *potatoes*; **patatine fritte** *french fries*; **piselli** *peas*; **puntarelle** *bitter salad vegetable usually served with anchovy sauce*; **rughetta** *rocket, arugula*; **sedano** *celery*; **spinaci** *spinach*; **zucchine** *courgettes*

Fruit & desserts

ananas *pineapple*; **anguria, cocomero** *watermelon*; **arance** *oranges*; **ciliegi** *cherries*; **fichi** *figs*; **fragole** *strawberries*; **mele** *apples*; **nespole** *loquats*; **pere** *pears*; **pesche** *peaches*; **uva** *grapes*; **gelato** *ice-cream*; **pannacotta** *'cooked cream', a thick blancmange-like cream*; **sorbetto** *water ice*; **torta della nonna** *flan of pâtisserie cream and pinenuts*; **millefoglie** *flaky pastry cake*

Miscellaneous

antipasto *hors d'oeuvre*; **primo** *first course*; **secondo** *main course*; **contorno** *side dish, vegetable*; **dessert, dolce** *dessert*; **fritto** *fried*; **arrosto** *roast*; **alla griglia** *grilled*; **all'agro** *with oil and lemon*; **ripassato in padella** *(of vegetables) cooked then tossed in a pan with oil, garlic and chilli*; **formaggio** *cheese*; **pane** *bread*; **sale** *salt*; **pepe** *pepper*; **aceto** *vinegar*; **olio** *oil*

Index

Sights & Areas

a
Abbazia delle Tre
  Fontane p156
Accademia di San Luca
  p95
Appian Way p151
Ara Pacis Museum p85
Aventine p117

b
Baths of Caracalla p117
Baths of Diocletian p101
Bioparco-Zoo p92
Borgo p139

c
Campo de' Fiori p67
Capitoline Museums p58
Castel Sant'Angelo p142
Catacombs of San
  Callisto p153
Catacombs of San
  Sebastiano p153
Celio p100
Centrale Montemartini
  p122
Centro, Il p56
Chiesa Nuova/Santa Maria
  in Vallicella p77
Chiostro del Bramante p77
Circus Maximus p58
Circus of Maxentius p153
Colosseum p58
Crypta Balbi p68

d
Domus Aurea p101
Doria Pamphilj Gallery p77

e
Esquilino p100
EUR p155
Explora – Museo dei
  Bambini di Roma p85

g
Galleria Borghese p92
Galleria Colonna p96
Galleria Nazionale d'Arte
  Moderna e
  Contemporanea p94
Galleria Spada p68
Gesù, Il p68
Ghetto, the p67
Gianicolo p138

h
Hadrian's Villa (Villa
  Adriana) p160

i
Imperial Fora Museum p61

j
Jewish Museum of Rome p68

k
Keats-Shelley Memorial
  House p85

m
MACRO p99
Mamertine Prison p63
MAXXI p99
Monteverde p138
Museo Barracco p68
Museo Carlo Bilotti p94
Museo del Corso p77
Museo dell'Alto Medioevo
  p156
Museo della Civiltà
  Romana p156
Museo delle Anime in
  Purgatorio p149
Museo delle Mura p153
Museo di Roma in
  Trastevere p128
Museo di Roma p79
Museo di Villa Giulia p94
Museo Nazionale d'Arte
  Orientale p101
Museo Preistorico ed
  Etnografico L Pigorini
  p156
Museo Storico Nazionale
  dell'Arte Sanitaria p142
Museum of Via Ostiense
  p122

o
Orto botanico (Botanical
  Garden) p129
Ostia Antica p156
Ostiense p120

p
Palazzo Altemps p79
Palazzo Barberini – Galleria
  Nazionale d'Arte Antica
  p96
Palazzo Corsini – Galleria
  Nazionale d'Arte Antica
  p129
Palazzo del Quirinale p96
Palazzo delle Esposizioni
  p101
Palazzo Massimo alle
  Terme p101
Palazzo Ruspoli –
  Fondazione Memmo p85

Palazzo Valentini –Domus
  Romane p63
Palazzo Venezia p63
Pantheon p76, p79
Piazza Navona p76, p79
Portico d'Ottavia p69
Prati p149
Propaganda Fide
  Museum p85
Protestant Cemetery p122

q
Quirinale p95

r
Roman Forum & Palatine
  p63

s
San Carlino alle Quattro
  Fontane p96
San Clemente p109
San Francesco a Ripa
  p129
San Giorgio in Velabro p64
San Giovanni in Laterano
  p109
San Gregorio Magno p109
San Lorenzo fuori
  le Mura p114
San Lorenzo in Lucina p85
San Lorenzo p114
San Luigi dei Francesi p79
San Marco p65
San Nicola in Carcere p65
San Paolo fuori le Mura
  p122
San Pietro in Vincoli p104
Sant'Agnese in Agone p80
Sant'Agostino p80
Sant'Andrea al
  Quirinale p98
Sant'Andrea della
  Valle p69
Sant'Ignazio di Loyola p80
Sant'Ivo alla Sapienza p80
Santa Cecilia in Trastevere
  p129
Santa Croce in
  Gerusalemme p110
Santa Maria del Popolo p89
Santa Maria della
  Concezione p94
Santa Maria della Pace p80
Santa Maria della Vittoria
  p96
Santa Maria in Aracoeli p65
Santa Maria in Cosmedin &
  the Mouth of Truth p65
Santa Maria in Domnica
  p110

ESSENTIALS

ESSENTIALS

When in Rome...

... let our locals guide you.

'Time Out's city guides are unsurpassable'
The Times

**TIME OUT GUIDES
WRITTEN BY
LOCAL EXPERTS**
visit timeout.com/shop